FEELS
RIGHT

FEELS RIGHT

BLACK QUEER WOMEN AND THE POLITICS OF PARTYING IN CHICAGO

KEMI ADEYEMI

DUKE UNIVERSITY PRESS   *Durham and London*   2022

Designed by Matthew Tauch
Typeset in Garamond Premier Pro by Westchest Publishing Services

Library of Congress Cataloging-in-Publication Data
Names: Adeyemi, Kemi, [date] author.
Title: Feels right : black queer women and the politics of partying in Chicago / Kemi Adeyemi.
Description: Durham : Duke University Press, 2022. | Includes bibliographical references and index.
Identifiers: LCCN 2022000024 (print)
LCCN 2022000025 (ebook)
ISBN 9781478016076 (hardcover)
ISBN 9781478018698 (paperback)
ISBN 9781478023319 (ebook)
Subjects: LCSH: Nightlife—Illinois—Chicago. | Sexual minority culture—Illinois—Chicago. |
Sexual minorities—Illinois—Chicago—Social conditions. | Communication and sex—Illinois—
Chicago. | Queer theory—Illinois—Chicago. | BISAC: SOCIAL SCIENCE / Ethnic Studies /
American / African American & Black Studies | SOCIAL SCIENCE / LGBTQ Studies / Lesbian
Studies
Classification: LCC GT3408 .A349 2022 (print) | LCC GT3408 (ebook) |
DDC 307.7609773/11—dc23/eng/20220317
LC record available at https://lccn.loc.gov/2022000024
LC ebook record available at https://lccn.loc.gov/2022000025

Cover art: Photo by Ally Almore.

Publication of this book is supported by Duke University Press's
Scholars of Color First Book Fund.

DEDICATED
TO EVERYBODY
WHO GETS DOWN
ON THE DANCE FLOOR.

CONTENTS

People who don't work on nightlife love to comment that my research must be so *fun*, a comment that often doubles as a suggestion that nightlife research isn't really research at all. This suggestion often comes with the ancillary assumption that people who participate in queer nightlife are also not doing anything of interest or consequence—they're all just partying, just having a good time. Sure, going out at night can feel like an incredibly fun release from the doldrums of daily life. But this expectation that the queer night is simply about pleasure is often rooted in a fundamental misunderstanding of the many kinds of work that it takes to get to and on the dance floor. If you have ever gotten up to dance in front of people (or if you tried to get up and dance but couldn't bear to, or if you've gotten up and danced and felt shamed or ignored for doing so), then you know just how much physical and emotional work it takes. Dance is a very intimate practice of putting ourselves in relation to other people, often strangers. We build feeling by putting ourselves in proximity to other people, we make eye contact, we share gestures, we share touch, we share bodily fluids.

Everything that is empowering about dancing among other people requires an intentional practice of vulnerability and, moreover, optimism— and the vulnerability and optimism that are required to become in alignment with other people makes dancing that much more difficult and exhausting. You must think, hope, or assume that the party is going to be amazing and that you'll feel good; that you'll meet new sounds, movements, people, and, potentially, lovers. You have to trust everyone around you to work toward a shared goal of feeling good. The demands of vulnerability and optimism feel intensified for nightlife researchers who put their bodies on the line as a condition of doing their work, which can be hard for me as a person who would generally rather that people not look at, talk to, or try to dance with me. My personal needs for the queer night had changed in my early and midthirties. I don't think I *needed* it in the way I had in my early twenties. Over the course of nearly a decade of working toward this book, I'd reached an age, which can be any age, when other modes of rest, relaxation, fun, and play simply felt better than those produced in the sociality of the bar or club: walks, daytime park hangs, dinner parties, watching TV, getting in bed at 9:00 p.m., and so on.

When I did go to parties, whether for work or play, everyone felt depressingly young; I would cross the threshold to the function and know immediately that I had aged out and that I couldn't (and maybe didn't want to) relate to the youth. Going out at night began to feel like a chore, yet I'd made going out a condition of my scholarly career. Going out had come to lose the spirit of spontaneity and, in turn, its charm, and this was shaping how I was approaching the party as a formal field site, as a place of work. Through my hundreds of hours dancing with black queer women, watching them dance with one another, and interviewing them about their experiences dancing, all I could see was that the hope for communal trust that the queer nightlife space depends upon almost always failed in some way; someone always fucks up the vibe somehow. As I lost my optimism about what the queer party could look and feel like, I withheld the very vulnerability that would require me to experience its expansive possibilities.

By the time I got to the E N E R G Y party, I was exhausted and not that much fun to party with. I had left Seattle for a summer research trip to Chicago in 2018, when I planned to collect final interviews with black queer women throughout the city and make final rounds at Slo 'Mo, Party Noire, and other parties and events I'd been visiting, thinking about, and writing about. I had been working on various permutations of this book for almost a decade at that point and I was tired of myself, tired of my project, and I was certainly very tired of being out at night. So I came to E N E R G Y, very late in my research process, with no intentions of taking it on as a field site. Doing so would extend my deadline for completion well over a year, and the process of conducting research would be difficult because the party is hosted every Sunday and I didn't live in Chicago anymore. These geographic and administrative restrictions made it so that I could go to E N E R G Y on any given Sunday without my "work hat" on, and I hadn't felt that way in ages.

I could show up exhausted from hot and humid Sundays of party hopping, or having convinced myself up and off the couch and into the night, and be immediately welcomed in by the organizers, Tori and Jae, who circle the room making connections to and across attendees. I could settle in to one of the low lounge chairs or sit at the bar to feel quiet, still, and observant—until I'd regained the resources to be up and about, chatting and dancing. The party helped me escape the gentrified hell that was (is) Logan Square, where I often stayed on research trips, and it felt *so nice* to be around that many unapologetically black queer and lesbian people in the tight quarters of Tantrum, where the party was hosted. The party and the people within it were largely new to me, and the process of entering the space reminded me of all the feelings and energies and hard work that it took to build my queer nightlife community when I first arrived in Chicago in 2008. This many years later, when I thought (and continue to think) of myself as a nightlife curmudgeon, E N E R G Y simply felt *fun*.

For all the ways that E N E R G Y reminded me of the value of simply partying without expectation, the party was just too good to pass up and I decided to make it one of my field sites. I continued to travel to Chicago to attend E N E R G Y and interview its organizers and attendees, and to try to remain connected to the city, parties, and interlocutors that I had developed relationships with over the previous decade. With that came the physically, mentally, and administratively taxing elements of long-term research endeavors. The travel wore me down and strained my finances, but when I wasn't in Chicago or at E N E R G Y I agonized that I was a "bad" researcher who wasn't committed enough to my project. I fretted that I wasn't adequately organizing my life and responsibilities to prioritize my research. I worried about whether I was sufficiently maintaining ties in Chicago, stressed that I wasn't on the ground, tracking the minute changes that can transform a party, or a city, seemingly overnight.

These anxieties, and the already-existing exhaustion they intensified, continued even when I *was* in Chicago to conduct research. E N E R G Y opened me to entirely different groups of people than those who'd been circulating through the scenes that I was already embedded in. Each interview I scheduled felt undermined by my anxiety about all of the interviews I could have (should have??) been getting with the innumerable amount of black queer women at any given E N E R G Y party as well as people I saw on the train, who walked past in my neighborhood, who I swiped on Tinder, who I saw on my Instagram explore page, etc. etc. etc. etc. etc. I was coming across a wealth of new lives and new stories and felt a desire and urgency to do more and more, but I was nearing a decade of the various permutations of what would come to be this book and I had simply burned out.

The tedious, draining work of doing research on queer nightlife, let alone hosting or participating in queer nightlife events, shapes every inch of this book's interests in how, when, where, and why black queer women dance in Chicago. Black queer women of course get on the queer dance floor to have fun and to feel good. It is also an intensely political space where they enact rigorous, detailed theories about the relationships between movement and feeling in a city that is entirely draining and on dance floors that are seemingly always threatened by many kinds of violence. This violence is rarely enough to stop the dancing, though. *Feels Right* looks at the queer dance floor through routine and spectacular moments of distress and discomfort so that we might take black queer women seriously as complex beings who adroitly navigate bad feelings and disagreement, and who do so in the pursuit of complex black queer community. We watch, we judge, we desire, we throw shade, we take it out on one another, we scheme to see one another, we flirt, we grip up on one another, we daydream about one another—all in one continuum. We do this against all odds, as spaces for us dwindle, as life for us feels as perilous as ever. We find one another on the dance floor even if we don't acknowledge or talk to one another. We're all exhausted but we get on the dance floor because we love each other, in some way. We believe in one another that much, want to be around one another that much. We want more for one another *that much*.

"Community" does not simply appear by virtue of sharing a dance floor. Our returns to the queer dance floor evidence black queer community as a practice, inflected by continual failure, but where failure feels like an invitation to possibility—and where possibility drives us back to the dance floor time and again. Black queer community is not an end point but is felt in the experience of returning to the queer nightlife function time and again in order to see and be around people who look and feel like us and who look and feel like who and what we desire. Black queer community is felt in the shared orientation toward the possibility that we might soon feel right together. This book is written in the meantime, as we fuss and fight and struggle and strive. It is written with deep exhaustion and a heavy dose of pessimism but also with an uncommon (to me) optimism tethered to my need to feel right among people who can reflect myself back to me.

ACKNOWLEDGMENTS

Not sure I'll ever find the right words to shower my parents, Ann Dates, Tony Dates, and Bruce Peterson, and my brother, Alex Peterson, with love and gratitude, so I'm not even gonna try. Love to Aunt Stella Brown, who always understood exactly what I was doing in the academy; to Grandma Irene Miller, who was a refuge; and to my aunts and cousins who always make me laugh the hardest.

Big shout out to my all-time BFF Grace Phương Thảo Trần. Couldn't have done it without the groupchats: ATL4EVA (Kareem Khubchandani and Summer Kim Lee), Gaycation (Grace, Rachel Cole, Brigid Dunn, and Collier Meyerson), Pizza Coven (Grace, Katy Groves, Alexis Koran, and Morgan Thoryk), and Sankofa (AB Brown, Kareem, Chris Lloyd, Mbongeni N. Mtshali, and Nikki Yeboah). Will Rawls, you have the best jokes (now say it back). Let's break out the chips and rosé, Julia Freeman, Eris Freeman, Steven Miller, Molly Mac, and Matt Jones. Jed Murr and Liz Bokan, aren't Cancers so great? Radhika Govindrajan and Jayadev Athreya: text me when you read this. I'll let you pick the wine next time, Jasmine Mahmoud. Hi, Autumn Womack. Christine Goding has one of my favorite brains on the planet. I only see Eric William Carroll, Sam Cassidy, Peter Bartz-Gallagher, Tucker Gerrick, Leslie Hammons, Heather McKerrow, Ashley Ryan, and James Taylor once or twice year but you always fill me up. Nathan Holmes, you're in the endnotes! My Seattle would be nothing without Rezina Habtemariam, Kia Pierce, Khadija Tarver, and Moni Tep. Emily Bock, Ally Burque, Elizabeth Cronin, Margaret Macmillan Jones, Ashley Stull Meyers, David Perez, Marie Snyder, and Jeanine O'Toole: what can I say other than you have seen it all, in so many ways, over so many years. shawné michaelain holloway, I'm so glad you found me at the club.

Many thanks to the Department of Gender, Women & Sexuality Studies at the University of Washington for letting me develop my competitive spirit in conversation with a feminist ethics: Angela Ginorio, Michelle Habell-Pallán, Bettina Judd, Cricket Keating, Nancy J. Kenney, Young Kim, Regina Yung Lee, Laura H. Marquez, Whitney Miller, Priti Ramamurthy, Chandan Reddy, Catherine Richardson, Luana Ross, Amanda Lock Swarr, Celine Waldmann, Sasha Su-Ling Welland, and Shirley Yee. You're listed together here as my department but I'm grateful to say that *I also like you as friends.* Northwestern Performance Studies prepped me for this life and for this book. Thank you, especially, to Ramón Rivera-Servera, E. Patrick Johnson, and D. Soyini Madison. I've gotten much-needed mentorship on how to hustle (in) the academy from Gianna Mosser, C. Riley Snorton, Kyla Wazana Tompkins, and Emily Zimmerman. Thank you to my editor at Duke University Press, Elizabeth Ault, for getting it even before I did; to Ihsan Taylor for shepherding the book into production; and to Sherri Barnes for the index. The Center for LGBTQ Studies, Royalty Research Fund, Institute for Citizens & Scholars, Walter Chapin Simpson Center for the Humanities, and Dean Catherine Cole gave me money, time, and space to do my work. I learned how to be mentored and how to ask for support while in the Mellon Mays Undergraduate Fellowship at Macalester College. My high school psychology teacher, Lydia Fitzgerald, is the only reason I knew about Macalester. Without her help finding and applying to schools, I'm not sure I could have gotten this far.

The biggest, most important thank you goes out to everyone in this book. It is no small feat to live a black queer life, a black lesbian life, a black trans life, a black gender nonconforming life, a black nonbinary life, a black genderqueer life, a black kink life, a black femme life, a black stud life, a black closeted life—to feel all these things in one black lifetime. It is daunting to write for you, knowing that you're so much more than what's in those terms and in these pages. I hope that what I've done feels right to you.

INTRODUCTION

In 2013, I stepped outside of a crowded, high-end cocktail bar in Chicago's Logan Square neighborhood to take notes on the white twenty- and thirty-somethings who were dancing to the DJ's catalog of late 1990s and early 2000s rap, an era characterized by baggy jeans, oversized white T-shirts, and hard rhymes laced over melodic, danceable beats. The crowd practiced bright, playful dance styles remembered from middle and high school years listening to Big Tymers, Outkast, St. Lunatics, No Limit Records, and Swishahouse Records on Top 40 radio stations, the regional inflections of Houston, Atlanta, New Orleans, and other black cities having a massive impact on popular culture nationwide. The night's black entertainment was increasingly common in this gentrifying neighborhood that young, white, upwardly mobile people were flooding to for its low rents, solid housing stock, accessible public transportation, and growing service industry. I was in the midst of taking notes on how black aesthetics shape the physical and social choreographies of such white, gentrifying city space when the DJ suddenly rushed out onto the sidewalk, breathless and frenzied as he explained to me that he had been in the middle of his set when

this black girl comes up on stage and starts scrolling through my iTunes and I'm like *Naaaaaw you can't do that* and she says, *All the music you're playing is about N-words and I'm the only N-word in here*, and then she POURED her drink on the mixer and ruined it! The whole room just STOPPED.[1]

When This Black Girl poured her drink onto the mixer, the music shorted out and the crowd immediately stopped dancing, confused by the abrupt sonic shift in the space but also suddenly attuned to the fracas brewing on stage. Bar staff rushed to physically remove This Black Girl from the stage, and in my note-taking I had missed her as she ran past me and jumped into a taxi. An hour later the bar was still buzzing from the drama. Crowded around someone's cell phone, bar staff tracked This Black Girl's activity on Facebook, where she referred to the event in a post, writing . . . *so I poured my very expensive cocktail on their very expensive mixer and am headed back to the South Side*. With that, This Black Girl physically and digitally absconded to the South Side, a conglomeration of neighborhoods south of Chicago's downtown area with a historically large black population, where she would, presumably, not be followed and where she was, potentially, landing in a space where the sound of hip-hop is more racially and ethically engaged.[2] She deleted her profile half an hour later.

In taking the stage to announce that it was improper for a crowd of white people to listen and dance to music that she had an authority over (an assertion she boiled down to the complicated utterance of the word *nigger*), This Black Girl called for people to be accountable to where they were in their dancing bodies, in this neighborhood bar, and in the city of Chicago writ large. Her intervention pointed specifically to how taking pleasure in black aesthetics in that bar was only possible through a conditional proximity to blackness: that the multiple forms of spatial, financial, cultural, and social value white dancers gained from reveling in the all-consuming black aesthetics that night was only possible because of the presumed absence of live black people therein. Indeed, the blackness that aestheticizes the pleasure economies of the gentrifying neighborhoods like Logan Square is often produced in direct proportion to the forcible removal of actual black people from them.[3] This Black Girl's protest against using black aesthetics in a neighborhood with a historically small black population (<7 percent) was framed by the broader push to expel working-class black people from the region. Her protest threw into further relief how gentrification was steadily displacing white ethnic communities who had long called the neighborhood home and the Puerto Rican communities who moved there in the 1970s and '80s after they were priced out of the adjacent Wicker Park neighborhood to the southeast.[4] Just under five miles southeast from Logan Square, the last of the Cabrini-Green Homes, a sixty-nine-year-old public housing complex home to a majority-black population, was demolished by 2011 to make way for an encroaching commercial corridor that is anchored by an Apple Store, an Apple-owned Chicago Transit Authority train station, as well as a Crate & Barrel *and* a CB2. The complex of seventy-eight low-lying rowhouses and massive towers was dogged by poverty, aggressive policing, and infrastructural decay and deterioration and was slated to be replaced by new, mixed-income housing that residents could apply to live in. As each building was razed, however, residents were given residential vouchers and dispersed to other areas of the city and suburbs. High-end condominiums were built across the street from the demolition site that was itself rather efficiently turned into a Target—no more housing, mixed- or low-income, has graced the lot.[5] The Julia C. Lathrop Homes public housing complex just east from Logan Square and north of the gentrified Wicker Park neighborhood faced similar circumstances. The units that long housed black, Puerto Rican, and immigrant families have been emptied through eviction and the complex has been redeveloped for mixed commercial use as well as market-rate and affordable housing—all on a property being developed to contain a river walk that will transform the landscape and raise property values. The changes in mixed- and low-income housing availability throughout the area have been further accompanied by shuttered social services like physical and mental health facilities, which have been replaced by ventures looking to take advantage of people's desires to buy food, drinks, and entertainment.

This Black Girl was not merely connecting the visible demographics of the room to the spatial politics of the broader city, though. She effected an entire, haptic reorganization of the space. She ruined the mechanics of sound production to halt all movement, disrupting the circulation of black aesthetics that were booming through the sound system and directly (re)shaping the physical and social choreographies of the white crowd. Her deeply performative critique was accompanied by a decrial of the literal cost of participating in this milieu (. . . *so I poured my very expensive cocktail on their very expensive mixer and am headed back to the South Side*). This Black Girl's active upheaval of the racialized network of music, movement, and feeling in Logan Square, and her subsequent flight to the presumed safety and reassurance of the South Side, mapped the raced and classed assumptions of how people move through certain kinds of city spaces. As she questioned not only *how* blackness moves us but *where*, she charted the racialized spatialized parameters around who is presumed to feel good in the neoliberal city.

Feels Right is interested in moments such as this that reveal how race and feeling are entangled with the geography of the neoliberal city and strives to document black queer women's incisive interrogations of these entanglements. In the Chicago neighborhoods that this book focuses on, private investments meant to wrench ever more value out of land, housing stock, and commercial, retail, and service economies are rationalized as providing people more opportunities to live easy, happy, healthy lives in areas full of stable housing, safe drinking water, abundant food, access to public transportation or plenty of vehicle parking, and diverse entertainment options. The question, of course, is which people? The access to good feelings that supposedly comes from inhabiting and/or consuming such gentrifying terrain often obscures the devastating effects that neoliberal economic policies have on the city and the black and brown communities who occupy it. As This Black Girl made plain, nightlife scenes serve as intensely political grounds upon which the dynamics of feeling—and feeling good, in particular—are inextricable from the racialized spatiality of these gentrifying neighborhoods and Chicago more broadly. In each chapter of *Feels Right*, we see how black queer women's practices of inhabiting queer dance floors pose similarly trenchant theorizations and palpable reconfigurations of how the city's neoliberal governance is an explicitly racialized regime of territorializing feeling and feeling good.

The book follows black queer women dancing through Logan Square, Hyde Park, and the South Loop, neighborhoods where economic and cultural capital has been concentrated in zones of (speculative) profitability to give wealthier, and often whiter, people many opportunities to simply feel good. It focuses on black queer women's movements in the small number of queer dance parties in these neighborhoods: how they get on the dance floor, move alone and with one another, hype up one another, sing along to the music, dance in playful competition, and dance to flirt and hook up. The queer dance party is not always an entirely pleasurable affair, however. Black queer women make a myriad of decisions to stop dancing because they're tired, to dance differently because they're receiving unwanted attention, or to get off the dance floor altogether because it's just not *right*. Their capacities to experience pleasure in any given party, bar, or neighborhood are seemingly always grounded by the difficulties of forging black queer life in a city that severely (and often violently) restricts their physical and affective capacities.

4

Black queer women's deft navigations of the dance floor are thus demonstrations of how they (re)shape a party's people, music, movement, and feeling to suit their immediate needs. The dance floor also serves as a site where they (re)theorize, (re)organize, and (re)narrate their relationships to the systems of neoliberalism that shape and overdetermine their lives once the function is over. For example, chapter 1 explores how, at Slo 'Mo: Slow Jams for Homos and Their Fans, in Logan Square, black queer women wield the pleasures of slow dance movements to contest the logics of acceleration and accumulation that define the neighborhood and the city, framing slowness as a distinctly black queer method of taking pleasure in sites bent on the rapid removal of black queer life. Chapter 2 examines how black queer women negotiate the choreographies of Black Joy at Party Noire, in Hyde Park, as they come to believe the party's deployment of such a racialized affect capitulates to the middle-class blackness of the neighborhood's gentrifying downtown core—which is set distinctly apart from the negative affects that shape the black geographies that surround the neighborhood.

Feels Right refuses the urge to narrativize black queer (night)life as a utopian outlet from neoliberal rule. Dance is ultimately a critical language through which black queer women articulate their spatial, embodied, and affective stakes of occupying neoliberal city space, and it is also a tool with which they imagine and enact black queer community in its midst—and both processes can seem impossibly difficult, look ugly, and simply feel terrible. However interested in pleasure this book is, it cannot avoid how utterly draining it is to throw, DJ, and attend queer nightlife parties. That's why *Feels Right* is full of frustration and disaffection. It's meant to reflect how good feeling is only ever temporary, if it arrives at all, amid the myriad of buzzkills that shape the queer party, whether they be bad music, whiteness, arguments between attendees and organizers, corporate greed, neoliberal capitalism, or just bad vibes. The stories of black queer women in this book circle far beyond the realm of good feelings to offer important insights into other, seemingly minor, sensorial registers through which black queer life is experienced. They are stories about the tedious stressors of going out into the night; of the dullness and boredom that can pervade the dance floor; of the frustration, failed expectations, and frequent disillusionment that can surround the queer dance floor and the black queer community it can only ever temporarily consolidate. The potentially productive outcomes of thinking with these lessor affects of queer nightlife come to a head in chapter 3 on E N E R G Y: A Party for Women + Their Buddies, held in the overdeveloped South Loop neighborhood. There, I consider how the extraordinary uneventfulness of E N E R G Y might help us take seriously other affective registers through which we might approach the doing (and the study) of black queer life in the neoliberal city. The burnout and exhaustion that circle the edges of each of this book's chapters—and that is perhaps the defining characteristic of life under neoliberalism, black, queer, and otherwise—comes full circle in the conclusion when the strain of using nightlife to build black queer community-building intensifies.

Feels Right continually complicates our hopes for and expectations that life at night, on the queer dance floor, or among black queer community simply "feels good." Of course, the goal of (queer) nightlife is largely to feel good and each chapter is ultimately organized around black queer women's efforts to secure good feelings at individual parties. Yet "feeling good" is seemingly always elusive in Chicago's queer nightlife spaces. I subsequently work to destabilize feeling good as a solid, achievable end point by holding it in tension with that much more difficult territory of feeling *right*: those hard-to-pin-down sensoria signaling that everything has clicked together. "Good" can be an unreliable shorthand because of the ways that it is subjective (one person's "good" night might look like hours of drunken debauchery to another). This is not to say that "right" is particularly objective. Indeed, "right" may certainly encompass "good"; the two flow in and out of each other. Something can feel right and also feel good, something that feels good can also feel right; something that feels right can feel far from good, something that feels good can feel far from right.

It is important to linger in the difficulty of defining and describing the messy lines between and across feeling "good" and "right" because black queer women themselves continually toggle between the two. People like Tracy narrate their relationships in and to queer nightlife, black queer community, and Chicago itself through the productively impossible matrix of feeling itself: a risky enterprise of agreeing that community or belonging has been registered not only because something feels good but because, when a constellation of effects sync up, it *feels right*. Tracy is in her thirties and has gone through several evolutions of partying within and beyond queer spaces. She finds herself aging into a new set of desires for her queer nightlife experiences and is especially interested in slower-tempo gatherings of smaller groups of people. As she explains what the composition of her ideal night might look like, she articulates the complex sensoria found throughout the book: "Everything is vibration," she explains. "The energy in a room, if it doesn't feel good, it doesn't feel good vibrationally. For me right now, if it's not a vibrational match I don't do it." Here, Tracy connects the potential for good feeling to "vibration," which requires a kind of focus and intention to read and interpret. Assessing vibrations requires an acute sense of one's own body and energy, as well as those of the people and objects in proximity. The emphasis is not on the individual enterprise of feeling good but on the cohesion between a personal investment in one's feelings and the holistic environment that makes such feelings possible.

Following Tracy, the framework of feeling right offers a closer, kinesthetic look at the interlocking systems that situate us in our bodies, among other people, and within the built environments that structure our movements *and* our energies. This book mobilizes the language of feeling right in order to continually account for the relational paradigms in which feeling, writ large, is produced in the queer nightlife party. There, something feels right when your vibrations are gelling with the room, as Tracy explains. A moment feels right when your improvisatory dance movements are sequenced in a way that sets you on a sustainable flow. It happens when everyone on the dance floor syncs up in shared gestures, that rush of bliss when everything clicks together, and it can last for only a few moments or the span of a whole song or a multihour set. Something like *feels right* emerges when you feel linked up to the energy (good or bad) of another person, held close on the dance floor or spotted across the room, and you feel that wave of "this moment could only happen right now right here because of *this* party." Issa vibe.

The search for feeling right on the queer dance floor always overlaps with efforts to feel emplaced in Chicago, where access to feeling right and access to legal rights are entangled and circumscribed by neoliberal spatial politics that overdetermine where black queer people go and how they feel. The city delimits where black queer women can and should take place and continually and violently strips the affective complexity of black (queer) life in the city. Blackness is produced as a disembodied aesthetic to be pleasurably consumed or it is a fully enfleshed terror, a scourge of the landscape. In turn, black queer women understand complex feeling as a right in and of itself that they should be afforded in the city; feeling good, feeling right, and the right to simply feel become things that they seek to possess as demonstrations of their right to take place in Chicago. Every time the black queer women who populate this book go out dancing, then, they actively embody and theorize the relationships between feeling and rights to the city and, in turn, feeling as an intense terrain upon which the formations of black queer community in the neoliberal city have to be staged.

THE NEOLIBERAL CITY MAKES EVERYTHING
HARD FOR BLACK QUEER WOMEN

Under neoliberalism, people, feeling, and landscapes are knitted together as the value of financial profit is bound to the accumulation of *certain kinds* of good feeling for *certain kinds* of people in *certain kinds* of places. Neoliberalism is a system of economic policies and political imperatives that solidified in the 1970s as governments and corporations colluded to produce an allegedly free market, which they did primarily through asset stripping, where publicly held goods and services are turned over to private corporations to own and operate.[6] Government oversight of institutions meant to serve the public good (such as public housing, education initiatives such as Head Start, free breakfast and lunch programs, healthcare programs such as Medicare and Medicaid, and job training programs) is scaled back and often contracted to private entities to manage, and government oversight of corporate industries is scaled back. Neoliberal economic policies that prioritize privatization often drastically reshape the social life of the city but also the physical landscape; zoning, taxation, and property laws that are meant to cultivate and protect people's abilities to secure resources for themselves give way to big business interests and multinational corporate investment. In Logan Square, where this book opened, the purchase and rental costs of the many two- to four-story buildings in the neighborhood have increased, pricing out longtime residents, at the same time that tax incentives reward private developers for building taller and taller, high-density buildings that stack increasingly wealthy people into expensive apartments sitting atop commercial space.

As neighborhoods and cities orient toward the kinds of private, corporate investment endeavors that traffic in economic profit—those that raise rents and property values, and encourage the influx of money laundered through service and creative industries—the use of service, arts, and cultural economies to produce "good" feelings also becomes good business. The chapters detailing the Slo 'Mo and Party Noire parties, for example, detail how private investments in the neighborhoods' housing and commercial stock in Logan Square and Hyde Park, respectively, have been accompanied by an influx of bars, restaurants, and retail that further transform the demographic and cultural milieu of the neighborhood. Developments aimed at incubating good feelings in the neoliberal city are often made possible only by removing certain people to the margins of the city's zones of profitability, especially low-income people, immigrants, black and brown people, and people who rely upon government support for employment, housing, education, healthcare, and food.

Neil Smith posits that neoliberal policies, particularly those that gentrify neighborhoods, should be understood as an explicit revenge plot against minoritarian subjects.[7] What he describes as the "revanchist city" reacts "against the basic assumption of liberal urban policy—namely, that government bears some responsibility for ensuring a decent minimum level of daily life for everyone. That political assumption is now largely replaced by a vendetta against the most oppressed," criminalizing people and behaviors that are seen to undermine the status and stability of the white middle class and get in the way of profit-minded development.[8] In using terms like *revenge* and *vendetta* to describe how neoliberalism operates, Smith offers important reminders that economic processes are not passive whims of the market but are produced and maintained through the active collusion of policy-makers, city managers, corporations, developers, think tanks, the police, and academics. Martin Manalansan similarly argues that neoliberalism is not a natural, organic, or inevitable transformation of capital but is in fact the result of people who make decisions about the status and capacities of people, neighborhoods, and the broader landscape that contains them. He argues that we use the more specific term "neoliberal governance" in order to underscore how such an active (and violent) process of resource extraction and management operates by rendering some people and places as "unprofitable" and needing to be "cleaned up."[9] To this end, throughout this book I use "neoliberalism" to refer to systems of economic and political policies and I use "neoliberal governance" to point to the ways that these policies directly and indirectly shape how we see, think and feel about, and move through our surroundings.

The economic and political imperatives of neoliberalism's assault on the most oppressed is just an intensification of Chicago's long-standing practices of gluing black people to increasingly disinvested areas of the city.[10] In twentieth-century Chicago, black enclaves were razed almost overnight to make way for the cosmopolitan image of what would become the downtown commercial core, The Loop. Scrubbing seemingly unprofitable black life from the speculated profitability of The Loop resulted in black neighborhoods on the city's south and west sides, which were maintained through the legalized segregation of restrictive housing covenants that prevented black people from moving *out* of these neighborhoods.[11] Many of the two dozen people interviewed for this book come from lower-, working-, and middle-class families who continue to live in these neighborhoods, including South Shore, Englewood, and Bronzeville. The racist aims and undertones of the revanchist city were evident across the United States throughout the 1950s to the 1990s as restrictive covenants that secured hundreds of years of state-sanctioned segregation were ignored, loosened, or struck down. In response to black people gaining slightly more choice in where to live, massive amounts of white people moved out of urban cores and into what would become the nation's first- and second-ring suburbs. This "white flight" was articulated through racist narratives that incoming black people were invading and wreaking havoc on white neighborhoods, ruining neighborhoods and driving down housing values. These narratives were enforced by an increasing, and increasingly violent, police presence in black neighborhoods; the defunding of social services, education, and job opportunities in black neighborhoods; and the construction and poor management of large and environmentally toxic public housing complexes that, all together, created a fine line between black life and death.[12] The collapse of the housing bubble beginning in 2007 and the related subprime mortgage crisis exacerbated ongoing struggles that black people faced in these neighborhoods, further indebting them or wiping out their abilities to stay out of debt, to keep their homes, and to transfer homes to family members in an effort to retain a modicum of generational wealth.[13] The rental markets within and beyond these neighborhoods remain fraught with unsafe housing structures, lead in the water, and absentee landlords and often have access only to subpar public school outlets, grocery stores, and public transportation options.

In light of this, for black queer women, questions of who gets to feel right in this difficult city are always entangled with questions of who gets to simply stay *alive* within its bounds. Throughout my time living in Chicago and researching and writing this book, the city's black communities dealt with brutal, unchecked police violence, undue surveillance by neighborhood associations, school closures, gun violence, and a fractured political system, just as the nation largely ignored the systematic murder of black and brown trans and gender nonconforming people nationwide—people's whose bodies and stories feel close to home for many of the people and communities discussed in this book. As LJ explains, "Any time I step out of this house, I'm going to be treated like I'm fucking invisible. Or I'm going to be hypervisible and it's going to be violent. . . . There's no way to describe black, queer existence without violence. And there's no way to define it without violence and displacement." For LJ, who has experienced houselessness, the violence of displacement is literal and they also gesture toward the widespread precarity that can come with living black queer life more generally. Their reflections speak to the experiences of other black queers in this book who are navigating the challenges of living black queer lives. Some have incarcerated parents and others occasionally deal drugs to maintain a basic quality of life for themselves and family members who they are formally and informally responsible for. Several of the people in this book have experienced or are currently experiencing violently upended social worlds as the result of their coming out, often leaving familial homes, forcibly and otherwise, and living in the wake of such turmoil. Black queer women's lives can be deeply stressful as they contend with regular, ongoing, state-sanctioned violence while navigating overlapping recessions, transitioning between cities, houses, jobs, and post-secondary education to try to secure resources, often saddled by various forms of debt.

The queer dance floor is not an apolitical site in these conditions. Black queer women's continued insistence on traveling the city to come together in gentrifying milieus in order to move and feel in shared space undermines ongoing efforts to contain racial and sexual "minorities" to particular, and particularly enclosed, regions of the city. The dance floor is just one of the highly contested zones where black queer women directly implicate their bodies as they assert their physical rights within and over the neoliberal city.[14] This is no small feat, to be sure. As Jasmine explains, "It's so hard to find space in the world that is made for black people, specifically black women. More specifically, queer black women, even in a smaller sense. The spaces get more and more limited, the platforms get more and more limited, the opportunities and everything." There are in fact few public social spaces— bars, nightclubs, event spaces, and the like—that are explicitly dedicated to queer women, black or otherwise, in Chicago and the United States more broadly. Indeed, much of the extremely small body of literature concerning black queer women has highlighted the importance of private homes to the formation of community.[15] The historical barriers to building ownership that black LGBTQ people, in particular, face contribute to the ongoing absence of something we might describe as a "black queer women's bar" in Chicago. The diminishing number of bars serving queer and lesbian women nationwide amid the proliferation of bars serving gay men speaks volumes about the ways that women have been historically marginalized in the public sphere and about the ways that the figure of the lesbian is not linked to the kinds of financial profitability or political sustainability that has been attached to gay male subjects.[16]

The economic, physical, and affective domains of black LGBTQ life have long been targets for removal to make way for spaces of convergence that generate profit and good feeling for white, upwardly mobile, heterosexual populations.[17] This was especially evident in the 1980s and 1990s, when zoning, tax, and police enforcement shut down sex districts in order to build New York's Times Square. The piers were cleared in Boystown, Chicago; Key West, Florida; and Chelsea, New York. There was at the same time more surveillance in the parks, alleyways, and corners that people used for intimate cover, and it became ever more expensive to open and maintain privately owned bars serving LGBTQ people who had been displaced from those sites.[18] These crackdowns on the very juncture of sexuality, feeling, and place identify and criminalize queer modes of connection that are not properly profitable within the capitalist logic of reproduction.

As capitalism is wont to do, some aspects of gay and lesbian cultures are absorbed and lionized as demonstrations of "good" neoliberal governance, perhaps most evident in the consecration of "gayborhoods" that encourage people to consume housing, commercial, service, and entertainment resources under the literal and metaphorical banner of LGBTQ pride.[19] One gayborhood on the North Side of Chicago, Boystown, part of the Lakeview neighborhood, has played an outsized role in black queer women's imaginations of queer life in Chicago. The symbolism of a sanctioned neighborhood where LGBTQ people live, work, and play together plays an important role in black queer women's searches for sense of self and community in Chicago. But Boystown has never felt quite *right* to black queer women. Professor-wrecks, a DJ in their twenties, gestures to the gulf between the image-ideal of Boystown and the material realities of circulating through its bar and nightclub scene:

> You grow up here as a queer kid and Boystown just is like the most visible space that people would see for anything gay. So that was just like, "I'm young, I'm in college, I can do whatever the hell I want. Let's move to Boystown!" without actually having that experience of, like, "What is it like to live in Boystown?"

For most black queer women in this book, the answer to the question is a resounding "horrible," colored by experiences of cis gay men's extreme inebriation and racism. Candace, in her late twenties, occasioned Boystown when she first moved to Chicago, often tagging along with an out, gay family member. As she found her own tribe in the city, though, she went less and less—especially as she became less and less interested in drinking. "When you go to Boystown," Candace explains, "you get hammered, you know what I'm saying?" Tess, 22, is just one year into legally drinking and some parts of the Boystown scene are appealing to her because "you know you're gonna have fun." The drunkenness is, however, on another level. "You get that everywhere, but in Boystown, it's just like, *come on*. There's always somebody throwing up, always. I've never been and somebody didn't throw up, or somebody being, like, step all over me or be leaning on you. I hate that. I hate that. I hate that." For Tess, Boystown's drinking culture is inextricable from the neighborhood's whiteness: the drunkenness and what she saw as simply bad dancing "was expected simply because being in white spaces, white people don't care as much as black people do. They don't care about nothing. If you come in there clothes-less, they don't care. You go that type to a black space and it's like, 'What you doing?'"

The nexus of intoxication, whiteness, cis men, and racism pushed Austin over the edge and they stopped going to Boystown altogether. Austin is in their early twenties and grew up in a black community on the city's South Side. As they came of age, they spent time in Boystown as they were learning the ropes of their adult black queer life in the city. "I stopped partying there but I actually went sometime last year and we had a bad experience. This white dude was trying to touch my friend's hair and we were uncomfortable. And I've outgrown the music too, it's whitewashed house music." While black queer people's personal preferences in music, socializing, and intoxication certainly shape their approaches to Boystown, their experiences of the neighborhood—and their decisions to stop frequenting it—are almost always shaped by their exhaustion with having to experience racist interactions therein. Many are like Erica, who puts it plainly: "I don't go out in Boystown at *all*. No. It's just, it's no, no, not at all."

Indeed, individual locations and neighborhoods that have been designated as "safe spaces" for LGBTQ people are rife with the same racism, sexism, misogyny, homophobia, and ableism that have long scripted neoliberal governance.[20] As Christina Hanhardt documents, the revanchist policies of the neoliberal city that demonize low-income people, people of color, and people with insecure housing have also been (inadvertently and not) espoused by lesbian and gay activists in their efforts to establish safe neighborhoods.[21] And because the spatial protocols that structure gayborhoods are also inextricably capitalist, sites like Boystown are subject to ongoing efforts to concentrate and control profit. Individuals, city councils, and neighborhood watch crusaders systematically police people—often black and brown youth, in particular—who do not directly contribute to the accumulation of wealth in neighborhoods like Boystown, variously alleging these people do not contribute to the neighborhood's housing market, do not pay entry fees and bar tabs in the service industry, and/or do not properly engage with the retail and commercial offerings of the gayborhood.[22]

The racialized territorialization of feeling occurs at the scale of the gayborhood and at the smaller scale of the individual gay bar, where the black queer women in this book regularly face overt and covert discrimination. Ca$h Era, who DJs throughout the city, points to the spring 2019 controversy that surrounded Progress Bar in Boystown, where many if not most of the black queer women in this book first encountered other black queer women and a broader black queer community. A leaked email revealed that bar management implemented a new "no rap" policy, a move that many saw as targeting the bar's black clientele. "Now," Ca$h laments, "the [black queer women's] scene is missing that again because I feel like, with Progress Bar doing that bullshit where they don't want hip-hop music to play anymore, you just had a whole bunch of people of color who are queer displaced. Whereas, like, anybody else who isn't queer gets to go to Boystown *any night*. Friday or Saturday, it doesn't matter: you can party." In this moment, Ca$h reflects on the multiple tensions that circumscribe Boystown and many gayborhoods like it: the racism and antiblackness of the gayborhood not only serves to protect the interests of nonblack LGBTQ attendees but also, significantly, heterosexual people.

Ca$h's comments underscore how, seemingly without fail, black queer women never quite feel right in gayborhoods like Boystown nor within the myriad of neoliberal spaces that frame and contextualize them. There are a variety of implicit and explicit policies that make it supremely difficult for black queer women to take place in, let alone feel right in, the neoliberal city. Their cultural, sartorial, embodied, and affective desires are suspect and their very presence is punishable by everyone from city officials to bar managers. In a dissertation concerned with black queer women's relationships to property ownership, which is to say, black queer women's abilities to sustainably take place in the neoliberal city, Sa Whitley writes, "Under the regime of neoliberal capitalism, the state and the financial industry *zone* black women for dispossession, displacement, and discipline."[23] The ways black queer women are zoned for punishing exclusion reinforce the presumption that they are not and should not be in the scenes and spaces that mark the neoliberal city. As Katherine McKittrick writes in a by-now canonical quote, "If *who* we see is tied up with *where* we see through truthful, commonsensical narratives, then the placement of subaltern bodies deceptively hardens spatial binaries, in turn suggesting that some bodies belong, some bodies do not belong, and some bodies are out of place."[24] The frameworks that McKittrick and Whitley use to understand black queer women's spatial geographies of dispossession are laced with affective meanings that figure them as always in excess to the neoliberal city: their ways of acting and feeling are not appropriate in gay bars or within or around larger gayborhoods like Boystown.[25] Progress Bar's refusal to play historically black musical genres in fact reflects and feeds into other, differently violent methods of regulating how and where black queer women take up city space. In 2006, a group of black lesbians traveled from New Jersey to hang out in Manhattan's Greenwich Village, long a haven of LGBTQ life. There, they got into a fight with a black man who used homophobic slurs to catcall, antagonize, and ultimately instigate a physical altercation that resulted in him receiving a nonfatal stab wound. Variously dubbed Killer Lesbians, a Lesbian Gang, and The New Jersey 4, they received between three and a half and eleven years in prison—sentencing that literalizes the incommensurability of black queer women's lives with the protocols of neoliberal governance.[26]

SOME PLACES WHERE BLACK QUEER WOMEN MIGHT FEEL RIGHT, THOUGH

Despite the risks, black queer women often desire to engage with varied options that parts of the neoliberal city can offer, be it capitalizing on the cultural milieu of the gayborhood or the housing and service economies of the gentrifying neighborhood. Serena lives in the Kenwood neighborhood on the South Side but regularly makes the thirteen-mile trek to Logan Square and braves the overwhelmingly white crowds to partake in the neighborhood's many bars and restaurants and to find black queer community at Slo 'Mo. "I might be going up North for the good cocktail, but as long as I got my people with me, I'm good." For Serena, consuming the gentrifying neighborhood has to be done with a critical mass of other black queer women who simultaneously act as a shield against unwanted white attention and a bubble in which she can fully inhabit a black queer space. She, not unlike This Black Girl, fully participates in the cultural economies of gentrification but in ways that critically engage the modes of racialized consumption that define how neoliberal city space is valued and inhabited. Their participation in, yet trenchant, embodied critiques of, the gentrifying neighborhood and larger city secure rights to feeling in what Kafui Attoh might call "strategically fuzzy" ways: they continually choose to participate in the consumptive practices of the neoliberal city, those that can feel *so* good, just as they interrupt, manage, and redirect the racialized territorialization of feeling in the neoliberal city toward the production of a sustainable black queer community in its midst.[27]

This book pays particular attention to three sites in which black queer women strategically forge black queer space in the midst of the neoliberal city that severely regulates their modes of thinking, moving, and feeling. These parties are part of a constellation of a diverse black queer women's scene that includes private homes and public engagements like sporting events; organizations like Affinity Community Services, which serves black LGBTQ+ people; bars like the Jeffery Pub and Club Escape, black LGBTQ bars in the South Shore neighborhood; itinerate parties on the North Side hosted by the now-defunct Chances Dances organization and LesbiFriends Cartel; and sometimes the handful of lesbian, queer, and "ladies night" parties that individual promoters host in more traditional nightclubs throughout the city.[28] The first party of focus, Slo 'Mo: Slow Jams for Homos and Their Fans, is a free, monthly event at The Whistler bar in Logan Square. The second, Party Noire, is not on a firmly set schedule but is held about once a quarter at the Promontory in Hyde Park, near the University of Chicago on the city's South Side. Party Noire is the only ticketed party in the book, though they offer cheaper tickets for people who purchase early, and they offer tickets priced on a sliding scale. The third party is E N E R G Y: A Party for Women + Their Buddies, a free party that is hosted every Sunday at Tantrum—the only black-owned venue in this book—in the South Loop.[29]

Feels Right is interested in the massive amount of labor that goes into creating black queer community on and through the dance floor. As discussed throughout the chapters, the party organizers and DJs are ultimately freelancers who not only throw the three events this book focuses on but host ancillary, related events (sometimes for pay) and often work full-time jobs (either at single locations or, more often, gigs that they cobble together). They are able, in other words, to host free events because of the paid labor that they do above and beyond their party organizing. Party attendees themselves put in a lot of work to party. Indeed, the politics of the black queer dance floor—and the political importance of the black queer dance floor—are embodied in black queer women's commitments to showing up and doing the fiscal, administrative, creative, and energetic work it takes to sustain a regular party. It costs time, money, and energy for attendees themselves to be out at night, whether it's once a year, once every few months, every month, or, for the brave regulars at E N E R G Y, every *week*. They plan their work schedules and family duties around attending these parties. They budget time to drive or use public transportation to get to the parties, money to buy tickets and to be able to afford the sometimes costly drinks at the bar, and energy to simply stay out late at night. The tedious work of getting to the function is rewarded when black queer women can revel in transformative senses of self and community.

When Ayana came out to her religious family and community, she couldn't stay home and was deep in the painful but hopeful process of transitioning into new ways of living when we met. She had just turned twenty-one and was coming into her own on queer dance floors. "It's like this is my time to release, to be myself and just breathe instead of what I usually go through during the week." When an opportunity to party comes around,

I don't know, it's like I call it the ratchetness in me just needs to get out, because during the week I'm, "Yes, oh my God, these are the reports, this is what I'm doing today." And it's just like "Oh, OK, now it's the weekend: I just want to be ratchet, I just want to be myself, I want to be black and carefree, just shake ass somewhere."

The queer parties in this book provide people like Ayana space to shake ass in a community with people who don't require her to define, explain, or defend herself. The work that is "done in the dark of the club," Jafari Allen reminds us, is a "reminder of selfhood for those whose historical (and paradigmatic) experience is precisely and uniquely marked by expropriated labor in chattel slavery, in which Black bodies were (are) not owned by those who inhabit them."[30] On the queer dance floor, black queer women stake claims to their own bodies and to the senses of community that they forge in the process of dancing—however temporary the senses of ownership and belonging may be. Allen quotes Bernice Johnson Reagon in telling us that the nightlife space is "sacred territory . . . the only way you know who you are sometimes has to do with what you can do when you go home from work, change clothes . . . and dance all night long."[31] Back queer women continue to pursue their queer nightlives despite the major and minor violence that can suffuse the neoliberal city, and they do so despite the ways that queer party spaces can be exhausting, intoxicated, fraught with conflict, and full of unsatisfied hopes for community and accountability. They continue to choose to put their bodies on the line and their vulnerabilities on display as they allow friends and strangers alike to see, smell, feel, move with, and at times taste one another because the parties in this book are often the only places that black queer women are able to *feel right* in their bodies and in the larger community.

Black queer women's shared practices of taking pleasure—of singing along to the music, watching people dance (and hyping them up), dancing themselves, and making platonic and sexual connections with one another—articulate their rights to occupy the landscapes of pleasure that the neoliberal city is organized around. But as black queer women move through neoliberal city spaces that are built around economies of pleasure, they also want and deserve access to the sets of feelings that are associated with these spaces. Their navigations of Slo 'Mo, Party Noire, and E N E R G Y further undermine the ways that neoliberal governance restricts black queer women's access to feeling in complex ways, "because we are able to," Jasmine deadpans. "And we have the right to adjust and have fun and enjoy ourselves in any space that we choose to walk into." Jasmine's concision highlights how black queer women see the constellation of sentiments that inhere in feeling, writ large, as valuable assets that are rights in and of themselves that they can and should be able to secure.

The right to feel good is a veritable political project that drives many black queer women to return to their nightlife scenes time and again, even as their pleasure is seemingly endlessly deferred on the dance floor and in the city. When they arrive at the parties, black queer women can still face the routine exclusions of the door, music, dress, and bathroom policies—despite the massive amounts of work that party organizers do to train venues in antidiscrimination practices. All kinds of administrative and emotional labor is expended in the major and minor conflicts that can suffuse the dance floor, from overly intoxicated attendees, to lovers' spats, to arguments over the music, to people dancing out of pocket (or not dancing at all), to criticism of party organizers, to anxieties about needy partygoers. Black queer women's negotiations of pleasure and conflict in these sites are further textured by the stress, anxiety, and uneasy, terrible, awful, painful feelings that they experience in their everyday lives. They have incarcerated parents, are surviving insecure housing, carry massive student loan debt, work multiple jobs (and are endlessly surrounded by white coworkers at those jobs). They take care of family, go to school, manage intimate relationships, and do all of this infused with the feelings of detachment, disaffection, disorientation, exhaustion, and other "bad" or ugly feelings, senses, sensations, and sentiments that are uniquely conditioned by the ways that neoliberal capitalism creates, depends on, and profits off of black queer women's precarity.[32]

Each chapter in *Feels Right* documents and contextualizes these conflicts in order to argue what should be a simple claim: that black queer women express the very ability to feel in complex ways, to feel beyond the limited binary of pleasure and terror that has long circumscribed black queer life, as a right in and of itself that they should be afforded. The conversations and conflicts that arise in their efforts to feel good on the dance floor are important staging grounds where they literally assert their complex physical but also affective rights to themselves, black queer community, the gentrifying neighborhood, and neoliberal Chicago itself. By putting their bodies on the line on the queer dance floor, black queer women not only imagine but actively construct environments where the spatial and psychic coordinates of black queer life in the larger neoliberal city might have more ethical and just arrangements.

THE FEELING PART OF RIGHTS TO THE CITY

Black queer women's orientations to the queer dance floor offer a way into much-needed analysis of embodiment to the question of rights that have been debated in the academy, in activist circles, and among urban planners and scholars of urban geography, especially those that engage Henri Lefebvre's discussions of what he called the right to the city.[33] Conceived in the late 1960s, Lefebvre's right to the city emerges from an anxiety over the transformation of urban life in the wake of capitalism's intensifying assault on industry, public space, housing, and radical thought alike. Subsequent conversations have generally conceived of the right to the city as access to the legal and economic means to shape how cities are governed and inhabited, especially for those who are most disenfranchised.[34] Insightful interventions into the largely class-based debates have focused on questions of race, gender, and sexuality and have forged important conversations about how minoritarian struggles around the right to the city are quite often struggles around civil rights.[35] Black queer women in Chicago are, for example, doing *immense* amounts of work around rights to the city. These efforts range from demanding accountability from the government and the police by activating marches and die-ins to protest the police cover-up of Laquan McDonald's murder to leading efforts to provide alternate social, cultural, and educational services to the city's black population through organizations such as Assata's Daughters and Black Youth Project 100.[36] Black queer women's political work approaches rights to the city as the combined effort to secure equal treatment under the law and to understand, imagine, and enact rights to senses of self and community that exceed formal, institutional structures.[37] Here, David Harvey's contributions to understandings of rights to the city are compelling for his suggestion that rights are more than issues of social and economic justice but necessarily encompass the question of desire.[38] For him, the right to the city is the right to determine and fundamentally reshape the forms and functions of urbanization,[39] but he understands that, under neoliberalism, this is not a right afforded to just anyone: one's right to the city is dependent upon the access and mobility that is conferred by property ownership, the security that is enabled by wealth accumulation, and is ultimately supported by "a neoliberal ethic of intense possessive individualism."[40] For Harvey, then, the effort to produce a more just city is a

> question of what kind of people we want to be, what kinds of social relations we seek, what relations to nature we cherish, what style of life we desire, what aesthetic values we hold. The right to the city is, therefore, far more than the right of individual or group access to the resources that the city embodies: *it is a right to change and reinvent the city more after our heart's desire.*[41]

This oft-quoted segment of Harvey's thinking underscores his investment in rights to the city as rooted in collective endeavors of the imagination and desire, and his language is useful for thinking about the multifaceted frameworks that black queer women use to identify their needs within the neoliberal city and advocate for themselves. As Bri explains, desire is perhaps *the* animating principle of black queer women's negotiations of rights, on and off the queer dance floor: "Desire to me is the only commonality that I see across all parties. There's desire to be accepted, a desire to see, and a desire to fulfill desire. And maybe desire to forget." Desire is the animating condition that brings black queer women like Bri to parties like Slo 'Mo, Party Noire, and E N E R G Y, and it is the root of their varied physical and affective entanglements on and off the dance floor—thus serving as an incredibly important root of many if not all of their struggles around rights to space and feeling within and beyond the party spaces.

But while Harvey invokes the powerful if ephemeral realms of imagination and desire in his conversation about rights to the city, he ultimately focuses on the mechanics of relatively organized movements such as the Occupy movement and landless rights movements that pair quality of life arguments with structural, economic ones. *Feels Right* refocuses the geographic scale of the conversation about rights away from such a systematized understanding of politics to look instead toward the informal actions of the dance floor, where the microgestures of the body and the language and practices of feeling serve as *the* terrain through which rights to the city are negotiated. Black queer women in Chicago are in fact quite suspicious of this formal political sphere, due in no small part to the well-known and widespread corruption of politics in Chicago. By 2018, a kind of state-wide political apathy had taken hold as newly elected Republican governor Bruce Rauner torpedoed the state's economy. The wealthy businessman-turned-politician faced a tall order trying to recover the state's financial status after Pat Quinn, accused of a corruption scandal wherein he misspent $55 million on a Chicago anti-violence program, had to take over from Rod Blagojevich, who was put in federal prison after trying to sell Barack Obama's senate seat. Troubles surround city politics as well. In 2011, Mayor Richard M. Daley, of the dynastic political family, closed his tenure by awarding a seventy-five-year, $1.15 billion contract that privatized the city's parking system before handing the reins over to Mayor Rahm Emanuel, who kicked off his first term by closing half of the city's mental health clinics and fifty public schools in efforts to privatize both.

For black queer women like Tracy, engaging with the formal political sphere is a futile affair because working within such a political system in order to change it assumes that government can or wants to change in the first place:

> It's hard for me to change the way people think I should change. "Go out and vote, do this!" That's not how I'm doing that. You can do that if that's what you want to do. You can play that game if you want to. I know that that's a game. I don't want to be a part of that game. I see that that game has never worked out for us. So, I don't want to play it.
>
> So, trying to fit the way I do things in this gimmicky scam of a fucking political structure, it demeans me. I don't feel safe. I don't feel secure. I don't feel right. I don't feel righteous about anything at all, because it's a setup. Now, the people that are in there working and doing what they can: more power to you. But it's not going to be right until you just tear the whole shit down. You got to tear it down from the root. It's just too fucked up. Honestly, there's no helping it. I mean, this whole tree is just spoiled. Do you understand what I'm saying?

Here, Tracy argues (not incorrectly) that the formal political sphere is a game that has been rigged against black people such as herself. This is not to say that she's *not* political, however. If we only look to formal, movement-based work as prime examples of how black queer women like Tracy advocate for their physical and affective rights to the city, we will lose sight of the mundane, everyday scenes in which they negotiate rights in the minutia of their everyday social interactions.[42]

Black queer women's navigations of the neoliberal city are not only or always signposted by, for example, overtly racist or homophobic events or marked expressions of institutional or state power. Their desires to make and remake themselves and the city are not solely crafted through formal, organizational responses to rampant deregulation, police violence, and incentivized privatization that constrict their abilities to pay rent and to be safe. Black queer women's practices of engaging with neoliberal governance are not always framed by or executed through formal political channels that are meant to provide people some control over how their cities are governed and inhabited, such as voting, calling upon their local aldermen, calling the police, signing petitions, or securing legal representation. Their experiences of navigating neoliberal governance are frequently shaped at the intimate registers of a conversation or dance movement, in that sharp awareness in the moment of seeing, as This Black Girl did, a crowd of white people take just a little too much pleasure in dancing to black music. Their political tactics are crafted in response to that one white guy who will not stop trying to dance with them when any given black rapper's music comes on or, as Austin describes dance floor dynamics in chapter 2, that "whole different feeling when it's a whole bunch of white people circling around you in a cypher, watching you, or literally saying, 'I like the way y'all dance.'"

Black queer women, in turn, conduct political work of negotiating their rights to the city every time they get on the queer dance floor and wield their entire sensorium as they directly implicate their own bodies and the bodies of those around them. In his ethnography of gay Indian nightlife cultures, Kareem Khubchandani explains that "queer dance at nightclubs and parties then is not merely an escape from politics, but a chance to revel inside them, letting power, meaning, bodies, aesthetics, and affects collide and find each other in new ways, inventing alternative realms to inhabit through sweat, sways, gestures, *jatkas*, and *matkas*, driven by the pursuit of beauty, sex, friendship, and intimacy."[43] Tracy may refuse to engage in the formal political sphere through practices such as voting but she asserts herself as a political being every time she decides to leave the house; she practices politics every time she steps onto the queer dance floor and, as we see in chapter 1, clears space for herself to take up space *as* black and queer. Certainly, black queer women strive to change and reinvent the city after their own hearts' desires, as Harvey writes; it just happens in perhaps less intelligible and codified, but no less powerful, ways of moving and feeling the body. Their struggles are not only over the right to physically take place in the city but to inhabit it on their own terms. It is a struggle over their physical *and* affective rights to the city.[44]

This was very much the case for This Black Girl. She did not solely lodge a formal complaint to, say, management that white people were taking too much pleasure in black music in the hopes of some form of administrative redress whereby the DJ or bar staff would, for example, change the music. She instead directly intervened into people's very abilities to absorb the hyperpalpable blackness that night and completely dismantled the conjoined kinesthetic processes and social choreographies that flowed from it. She destroyed the production of racialized sound in the bar, sabotaging people's very abilities to sense and respond to it, and renetworked the related practices of white communality through a deeply performative critique of how the kinesthetics of neoliberal city space are circumscribed by logics of race and feeling—and, specifically, the spatialization of blackness and pleasure. This book follows hers and Tracy's cues and pays close attention to how black queer women interface with and remap the racialized territorialization of feeling in Chicago. Their acute awareness and adroit *management* of the racialized networks of music, movement, and feeling on the queer dance floor are an incredibly important part of how they understand their place in the larger neoliberal city—and, moreover, how they reconfigure not only their physical but their affective rights to and in it.

Black Queer Method(s)[ologies], Black Queer Politics

In its rich attention to the body, Performance Studies has given me a wealth of tools to effectively document how black queer women demonstrate this awareness and management. *Feels Right* takes a particular cue from the Performance Studies scholar Dwight Conquergood, who was critical of how the academy's reliance on empirical observation and quantitative analyses often obscured the alternate ways people have of experiencing, understanding, and narrating the world around them. "Marching under the banner of science and reason," he explained, "[the academy] has disqualified and repressed other ways of knowing that are rooted in embodied experience, orality, and local contingencies."[45] For Conquergood, performance ethnography's emphasis on the body had the radical potential to uproot traditional ethnography's roots in racist, colonialist, and sexist gazes. Social scientists have long been installed as "experts" speaking for and about their interlocutors, often wielding allegedly "objective" data against the very minoritarian subjects they've solicited participation from.[46] In the interest of reframing this power dynamic, Conquergood implored scholars to remain attentive to how gesture, affect, intonation, and other embodied modes of expression reveal the deep meanings and perspectives of those we collaborate with in the field, and he was especially interested in "meanings that are expressed forcefully through intonation, silence, body tension, arched eyebrows, blank stares, and other protective arts of disguise and secrecy"—especially as these acts demonstrate a justified suspicion of social scientists themselves.[47]

This attention to embodied ways of knowing demands researchers engage "in active, intimate, hands-on participation and personal connection" with those in their field sites.[48] Such an approach to performance ethnography requires self-reflexivity and is a deeply vulnerable, embodied process of asking people, often strangers, to share themselves with you. *Feels Right* heeds Conquergood's call for renewed intimacy between researchers and the people who lend us their voices and experiences by self-reflexively contextualizing the act(s) and ethics of conducting research. In doing so, the book contributes to and builds upon the work of black feminist ethnographers who have long demonstrated the relationships among identity, methods, and politics, including but certainly not limited to Aimee Meredith Cox, Jasmine Mahmoud, D. Soyini Madison, Mignon R. Moore, Savannah Shange, Brandi T. Summers, Gloria Wekker, Nikki Yeboah, and, of course, Zora Neale Hurston, whose dogged and long-unappreciated work made ours possible. Diverse black feminist methods are brought together by the belief that the researcher's identity is always imbricated in the work that we do; for ethnographers, this means that our positionality always shapes and is shaped by the people and environments that we work in and always shapes our interactions in the field as well as the ways we reflect upon and analyze them. My own positionality as a black queer woman "mak[es] it impossible for me to think of my study in a detached manner," as Kai M. Green writes, "because in many ways what I say about the people I study, is also what I say and believe about myself."[49] And what I say and believe about myself is that I'm much more complex than I have been thought about, written about, and depicted in academia and in popular culture. This black queer feminist ethnography is committed to what Zenzele Isoke describes as "the impossibility of our wholeness"; it is an impossibility that is structured by ongoing violence that delimits our capacities but that is also an open question that we need to continually mine as evidence of our ongoingness in the face of that violence.[50] In this final stretch of this introduction, my self-reflexive discussion of methods necessarily bleeds into and lays the groundwork for this book's larger interest in the politics of researching black queer life and specifically serves as a kind of plea for a more rigorous, complex rendering of black queer women's practices of living. Here, then, I begin this book's work of embracing methodological complexity in lieu of a coherent, stable, locatable black queer method or politics—a methodology capable of documenting how black queer women's geographies of feeling right are always on the move and are continually entering new formations that are especially imaginable and palpable on the queer dance floor.

ON METHODS

Without a doubt, this book documenting the complex sensoria of black queer women's nightlives could not have happened without me simply being in intimate space with them at Slo 'Mo, Party Noire, and E N E R G Y. I attended these parties from 2009 until the middle of 2016, when I moved to Seattle for a job in the University of Washington's Department of Gender, Women & Sexuality Studies, though I returned frequently for days, weeks, and summers to attend parties, conduct interviews, and write this book. I balanced fully participating in these events—dancing, socializing, and at times socially drinking—and taking breaks to step back to observe in more critical detail the happenings around me. While in my field sites, I took constant, brief notes charting my experience and observations during any given party and would sit down for the tedious work of fleshing out my notes in detail the morning after. My research practice would continue after the party had ended as well, spilling out to the street in the immediate aftermath of closing time and also extending into the days and weeks after any given event, as I would run into people out and about in the city, at other events, and, especially, on social media, where black queer women post their experiences. These experiences that circle the queer dance floor are just as important to queer nightlife as the dance parties themselves, and they were often the first points of contact I had with black queer women who I later asked to interview with me.

Most important to this book are the formal and informal interviews I conducted with black queer women who circulate through the parties in question. I conducted formal, in-depth interviews with each of the five organizers of the three parties and with twenty-four black queer people I met while researching. Except for three, these people and I were largely strangers before I introduced myself and my project, which would typically happen in the early hours of a party, on the edges of the dance floor, or as a party spilled out onto the street. I would briefly introduce myself and a generalized account of my project ("I'm writing about black queer women's experiences at parties like [this one we're currently at]") and would ask if they'd be interested in having a conversation about their experiences. We would follow up over email, text, and/or social media direct messages and set a time and place to talk. The interviews were semi-structured and lasted between one and three hours. I would record and transcribe them, and in most cases I invited interlocutors to expand, revise, or redact their interview content as they so desired. Most returned the interviews without edits or annotations, simply OK'ing them, though a couple of interlocutors used the space to think longer and expand upon their words. I use pseudonyms throughout this book, and people were given the opportunity to choose their own pseudonyms if they liked. I use the real names of public figures of the parties in question (organizers and DJs). This option for collaboration allowed the people who so generously gave me their time the last say on their own words.

I also traded stories with these and other black queer women in informal settings: while we waited in line for the same parties, while we danced to our favorite songs, ran into one another on street corners and in coffee shops, and made plans to meet up at events run by people we had in common. These experiences of the expanded social world of the queer nightlife space, and of the ethnographer-interlocutor exchange, point to the more visceral and ephemeral ways of navigating the neoliberal city and of doing research that cannot always be captured in interviews.

My methods of conducting and using interviews for this book are rooted in Conquergood's ethics of dialogic performance: "a way of having intimate conversation with other people and cultures. Instead of speaking about them, one speaks to and with them."[51] Dialogic performance is invested in the fundamental dynamism of interpersonal interaction that shapes the ethnographic encounter, and which can be stripped in traditional ethnographies, and it contains an ethical commitment to bringing our interlocutors into presence. As D. Soyini Madison explains, the emphasis on dialogue moves the ethnographic encounter out of a stagnant, always-past-tense engagement that fixes the interviewee in time (and thus makes them susceptible to misreadings): "This conversation with the others, brought forth through dialogue, reveals itself as a lively, changing being through time and no longer an artifact captured in the ethnographer's monologue, immobile and forever stagnant."[52] *Feels Right* is conceptually and technically organized around this commitment, evident in my methods of collecting interviews as well as in the literal page space that I give black queer women. Each chapter prioritizes their own words in narrating what happens on and off the dance floors, and I try not to burden their voices with the academic literatures that I put them in conversation with. Instead, scholarly citations serve primarily as supplements that flesh out black queer women's experiences and add deeper context and complexity rather than the other way around: using black queer women's lives as "evidence" that simply bolsters conversations by, among, and for academics. Black queer women subsequently emerge as authorities of their own experience but also as skilled interlocutors whose intellectual and rhetorical skills match and at times outpace those of traditional academics.

While a key goal of dialogic performance is to bring "others" into continual presence, it is as much about the ethnographer's own self-reflexivity. Dialogic performance, in other words, demands ethnographers such as myself account for our presence within the ethnographic encounter, especially as the systems of power that frame academic research can greatly affect how people talk to us and about what. My own experiences as a black queer woman who lived, worked, and partied in Chicago for nearly a decade certainly shaped black queer women's comfort levels sharing their lives with me for an academic book. There are many ways that my interlocutors and I had similar experiences of race, gender, sexuality, family history, class, and/or regional backgrounds, which created an ease in conversation and thus an abundance of interview content. Our points of connection also led to shared understandings of plenty of terms, phrases, statements, sentiments, and descriptions of experiences and there were many times in interviews when I did not push for clarification or definitions that might lead to a more "comprehensive," data-driven interview transcript. I instead let my interlocutors tell me what they wanted when they wanted, due in part to the fact that I was raised in small-town Minnesota where we don't ask a lot of questions and because I simply tend toward concision. As my interviews and this book are an extension of my personality, there were things that, based on the energy of the interview, I simply did not solicit further elaboration on, and there are plenty of things that were discussed and inferred that you simply will not find in these pages. This is certainly the case for some of the commonsense vocabularies and experiences that my interlocutors and I share(d) as black queer people navigating Chicago and its queer nightlife scenes and that I don't believe need to be commonly available to everyone reading this book. Sometimes the dialogic, ethnographic encounter does not need to make it into the pages of a book—its power lay in the moment of its passing, how it is enfleshed only for the black queer women catching eyes as Aaliyah pumps through the sound system, as we elbow our ways through crowded bars, and in the playful way we pull one another into a circle of dancing friends and strangers.

ON TERMINOLOGY

I use the phrase "black queer women" throughout this book, though "black," "queer," and "woman" are highly unstable terms that cannot contain the lived experiences of the people in this book. All of my interlocutors have had a lived relationship to the category of "woman" but this relationship can and does shift over a person's lifetime. Most of my interlocutors identify as women and several identify as trans, gender nonconforming, nonbinary, genderqueer, genderfluid, androgynous, or prefer not to identify at all. Party organizers have themselves adjusted the language of gender and sexuality to reflect the expansiveness of their attendees. For years, Slo 'Mo's byline was "For Homos and Their Fans," and E N E R G Y's byline was "A Party for Womxn + Their Buddies." By the time of publication, Slo 'Mo described itself as "Slow Jams for Queer Fam," and E N E R G Y explained that "'Womxn' was used to be inclusive of trans and gnc [gender nonconforming] folks. Recently there has been a social push to revert to 'women' and we agree so going forward it will be 'A Party for Women + Their Buddies.'" As we see more in depth in the third chapter, Party Noire has also experimented (and at times struggled) with how to name and describe their focus on diverse genders and sexualities at their events, which helps us see how black queer community is sometimes forged through language that often fails.

The people in this book also have shifting relationships to "black queer woman" and they deploy its vocabularies differently and strategically depending on where they are, who they are among, and how they are feeling. All told, their experiences and definitions of blackness, gender, and sexuality shift and adapt in conversation with how they feel in their physical bodies and what they want to project to others, and they variously present as masculine-of-center, butches (soft and hard), bois, studs, femmes (high and low), stemmes, andros, and other modes of self-fashioning that push against rigid gender categories.[53] The language I use throughout *Feels Right* is attentive to the detailed particularities of each person whose voices appears in these pages: I use the pronouns they used during our interviews and largely refrain from describing their physical attributes, knowing that these details can change. I updated people's pronouns as needed as this book neared completion, and people's pronouns may have changed by the time you're reading this. My own use of "black queer woman" in this book is adaptable: there are some places where I use it frequently, and other places where I use "black queer" or "black queer people" alongside context clues that draw upon the complex beings of the people I'm referring to.

My use of terms like "woman" and "black queer woman" in this book is subsequently not meant to stabilize the language or practice of identity, nor to center people who were assigned female at birth and identify as women. Instead I aim to think through the ways that terms like "woman," "black woman," and "black queer woman" often organize people's experiences of their bodies and identities but also their experiences of queer nightlife and the possibilities of black queer community in Chicago. My interlocutors' relationships to gender and sexuality often play out in direct conversation with the perceived utility of a phrase like "black queer woman," as well as its component parts. Taylor, for example, reflects on how we live in a racist, misogynist, and transphobic society where "black woman" is one of the few commonly available frameworks through and against which we are read. They moved from a southern state to Chicago in their early twenties, as did several people in this book, and have spent many years understanding (and pressing against) how strict gender roles play out in their family as well as in their friend-based community. Taylor is very aware of the ways that other people's expectations and assumptions about their physical body shape and their experience of identity and politics:

> I think, and not that being a black woman is its own gender, but I feel there are certain things that being a black woman, and experiences that only black women have, [that are] different from being a woman. So, I have those conversations with people as a "black woman" so they understand my experiences—although I identify as being genderqueer and that my gender is, like, all of them. Just everything rolled up into one; however I feel, it is what it is. But as far as I get explaining experiences to people: my experience is being a black woman because that's how the world sees me. Before I open my mouth and tell them anything, the world sees me as a black woman. It's something I have to acknowledge, and I can't just push it to the side because I don't want "woman" to be attached to me daily or something. It's a real thing and it's something I have to accept, that that's how people see me.

Taylor details how the visual, racialized logic of "black woman" scripts their body and everyday life in ways that are extremely limiting to their expansive notion and experience of gender. "Black woman" is a category that does not neatly describe their lived reality but the term and the ideas and the beliefs that are entangled with it deeply condition and at times overdetermine how they relate to their surroundings and how they become legible (and not) within them.

While Taylor sidesteps the idea of "black woman [being] its own gender" in their theoretically complex statement, their comments resonate with black feminist theorists arguing just that. Taylor is in fact in productive conversation with the historian Saidiya Hartman, who describes how "the purportedly intractable and obdurate materiality of physiological difference" is continually reinforced through violent physical, rhetorical, and conceptual regimes that render certain bodies legible as "black woman."[54] Categories of race and gender are inextricable from one another, and they are mutually constituted through a matrix of violence that continually reinforces "black woman" as a seemingly stable and unchanging category.[55] This violence is perpetuated by religious, carceral, educational, and medical institutions, and it impacts the everyday experiences of people like Taylor who are both constrained by the terminologies of "Black Woman" even as it affords them a kind of shorthand, if not communion, around "experiences that only black women have," and that they want to honor.

Many black attendees use "queer" to identify their fluid sexualities and their resistance to the protocols of heterosexuality, and as a shorthand that identifies their broad-based commitments to equity and justice. But my interlocutors' definitions of *queer* are often routed through theories of race that complicate the term's perceived stability. For people like Tess, "queer" operates in direct tension with "lesbian," and they draw upon the specific racial and political connotations of each term in order to make themselves adaptable in different social contexts. Tess breaks down how "queer" and "lesbian" do different kinds of political work, and they often shift between the two (and just as often prefer to not identify at all):

> I feel like they're interchangeable, simply because for me, queer is someone that's free, you don't really want to label yourself. For me, people always ask, "What's your pronouns?" It's like for me, it doesn't matter to me, simply because there's no need to label me. I am who I am, as I am. So, to be queer is to be free. So, I say, "Oh, I'm queer," but sometimes people don't understand what that means, so I say, "Oh, I'm a lesbian," to help, depending on the space.

Tess clarifies that "lesbian" is especially productive: "Honestly, in black spaces. In black LGBT spaces, definitely—because you'll say queer and they'll be like, 'What's that?'—or black-specific lesbian spaces. . . . A lot of the black gay spaces: you're either gay, bisexual, or lesbian. That's it. That's all you can be." Here, Tess maps out how terminologies of sexuality map differently in Black spaces, where "lesbian" is part of a commonsense, if (to some) limited, vocabulary of sexuality. They position queer as a kind of open field for experimentation, as does Jayla, who explains, "When I think 'queer,' I think of just, like, eccentricities. And then when I think of 'lesbian' I think like not just a preference, but just an identity as well." Many in this book strategically distance themselves from "queer" when they want to point to the term's roots in white lesbian and gay communities and the ways that the term is increasingly divorced from a politics of sexuality ("everybody is queer these days") and of race. As Tracy explains, "With a lot of queers that are white, they think they can get away with certain things because they're queer. It's like, no. I see your whiteness underneath your queer blanket." Tracy sees "lesbian" as useful for people who are "wanting to be attached to something that says, 'I'm still black. I'm rooting for black people.'" Tracy thus works to put queer and lesbian in conversation in how she herself identifies as an expressly *Black* political subject: "I want to be a part of the Black Queer Lesbian movement, because I very much fuck with queerness. I am queer myself—and that's not just in the sexuality department, that goes with morals and values and political views and things like that." The dance floor is the site where black women and gender expansive people negotiate the intersections between sexuality and "morals and values and political views" that privilege and prioritize black life—and, across the chapters, we see them grappling with the ways in which something like "black queer" might not be able to hold them together.

In order to further signal the challenges of cohering under experiences of race, gender, and sexuality on Chicago's queer dance floors, I largely use the lowercase "black" throughout this book. Academic and journalistic standards have shifted to using the capitalized Black to describe the shared cultural identity of this group of people—to distinguish people from, as is usually invoked, "a color in a box of crayons." These are necessary and valid changes to make, as they acknowledge the physical and discursive violence that Black people regularly face in the United States; the black queer women in these pages are of course united in the ways that they are subject to the violence of racial organization. I use the lowercase "black," however, to continually underscore to the fact that the very notion of, possibilities for, and shape of a shared cultural identity and history is precisely what black queer women are negotiating at Slo 'Mo, Party Noire, and E N E R G Y. In each chapter we see how people adjust and modify the terms of racialized, gendered, and sexualized identity as part of the process of attuning themselves to people they want to be in community with. Their methods of navigating the queer dance floor, and their desires that this space organize commonality and communality, are key to their efforts to secure black queer community. This process is often fragile, inconclusive, and absent of consensus or coherence. *Feels Right* thus uses the lowercase to destabilize or delay the kinds of political forms, methodologies, and expectations that become attached to capitalized words, and to document how the desires for and movements toward black queer community are an always ongoing *process*.

Over the course of the book, we ultimately see how "black queer," "black queer woman," and "black queer community" do not neatly secure the political or cultural goals of the people in this book, the parties in question, nor, to be sure, the analytical goals of this book. The black queer women in these pages very much want to shape collectives rooted in shared identities as black and queer people. They at the same time express desires for and work toward modes of collectivity that are rooted above all in shared practices of thinking, communicating, feeling, and, of course, dancing that often press the limits of strict identitarian categories and the politics they assume. *Feels Right* allows us to think with terminologies that don't quite work because they point to politics that are kind of shaky, and ends and means that don't quite sync up. The linguistic, physical, and affective adjustments black queer women make on these unstable grounds chart the very experience of living black queer life under neoliberalism.

Where Methods and Terminologies Get a Bit Sticky . . . in a Good, Productively Challenging Way

All of my attention to the methods and politics of a rigorous, queer, black feminist performance ethnographic practice lowkey flew out the window the minute This Black Girl ran out of the bar, though. The moment is theoretically compelling because it demonstrates how dance is a highly political arena with explicitly geographic acts that speak to the racialized sociality of the city and propose alternative spatial realities-cum-practices to it. But my use of that moment flies in the face of ethnographic traditions of opening a text with an example that is the seemingly perfect microcosm for the larger arguments to be made. It's actually a pretty bad example to start this book with, due in no small part to the fact that I was never able to find and interview "this black girl" and so their pronouns and sexuality remain undefined to me and to you. This Black Girl may not identify as a woman or as a queer subject at all—and might vehemently refuse the infantilizing of "girl." To top it off, their actions were not even staged in a particularly queer nightlife setting. The anecdote usefully underscores, however, the political resonances of how black gender becomes mapped onto bodies and space. I subsequently conclude this introduction by tracking how the person who opened this book becomes produced as "This Black Girl" at the nexus of race, gender, space, and, importantly, the racialized political expectations that bring the three together. This meaning-making process reflects how the black queer women throughout this book become legible and not within neoliberal Chicago.

This Black Girl's intervention into that hip-hop party remains the most astounding upheaval of a dance floor that I encountered during and after my fieldwork collection. One of the reasons that the moment has stuck with me for so long is because it is such a fierce dismantling of the white spatial imaginary that values (profitable) forms of leisure that depend on the removal of poor and nonwhite people from the landscape, and a calling out of how this white spatial imaginary depends on blackness for its survival.[56] It is moreover within "a black radical tradition of gendered fugitive practice" that Sarah Haley describes as activated through sabotage, through "ruining, destroying, and disabling intentionally" those mechanisms of control that have imprisoned black women and demanded their labor and subservience.[57] This Black Girl's sabotage followed by *I'm headed back to the South Side* mapped the desire lines that emanate outward from the mundanely oppressive geographies of the gentrifying neighborhood and toward other sites where This Black Girl's possibilities of feeling, feeling good, or at least feeling more comfortable may fully bloom.

In her flight from the bar, This Black Girl's sabotage fits neatly within a genealogy of Black political thought and practice that is organized around geographies of just beyond the here and now, including Afrofuturist space trails, underground railroads, the out of field and out of doors, the undercommons, and more. These geographies may have different inflections, methods, and end points, but in what Kara Keeling describes as "radical Elsewheres" we can ultimately imagine and work toward different coordinates of black life "that might support alternative forms of sociality, forms that are not necessarily predicated on familiar modes of exploitation and domination."[58] These radical Elsewheres are similar in that they are almost always approached through fugitive movement away from *here* and toward *there*. The differences in how, exactly, *here* and *there* are located in real and imagined space says much about how we understand the constraints around, and possibilities of, living within our current surroundings.

This Black Girl's departure from Logan Square to other desired sites generates complicated questions about the terrain of doing and imagining black queer life and politics within the heart of the neoliberal city. Her flight to the radical Elsewhere of the South Side certainly mapped an alternate geography of black life—but she did so by reinscribing a cultural logic of racial authenticity that depends upon and reinstantiates the imperceptibility of black people within the gentrifying neighborhood. Her black politics worked by coding a historically black music genre as the privileged domain of black people (*All the music you're playing is for niggas and I'm the only nigga in here*) and, in locating the South Side as a space of refuge for her black subjectivity, spatializing black people as excluded from Logan Square and the broader North Side. In other words, while This Black Girl productively critiqued the racial contours of the hip-hop night, the bar, and the neighborhood, she simultaneously reproduced the very logics of the neoliberal city that argue that black people do and perhaps *should* exist outside the boundaries of the gentrifying neighborhood. This Black Girl's complex movements (stopping movement in the bar, her own movement away from the bar) reiterated the boundaries around the racialized territorialization of feeling in the city. This Black Girl had to leave the space in order to contest it and in doing so she argued that one cannot practice black politics and stay in the gentrifying neighborhood—that life must exist in its fullness beyond it. This geography of the just beyond has very particular consequences for how black people actually become perceptible and not in the gentrifying neighborhood. As This Black Girl called upon her own visible body to hold the room accountable, an accountability activated as she authenticated her own sovereignty as *the only nigga in here*, she foreclosed the possibility that there was another nigga in the bar that night: me.

What might it mean that This Black Girl didn't see me in the cramped bar? What other sets of questions must be raised when we consider that she may have seen but simply not cited me in her radical disavowal of the white sociality of the scene? That she saw me but could not figure me into her dissent from it? These questions remain largely unanswerable as I've been unable to find This Black Girl, to interview her, to allow her side of the story to be present in these pages. She has always remained out of view, eluding my efforts to find her on social media and through connections to other people who were in the bar that night. My desire to find her presses against my belief in the power of opacity, dissemblance, and subterfuge in the doing of black feminist politics: that she has a right to remove her physical and psychic self from view, and that doing so has long been important to maintaining a sense of self (and a semblance of sanity) in a Western political field that demands the hypervisibility of black women.[59] Yet the scant information and the gossip and speculation that came out about This Black Girl in the days and weeks after the sabotage raise important questions about evidence and ephemera in the doing of and theorizing about black queer life in the neoliberal city—and raise important questions about how performance ethnography, a field that regularly deals with the ephemerality of the body, might grapple with them. Narrating This Black Girl as a real person and a symbolic figure demonstrates how performance ethnography can balance an ethics of care rooted in (real, perceived, and speculative) shared identities with a commitment to detail, despite the fissures such detail may reveal. It's important to render the fully enfleshed complexity, if not messiness, of the terms and fields that black queer women operate in to most fully represent the deft skill with which they navigate the tricky politics of and beyond the queer dance floor.

The night of her sabotage, This Black Girl was on a date with a white man who owns a small business; a man who, in the aftermath of her flight, shrugged and exclaimed to the bar staff, "Some sauces are just spicier than others!" Later, in a now-deleted Facebook post, he wrote, "First time dating a Puerto Rican woman!" an exclamation that simultaneously gestured to her act as a kind of exotic flair stereotypical of women in the Caribbean and diminished the seriousness of her critique of the hip-hop party. This information was collected in informal conversations I had in the days and weeks after the event, and in informal conversations (re)collected over the course of writing this book. While I was able to track down the man in question, years later, he didn't remember This Black Girl other than the fact that they had met earlier that night.

Read through the optics of her speculative biographical data, This Black Girl's sabotage of the hip-hop party and her later mis- and unnaming underscore the historical intersections of race and nationality in neighborhoods like Logan Square (and Humboldt Park) that have strong roots in Puerto Rico and reflect how black and Puerto Rican political identities have often intersected.[60] Scholars of Puerto Rican life in Chicago have discussed how Puerto Rican political identities are sometimes shaped in conversation with how African American people are imagined as always organized around resistance.[61] We can think of how This Black Girl's mobilization of blackness in her sabotage, read in conversation with this literature, speaks to the ways that Puerto Rican activists have sometimes selectively taken up blackness to articulate resistance to the state and to establish cultural capital in Chicago.[62] This Black Girl's sabotage gestured to the strategic though sometimes tense racial, national alliances that have been forged within and across Puerto Rican communities in Chicago and in Puerto Rico, generating fruitful opportunities to theorize the complex ways in which blackness and black political identities can be politically activated in a diverse Logan Square milieu.

I am not interested in the "truth" of This Black Girl's identity but I am interested in thinking about how the mechanisms of foreclosure, the shutting down of complexity, that This Black Girl enacted rendered an unambiguously Black (*I'm the only nigga in here*) politics attached to an unambiguously Black territory (*so I'm headed back to the South Side*)—an enactment of unambiguousness that was further solidified in the immediacy of her being named "This Black Girl." What happens when we understand This Black Girl's sabotage as perhaps not all that radical, but reflective of a familiar and commonsense Black politics that depends upon the hypervisibility of the sovereign body? In what ways might this Black politics reproduce the demands neoliberal governance places on individuals to be particularly visible in order to demand, let alone secure, rights? How might such an embodied politics reinscribe a restrictive geography of feeling in a segregated landscape? Perhaps this is a Black politics that is stripped of affective complexity as it virtually demands that black people's pleasure only cohere in territories such as the South Side that have been deemed decidedly Black, no matter their relatively ambiguous borders and demographic diversity.

Speculating on This Black Girl's very presence as a black Puerto Rican woman moving between the South Side and Logan Square suggests that the socio-racial organization of the city's segregated, gentrifying landscape is fundamentally more ambivalent than the physical and affective black-white binary her sabotage was contextualized by. Maybe she came to be at the bar because she was part of, if not wholly integrated into, a larger social and cultural network that is organized in and around the residential, commercial, and service options that mark the neighborhood's gentrification. While the South Side has been home to a historically large black population, it has also long been home to diverse white ethnic communities—Irish Americans, in particular—and is increasingly home to Latin and Central American migrant populations. Her sabotage marked the racialized expectations and assumptions structuring the very possibilities for pleasure at that hip-hop party just as her flight obscured the multiple paths of arrival, methods of taking root, and processes of self-reflexivity that people of color enact within scenes and spaces where their presence is seemingly unexpected.

Feels Right presses against the imperative that black politics be organized around a geography of the just beyond and takes its cue from the idea that This Black Girl's most radical act may not have been her leaving the bar but her making it physically impossible for other people to reproduce the expected sociality of the gentrifying milieu. This book pauses in the moments before This Black Girl leaves the bar, idles when the music cuts out and people have to awkwardly take time to reorient themselves to the sights, sounds, movements, and feelings of the dance floor. This time-space of negotiating one's own body's relationships to the structures of feeling that enmesh it is a potent site of knowledge production, and it is a potent site that black queer women wield to articulate their personal and political investments in the racialized sociality of the queer party and the city that surrounds it. While This Black Girl must seemingly be in flight away from the dance floor and toward another place so that her black politics can become perceptible, the black queer women throughout the rest of this book refuse to leave the party or the gentrifying neighborhood and instead work to remake the very frameworks of black queer perceptibility itself.[63]

They do so by putting their individual bodies on the line, as This Black Girl bravely did, but always with an eye toward the possibilities of the larger collective's staying power. This isn't to discount the important personal and political work This Black Girl did in leaving the function, especially as her work was articulated through extreme vulnerability and risk. The goal is to just remain on the dance floor a bit longer and see what happens. The chapters look to the microgestures of presence that are enacted when black queer women take public transportation from their black neighborhood to the function across town in a white neighborhood, when they choose to pay entry fees and buy drinks and food at a party, in the decisions they make to get on the dance floor or jump in the middle of a cypher, when they grab onto one another and move together in the dark heat that is club-life. In spaces where sight and language are often made impossible in the cramped, dark loudness of a Slo 'Mo party, the possibilities of black queer politics and of black queer community consolidate around hearing a particular song and moving to it, in gripping the dancing bodies around you, and at times getting up on stage and screaming at them. These possibilities accumulate in the rush of four hundred people Swag Surfing at Party Noire or the dissonance of finding that a potential lover cannot keep up with your twerking at E N E R G Y, which helps you decide to come back next week to try again with someone new.

These are modes of aggregating that cannot rely upon sight, the sovereign body, or the explicitly black territory but that coalesce through touch, in the indistinctness between a single dancer and the cypher that hypes her up as she dances, and in that one very black queer night that you have that helps you face the sea of whiteness when you wake up in the morning. This is black queer politics rooted in the depth of what the body marked by black queer gender and sexuality wants and sometimes feels but may never fully attain, because its attainment would spell the end of the world as we know it—not that this book isn't invested in that. It is just, in the meantime, dedicated to the task of defining and describing the plain hard work that black queer women put into making lives worth living, loving, and knowing in the neoliberal city.

ONE
SLO 'MO AND THE PACE OF BLACK QUEER LIFE

Tracy is yelling *The kids don't even know! The kids don't even know!* as she jumps up to dance to the Luther Vandross song "Never Too Much." She clears space for herself in the cramped walkway between the Slippery Slope's bar and the red vinyl booths that she had been sitting in across from it. She and I have been edged off the packed dance floor of the queer dance party Slo 'Mo: Slow Jams for Homos and Their Fans, held in the rapidly gentrifying Logan Square neighborhood.[1] From its inception in 2011, the monthly Slo 'Mo party has brought upward of one hundred black queer people, particularly women, together from around the city of Chicago. Tonight, however, the party's regular black queer attendees have struggled to maintain space for themselves amid the mass of straight, white people swarming the bar.[2] *The kids don't even know!* Tracy shouts again as she begins clapping on every beat and dance-ushers away a clump of hipster bros, a permutation of white, upwardly mobile, urban dwellers whose desires to access and participate in the cultural capital of "cool" gentrifying neighborhoods intersect with the aggressive whiteness, heterosexuality, and macho physicality of "bros" whose higher income brackets and upper-middle-class tastes have been encouraged in the gentrification of Logan Square.

Other Slo 'Mo attendees almost immediately notice the small clearing Tracy makes and come to her from the corners, booths, and bar stools they'd been pushed to. "This song comes on and all the black people be like *gaaaaaaaaah!!!!!"* screams Andrew, throwing his hands up and shaking his head in mock fervor. I myself jump up to join the group of five black queer thirtysomethings dancing variations of Chicago-style stepping, which balances a measure of smooth rigidity in the upper body and through the torso with a graceful, shuffling, two-step. We loudly sing along as Luther croons the chorus, "Oh my loooooove," trying to reproduce his melisma before physically marking the staccato phrasing of the next line, "a thousand kisses from YOU," by shooting our arms out, snapping our shoulders back, or jutting our chins left and right. The surrounding crowd vying for the bartender's attention pays us no mind as we playfully lock eyes with one another, collectively connecting with Luther as we sing-shout "is never too muuuuuuuch." When the song ends the circle collapses and each dancer is swallowed back up into the mass. Tracy returns to her seat in the vinyl booth, Andrew elbows his way onto the dance floor, inspired to keep working at finding a space, and I head for the exit.

This moment of connection through and with the queer icon of Luther Vandross interrupted an otherwise terrible night at Slo 'Mo. It was, in fact, to be the second-to-last installment of the party's residency at the Slippery Slope bar as Kristen, the party's femme, white, queer organizer, had been fielding complaints from the party's regulars who felt watched, harassed, and generally made to be uncomfortable by the bar's largely white, male, and heterosexual clientele. The party emerged as a queer nightlife force on the city's North Side as it concentrated exclusively on "slow jams" that encompass a wide range of midtempo music that is sultry and often laden with references to sex and romance and is typically sung by black artists. Focusing on the R&B, Disco, and Quiet Storm formats from the 1970s to the early 2000s, the party spotlighted classics from artists like Dinah Washington, Chaka Khan, and Sade, as well as mixes of more contemporary R&B power-players ranging from Mary J. Blige and Ginuwine to Frank Ocean.

When the party moved in 2014 from the small, intimate space of The Whistler to the new, larger space of the Slippery Slope less than a block away, however, the demographic changed and the music got louder and faster, which affected the capacity of the party's regular black queer clientele to take pleasure in the party, to be sure, but also in a neighborhood with a historically small black population and a larger city long organized around whiteness. For many black queer women, Slo 'Mo's move reflected a kind of selling out: a feeling that the party was capitalizing on the cultural capital of blackness and queerness in ways that secured a brand of pleasure that was wholly antithetical to the black queer lifeworlds that it had, until then, cultivated. The battle between hipster bros ordering drinks at the Slippery Slope and black queers trying to dance at Slo 'Mo is not only about what kinds of people take pleasure in the nightlife cultures of Chicago's gentrifying neighborhoods, but how, exactly, they do so. Indeed, pleasure is *the* currency with which territory is gained and lost in the venues that Slo 'Mo is hosted in, and for many of the party's attendees, hipster bros throughout the city exercise their seemingly inalienable right as white men to take up space and take pleasure wherever and however they please. Tracy clearing space for herself to dance to Luther, then, was more than the simple exercise of her right to inhabit a bar. In her two-stepping that recalled the black vernacular styles of her upbringing on the city's South Side, and in her playful, clarion call to the rest of the black queers in the bar ("the kids"), Tracy asserted a black queer practice of taking pleasure in and from spaces like the Slippery Slope that capitalize upon black queer aesthetics while catering to the crowds of white men and women that were the bar's primary clientele. Her interfacing with slowness, responding to Luther's song with the measured movements of two-stepping, reveals a particularly black and queer theory, method, and a mode of critique within the Slo 'Mo party and the larger neighborhood it is staged in.

In this chapter, I highlight slowness as a key framework through which black queer women understand their relationships in and to a party, neighborhood, and city that are increasingly entangled with the imperatives of accumulation and acceleration that are characteristic of neoliberal governance, and that are at odds with how they seek to secure black queer communality. Slo 'Mo took root in Logan Square when the neighborhood's hipster gentrification was becoming more entrenched as a younger, whiter population contributed to a myriad of structural efforts that priced out the Puerto Rican, Cuban, and Central and Latin American populations that made up over half of the neighborhood's population since the 1980s. As Chicago's economy began to rebound after the housing collapse and related recession in the early aughts, low-value buildings in Logan Square became increasingly attractive to residential and commercial developers who negotiated with local alderman to obtain building permits for new construction, revise zoning designations to incorporate more retail into residential districts, and to procure the tightly controlled liquor licenses required to open bars and restaurants. These (re)investments have been made possible by designating parts of Logan Square as a Tax Increment Financing (TIF) district, a long-term urban renewal initiative that directs a portion of rising property tax revenues toward public and private projects. Chicago has utilized TIF funds to make much-needed improvements that, for example, modernize train stations and tracks. TIF money is (perhaps more) frequently diverted into subsidies meant to lure and support the private development of stadiums, high-density housing, and entertainment venues in areas that don't necessarily need them.[3]

In 2000, the roughly three-mile stretch of Milwaukee Avenue extending from the heart of Logan Square to the western border of Wicker Park was designated part of the larger Fullerton/Milwaukee TIF district based on "the presence of age, deterioration of buildings and surface improvements, depreciation of physical maintenance, obsolescence, presence of structures below minimum code standards, excessive vacancies, and lack of community planning."[4] These qualities characterized the region as "blighted."[5] Over the course of twenty-three years, a projected $40 million was to be used to develop housing and commercial stock, stabilize economic governance, and generally beautify the area.[6] A series of amendments would enhance the scope and timeline of redevelopment, and bump projected costs to $52 million in 2004 and to $136 million in 2011.[7] Developers can also request some TIF funds to cover or assist in the cost of redeveloping historically important buildings, as did the real estate company M. Fishman & Co., which holds a vast amount of properties in Logan Square, when it requested $1 million of TIF assistance to redevelop the Logan Theater. Other private development projects included rehabilitating the Hairpin Lofts building to the north of the theater to include mixed-income apartments, retail outlets, and an art gallery. These TIF funds have also been used to subsidize the rapid development of the neighborhood into a profitable bar, restaurant, and nightlife district that hails people from the surrounding neighborhoods like Avondale, Wicker Park, Bucktown, and Humboldt Park. From 2005 to 2014, around twenty *new* bars and restaurants opened on Milwaukee Avenue, with another dozen or so opening nearby. Many if not most of these entities were not opened by small business owners but by large, corporate restaurant groups with multiple holdings throughout the city.[8] The area's rising property values (which dumped even more money into the TIF, allowing for even more distribution of revenue to private investment) contributed to an increasingly expensive rental and housing market, creating housing instability for longtime residents and drawing new residents who are capable of affording the market.[9]

The Whistler, where Slo 'Mo is hosted, sits in the middle of the stretch of Milwaukee Avenue that anchors much of Logan Square's commercial and service industries and anchors, in many ways, the neighborhood's hipster gentrification. As Slo 'Mo picked up steam as one of, if not the, hottest queer parties in the city, anti-gentrification activism in Logan Square often centered on the financial and cultural threat that hipsters were seen to pose the neighborhood. One of the biggest issues activists confronted was the rapid and opaque process through which developers could secure new zoning designations that would allow larger and taller buildings to be built in a neighborhood composed largely of two- and three-story buildings without the consent of, or conversation with, neighborhood residents.[10] Hipsters were the focus of criticisms of a sixty-three-unit, "transit-friendly" microapartment development; of the "Twin Towers" development (ultimately branded as MiCA) that would bring two twelve-story buildings to Milwaukee Avenue; and of a massive apartment building that would replace the Mega Mall, a small-business-focused retail space worked and populated by many people from Central and Latin America, as well as the region's large Puerto Rican population.[11] The Save Our Boulevards organization posted flyers throughout the neighborhood that criticized the development by highlighting how its construction would disrupt the existing social fabric of the neighborhood by encouraging hipsters to move in. "Most of us don't ride our bikes to work," they write in one poster, gesturing to the stereotype that hipsters ride fixed-gear bicycles. "The media calls Alderman Moreno the 'Hipster Alderman.' Tell him to stop representing the hipsters who don't live here, but want to move her[e], drink fancy cocktails for a few years, and then move to the suburbs because it's too congested and their friends can't find a place to park." The flyers highlight the growing perception (and anxiety) that Logan Square is "Now the Hipster Mecca of the Midwest."[12]

The rapid development of the neighborhood frames the conditions in which Slo 'Mo's slowness takes on significance. Under neoliberal capitalism, Nick Salvato suggests "speed has made itself felt as one of the most pressing, if not alarming, attributes."[13] Neoliberalism's set of free-market economic policies that encourage deregulation and privatization purport to increase quality of life by providing the individual with increased choice and agency over where they live, how and where they work, and how and what they consume. As has always been the case of life under capitalism, the sense of rapidity that neoliberalism conditions is deeply racialized and territorialized and depends on the exploitation of those who *cannot* afford to take time. Sarah Sharma argues that, in fact, the pace of life has not actually increased under neoliberalism. Our emphasis on speedup merely masks what Sharma describes as the temporal inequities between people whose hard and fast labor is exploited for cosmopolitan elites who can afford the time, space, and money to unplug and slow down in spaces like upscale condos or in the latest craft cocktail bar, and through activities like yoga and the slow food movement. That is, participating in spaces and activities meant to alleviate the stresses of a life with seemingly less and less time risks merely "confirm[ing] and maintain[ing] the same structures of power that drain, tire, and exploit other people's time, while elevating one group's sense of temporal importance."[14] Moreover, if slowness provides a moment of breath from the pressures that neoliberalism brings to bear on the physical and psychic landscapes through which we circulate, it is often only to gather the reserves to *re-enter* the "real world" as newly centered and thus more efficient worker-subjects. Insufficient attention to what Sharma calls this "biopolitical economy of time" subsequently risks affirming the "appropriate temporal order" of neoliberalism.[15]

This is not to say that desiring or enacting slowness at Slo 'Mo is equivalent to participating in the same exploitative cycles Sharma examines, or that black queer women dancing to slow jams does a kind of violence that is equivalent to, say, M. Fishman & Co.'s gutting of Logan Square. Slowness is an optic through which we can sense other ways that people negotiate the very real pressures of making-do in environments where they are at times slowly and subtly, and sometimes quickly and violently, removed. Black queer women like Tracy use the discursive and embodied language of slowness to perceive, reflect, and intervene into this pace of neoliberal governance and how it is seen to cater to a class of white people who can afford the financial and temporal resources to participate in Logan Square's economies of pleasure. Black queer women's haptic negotiations of ownership in and of the party—their embodied negotiations of who gets to feel what, where, and at what pace—reveal the enduring potential of slowness as a racialized queer aesthetic and practice that provides them the theoretical language, surrounding, and scaffolding for embodied interventions into the normalizing spatiotemporalities of neoliberal urban governance. In their articulations and theorizations of slowness, black queer women carry a longer history of how black people have negotiated time, speed, and tempo as they have recalibrated their bodies in order to make do in, yet speak back to, the temporal expectations demanded by capitalist labor systems that structure work and play alike.[16] At Slo 'Mo, slowness is a textured theorization of a specifically black queer aesthetic and embodied resistance to how neoliberal governance shapes Logan Square and seeps into the fabric of the Slo 'Mo party.[17] Their abilities to register belonging and a measure of control over their bodies within a party that is increasingly defined by rapidity is staged in direct conversation with their abilities to manage speed beyond it, in a city also increasingly defined by speed. Slo 'Mo's choreographies of slowness are subsequently linked to black queer women's abilities to refuse the racialized logics of acceleration that govern Chicago more broadly, underscoring how valuable the haptic and affective capital of feeling good are to black queer women as they assess and assert their rights to the landscapes that they move through.

The Slowness of Slo 'Mo

As one of the only, if not the only, queer parties in Chicago's Logan Square neighborhood to draw a significant number of black women and trans people through its doors, Slo 'Mo has fostered an enormously important queer scene since 2011.[18] From its inception, slowness infused the entirety of the Slo 'Mo party, from the title and the sonic theme of the party itself to the long and lasting line of people waiting to get into The Whistler (a seventy-five-person-capacity bar). The sensations were amplified by the conversations taking place at the small, candlelit tables that surround the dance floor. Slo 'Mo began when Kristen, tired of attending queer parties that play high-energy music that attracts seemingly younger and more energetic crowds, endeavored to fashion a scene that, she explains, is "a little bit more low key . . . just a little bit more grown up." Slo 'Mo almost immediately drew a critical mass of black queer women, most of them in their late twenties, in their thirties, and in their early forties, who traveled from around the city to The Whistler, located on Milwaukee Avenue's growing entertainment district, just a short walk from two train stops and accessible by three major bus lines.

The venue can, however, be quite tedious to reach from the city's north and south sides, and attendees often arrive by car services like Uber and Lyft or carpool with friends, as Alisa tells me at one event. "It's my first time!" she exclaims when I ask if she's been to Slo 'Mo before. "I can never get friends to go but tonight I got a group of friends to come." She and her friends came from Rogers Park, a neighborhood to the northeast of Logan Square that is at least forty-five minutes via the city's public transportation, and requires at least one, sometimes two, transfers. "I have a car . . ." she adds, giving me a knowing glance that signaled there was no way she'd make the long trip taking the train to the bus to get there. Still other women come from further reaches of the city, as Tyanna, who drove nearly an hour to The

Whistler from her home on the city's largely black southwest side one night; on the way, she picked up her friend living in the historically white ethnic and Mexican neighborhood of Pilsen just south of Chicago's downtown, which poses similar public transportation difficulties.

Black queer women's efforts to attend Slo 'Mo reflect the real hole the party filled for those not wanting to engage Boystown, a gayborhood in the Lakeview neighborhood that is perceived as a largely white, male, middle- and upper-middle-class space. While Boystown offered many black queer women important opportunities to experience life as out, queer people when they were younger, and introduced them to LGBTQ party scenes more generally, most also sought forms of nightlife community that did not center around (or even involve) cishet gay men. Slo 'Mo also became an important alternative to parties such as Formerly Known As (FKA) in the Rogers Park neighborhood and, before it ended, Chances Dances in Wicker Park, to the southeast of Logan Square. While the latter parties may have included many women, gender nonconforming people, and trans people, Slo 'Mo's attendees felt aged out of FKA's younger, early-twentysomething crowd and alienated from Chances' at-times overwhelmingly white crowd. Chicago's south and west sides are scripted as historically black neighborhoods and there are a handful of black lesbian and gay nightlife events that are regularly held there. But there are a variety of reasons that the black queer women in this book do not frequent those events—namely, that the events were simply unknown to them, were geographically distant from where they lived, or because they felt unsafe in their queerness in these spaces. Slo 'Mo, in other words, fulfilled many of the geographic as well as cultural needs of black queer women whose communities are staged in and around Logan Square.

To take full advantage of Slo 'Mo's black queerness, party regulars often arrive at The Whistler at 8:30 or 9:00 p.m. in order to avoid the line that is often forty people deep by 10:00 p.m. In this window of time, Kristen and the party's DJs are typically setting up while an older, whiter, more affluent crowd is finishing their happy hour cocktails. As Kristen laughingly relates, those finishing their drinks around this time would typically react to the growing crowd of black queer women in one of two ways: "either by finishing their drinks and leaving, or sticking around to see what the fuss was about." During their setup, Slo 'Mo posts "gender neutral" signs on the doors of the bar's two bathrooms, often posting additional signage explaining the meanings and implications of gender neutrality as well. For bros "in Polo shirts and khakis," Kristen explains, a growing presence of self-assured queer people of color and new signage resetting the rules of the space can be, "frankly, kind of intimidating to them." Early in the night, these people began to take over the barstools and tables, to crowd behind the DJ booth on the stage, and to stalk space on the intimate back patio, strung with white lights, where people can smoke, drink, and catch snippets of the music playing inside.

While the party has never explicitly marketed itself as a *black* queer party, the racialized aesthetics of the party mixed with black queer people's abilities to physically take over the small space each night contributed to early understandings of the party as a space for black queer women, and for black queer people across the gender spectrum. Kristen is careful to acknowledge how her background as "a white girl from Vermont" impacts her capacity to host such a space; ultimately, she explains, the depth of the music played has a particular draw for black queer people because it calls into being the network of friends, family, home, and community that they don't often find in other queer dance parties in the city's white, north-side enclaves. The party quickly attracted black queers who gathered around a soundscape grounded in shared listening histories, as Adrian explains:

> Slo 'Mo, like, connects me to a memory growing up; of like sitting in my room and, like, listening to slow jams and that was like my TV, you know. Dreaming about one day, like, having a boo and listening to Marvin Gaye and some shit . . . Some of those old jams that they play, my mother, like, raised me on them. You know: *records.* You know: Prince, the O'Jays, Ohio Players, all that stuff; the Isley Brothers.

Apart from the draw of music rooted in family and community history, the party provided many a welcome respite from the networks of music and dance found at other queer parties where movement is virtually compulsory. "I hate the music sooooo much at . . . Every. Other. Dance. Party," Caroline tells me, slamming her right fist into her left palm to punctuate each word. "It's just, like, not very cohesive to me as someone who's not a DJ, right. But to me as a dancer, it's just not cohesive and it's just like the same kind of beat." With a bored look, she puts her fist in the air and pumps it rhythmically to mime the pounding *mmph-mmph-mmph-mmph* bass line, her long locs rocking back and forth as she embodies the "four-on-the-four" beat. She continues,

> It's like: aite, let's do something that we can actually dance to. And, like, sing! I just love singing along to things . . . at Slo 'Mo that's all you get! You get really nice dancing beats and stuff, you know, so you can sing

along to it. All the other parties are just like . . . sometimes the music is fine; sometimes it's good, or sometimes it's OK. But at Slo 'Mo it's the best one, the best music.

The familiarity of Slo 'Mo's music allows Caroline to reflect on how she wants to engage in queer club spaces, and it similarly allows this reflection for Francine, for whom Slo 'Mo's musical emphases recall her roots in an all-black community on the East Coast, a measure of control over her movement repertoires:

> What I like about the music, personally, is that it's all music I know and I grew up with and am familiar with; music that I'm comfortable with. I don't have to get out and do a weird new dance or something like that, you know what I mean? Like, I don't have to sit down because I can't do the weird new dance. I can just go and dance if I like, and not, if I don't want to.

Though Francine self-describes as a partier who "likes to drink and have fun," she finds there is pressure at many clubs, queer and not, to demonstrate technical proficiency with particular dance styles that accompany many contemporary hip-hop songs. She describes her own dancing as "real wild" and she would rather not feel policed or judged for moving outside the expected repertoires during a given song. To this end, "I usually tend to dance alone," she explains, "but that doesn't always work because dance . . . is a pretty communal thing." She is always looking for opportunities such as those presented at Slo 'Mo where she can show up with friends, but "we'll just split up [and dance alone] and we'll see each other in a couple of hours." Most of the time Francine would rather circulate the dance floor alone, and she finds that Slo 'Mo is a nonjudgmental space where she is not only free to move her body as she pleases but also feels comfortable moving through the space as a single person.

Francine's relief from the pressures of keeping up and demonstrating technical proficiency with dance trends resonates with an overarching dissatisfaction with how queer club spaces can force the same kinds of dance moves which, ultimately, force the same kinds of (non)connection to other people. At the time of our interview, the contemporary pop and hip-hop landscape was dominated by songs that were soundtracks for particular dance fads such as the Nae Nae. Dance floors that are organized around shared knowledge of these audio-physical repertoires require in part the hyperawareness and consumption of the latest fad; one must be aware not only of chart-topping songs but also of the music and viral videos that demonstrate the related dances, which are then carried onto the dance floor space in sometimes exhausting ways. For Francine, then, slowness not only allows for an expanded range of available movements but enables a refusal of a consumption style endemic to (assimilation under) neoliberal capitalism.

Slowness opens up important, alternative forms of nightlife intimacy that, for Adrian, are uniquely and importantly nonsexual:

> I just feel like in [gay club] spaces it was just like, 'how can I simulate sex,' you know what I mean, 'while dancing with this person.' [A queer-safe space like Slo 'Mo] is being able to have space to hold conversation to actually connect. It's like we're dancing and having a good time, but at the same time it's like we're just like watching, we're like kiki-ing, you know what I mean. It's not necessarily this very sexual like *act* where's it's like, 'OHHHHH WE GOTTA GET IT IN,' you know. Like taking out all this aggression on someone [*laughs*].

Slo 'Mo's midtempo music allowed attendees like Adrian and Francine to move their bodies in ways that were not predicated on virtuosic, skilled, or hypersexual movements or, as for Caroline, boring and repetitive ones. The particular musical aesthetic of slowness subsequently attracted many people uninterested or unable to physically participate in queer party scenes like they used to. Erin was a longtime Slo 'Mo regular who would eventually come on as a DJ and co-organizer, DJ Audio Jack. She explains that she could dance and socialize all night "when I was younger and could keep up." Now, she exclaims, "I can't move like I used to! My knees hurt, my feet hurt." A decade into participating in queer dance nights came with not only new limitations on her range of motion but also a heightened awareness of how little she and those she saw monthly actually knew about one another. As a self-defined "older" queer partier (she was just thirty-one during our interviews), she feels less pressure to dance at Slo 'Mo, which has, in turn, opened space for more and more fruitful connections with other black queer attendees whom she's met on the sidelines of the dance floor. Whereas the physical labor of moving one's body is often seen as a virtual requirement of participating in a traditional dance or club space, the foregrounding of slowness at Slo 'Mo allowed for productive recalibrations to a neoliberal order that governs and rewards the ability to "keep up," whether that means staying on top of what dance fads are out or being able to physically execute them.

The party certainly affords many opportunities to dance but black queer women long found the party special for the ways that it expanded the range of connections, intimate and otherwise, that they could have within a night-life setting. Indeed, many of the social practices at Slo 'Mo at The Whistler were in fact staged off the dance floor, even if oriented toward it. While people certainly took to the dance floor en masse, it was common for there to be equal amounts of people talking for hours on the patio or sitting at the low, candlelit tables having conversations, watching other people dance, and chair-dancing themselves. The particular importance of slowness itself as key to Slo 'Mo's black queer lifeworld—of the alternative networks of communication, community, and movement that slowness opened up in and around the dance floor—became especially visible, however, when the party left The Whistler bar and began experimenting with hosting satellite parties in venues in the city.

A Change in (S)Pace

The black queer pleasure that was carved out at Slo 'Mo at The Whistler was fundamentally altered when the party moved to the Slippery Slope bar in early 2014 and began experimenting with hosting satellite parties throughout the city. Whereas the intimacy of The Whistler provided a safe space for black queer women to both commune with a larger room of black queer women and/or simply listen and dance alone, Slo 'Mo entered into new spaces where black queer women were suddenly hypervisible and subsequently unwilling or unable to inhabit the black queer space they'd become accustomed to. The physical, cultural, and sonic changes that Slo 'Mo underwent while adapting to the physical space of the Slippery Slope, in particular, fundamentally changed black queer women's abilities to listen and dance to slow jams. In the larger space of the Slippery Slope, black queer women found themselves listening to more up-tempo music, squeezed off the dance floor, physically disconnected from other Slo 'Mo attendees, and having to attend with oftentimes aggressive white men who pervaded the space. As Slo 'Mo's black queer women discuss the difficulties of maintaining a black queer space within the Slippery Slope, they simulta-neously examine the racialized logics of pleasure and consumption that are privileged in Logan Square.

Encouraged by winning several awards naming Slo 'Mo the best dance party in the city, but anxious about the growing line of people hoping to get a spot inside The Whistler's small space, Kristen and DJ Tess moved the party to the Slippery Slope just one block north of The Whistler on Milwaukee

Avenue with a three-hundred-person capacity. The Slippery Slope is one venue on the longer stretch of the diagonally running Milwaukee Avenue that, by early 2014, was in the throes of redevelopment. The one-block span between California Avenue to the southeast and Fullerton Avenue to the northwest had been experiencing a rapid turnover in building use since 2012, as a high-end coffee shop, the Slippery Slope, a vegan restaurant, a local beer brewery, a high-end juice bar, a 4 a.m. bar, the second location of an arcade bar, a German beerhouse, an art gallery, and a used science fiction and horror bookstore opened. As part of this rapid development, the Slippery Slope marketed itself as a venue with DJs every night and quickly became a midpoint stop-off for people bar hopping between Wicker Park and Logan Square.

The first Slo 'Mo party coincided with the bar's third day of being open, and while Slo 'Mo attendees didn't have to wait in line to get into the larger space, they were immediately critical of the bar and the party therein. Confronted with bar goers who were largely white and male, Slo 'Mo attendees were confronted by a radically different Slo 'Mo culture. "Who *are* these people?!" Aisha exclaimed, her eyes agape in mock terror. "They're the people who didn't get in [to The Whistler]!" Sasha laughed in reply. "They never got in!" Aisha laughingly shrieked back. At the Slippery Slope, party regulars felt an acute loss of ownership over the party as the palpability of their black queer presence was swallowed up in the bar's largely white, male, and heterosexual clientele. As Elsa describes, "Of course there were, like, 'Chads' and 'Todds' [at The Whistler]," she says, using names often used to describe stereotypical hipster bros. "But, for the most part, the people who took up the most space were, like, *us.*" In the tight space of The Whistler, Slo 'Mo attendees felt the power of their black queer critical mass throughout the space. There, black queer women like Elsa felt they could contend with the occasional white dude who was taking up a lot of literal and figurative space. With a much larger capacity, however, another interlocutor describes the Slippery Slope as "too big for the gays to take over!"

Just as quickly as the Slippery Slope opened, it gained a reputation as not only a place where hipster bros go, but a place that seemingly brought out their worst stereotypical characteristics: that they are loud and aggressive, rude and demanding, and seemingly oblivious to the personal space of the people around them. Hipster bros on the Slo 'Mo dance floor at the Slippery Slope often enacted space-taking behaviors that diverged greatly from how black queer women experienced the party when it was hosted at The Whistler. The floor was often filled with hipster bros dancing with women in overtly sexual ways, or in group circles that took up a lot of room. Moreover, hipster bros who were very drunk were not typically conscious of how they were moving their bodies or whom they were slamming them into. Their behavior was extremely off-putting to black queer women who felt like Slo 'Mo at The Whistler was one of the few spaces where they were allowed a measure of protective space. "Since they've relocated [to the Slippery Slope] it's like . . . *pheeeeew*," Elsa sighs. "I've just never had to fight for space so hard for something that's supposed to be a dance party for *us*."

Much of the troubles at the Slippery Slope had to do with the venue's shape. Walking into the long L-shaped bar, one encounters three Skee-Ball games to the right and a small concessions stand to the left. The dim red lighting complements the three large red vinyl booths that line the left wall and that face the heavy wood décor of the three-hundred-foot-long bar, giving the space the aura of a classic supper club. Walking down the narrow walkway between the booths and the bar, one emerges on the dance floor where the DJ booth on the left is on a raised stage that is wrapped in chicken wire. Across the dance floor from the booth, bleachers line the opposite wall that are typically used by dancers wanting to showcase their own moves on an improvised stage, drawing likeness to a go-go stage. Despite the potential for this space to be used for seating, the bar generally did not allow people to congregate and commune around the dance floor, as happened at The Whistler.

Slo 'Mo's cultivation of slowness changed as DJs struggled to wend their sound throughout this space with a lot of distance between the official dance floor and the rest of the room. In the effort to increase the energy within and between songs in the twin hopes of drawing more people to the dance floor and more fully engaging those at the margins of the room, the DJs turned the volume up and played faster and more upbeat songs, (re)mixing the slow jams they *did* play in the style of contemporary electronic dance music (EDM) that emphasizes the repetition of short words, phrases, and drum patterns. As a result, the expected arrangements of Slo 'Mo's black queer sociality became subsumed under what Robin James describes as the musical conditions of subjectivity under neoliberalism. Looking to artists ranging from Rihanna to Skrillex, James describes how there is a point in any given EDM song where the repetition of a single vocal phrase or rhythm becomes intensified: the repetition is increased, the volume is raised, and the frequency is generally amplified. This amplification of sound (and the related dance movements) is always tempered, however, by the knowledge that the bass line will soon return and ground the song and the dancer back in the rhythm.[19]

In this, EDM pushes listeners to the limit only to release them with the finality of the beat finally dropping back in. "Riding the crest of auditory or machinic burnout," James explains, "these songs mimic, in music, the generalized affective experience of privilege in neoliberalism . . . EDM lets listeners experience what *feels like* risk, indulgence, and excess but is actually very tightly and carefully controlled."[20] But black queer women whose everyday lives within and beyond the gentrifying neighborhood already feel risky, precarious, and unstable don't necessarily *want* to experience their bodies being pushed to the edge within the span of a three-minute song, or over the course of a multihour queer dance party. The changing musical and social culture of Slo 'Mo at the Slippery Slope subsequently raised intense conversation among black queer attendees about what a black queer space can and should look like in a neighborhood where particularly black queer community is increasingly difficult to find and maintain.

The party's move to the Slippery Slope revealed much about the demographic and musical expectations of the party. The move also revealed how the party's soundscape, and the movement vocabularies it structured, was intimately entangled with the racialized queer politics and stakes of convening the party in the first place. One August night proved to be a tipping point where the method of nightlife convening long fostered at Slo 'Mo—a method organized around racialized gender and sexuality and attentive to the social and racial justice aims of its clientele—had to contend with the white obliviousness of the Slippery Slope. The summer of 2014 featured the high-profile murders of black people throughout the United States, including Eric Garner and Michael Brown, who, on one late-August night, Slo 'Mo commemorated. The dance floor was filling midway through the night when Kristen got on the microphone to make an announcement just as DJ Tess cut the music. Standing in the raised DJ booth, Kristen welcomed us to Slo 'Mo and thanked us for our presence, as she did every month. Those of us in the crowd took this moment of rest to sip our drinks as she began to voice her outrage at the events in Ferguson, Missouri, where Brown had just been gunned down and left to rot in the summer heat of a parking lot. Calling for a moment of silence, she worked to quiet the crowd of hipster bros gathered along the thirty-foot-long bar that is perpendicular to the dance floor, shouting into the microphone for them to be quiet in this grave moment and eventually repeatedly shouted a bartender's name into the microphone, asking him to quiet the bar crowd—which he also tried in vain to do. Kristen ultimately gave up on the task of quieting them and turned to focus on the crowd of nearly 100 queer women, trans, and gender nonconforming people, many of them black, clutching one another's hands, elbows, and shoulders.

Kristen then began a ghostly roll call of those who had been killed by the police, an unfamiliar practice that would come to be de rigueur in short time. The names she read were heard in concert with our collective memory of the pain that rang out when two beloved performers in Chicago's queer community went missing under separate circumstances that summer as well, resurfacing, thankfully, within weeks. She continued her roll call, calling the name of Vernita Gray, a black lesbian activist in Chicago who had passed away in March, and the names of Mia Henderson and Kandy Hall, black trans women who were killed in Baltimore, just as the presence of the hipster bros became suddenly indomitable. The hipster bros' voices had not only risen to a fever pitch, but they had themselves been slowly making their way to the dance floor on which we stood in silent remembrance. DJ Tess took the initiative to cut the memorial perhaps shorter than Kristen would have wanted, queuing up Chaka Khan to assuage a potential confrontation between the oblivious bar goers and the concentration of queers there for Slo 'Mo who had become quite agitated.

As Chaka sputtered over the sound system, the gathering of queer people of color who had earlier surrounded me in respectful silence suddenly whooped, shouted, and sang along to the song as they danced, relieved to shake off the gravity of the previous minutes and anxious to stand firm in their occupation of the dance floor. Soon, however, the hipster bros were drunkenly spilling their drinks down our backs as they danced with their elbows high in the air, holding their drinks above their heads while they marched to the music. It seemed they had no sense of bodily awareness as they rattled our bones pushing and squeezing their way between me and my friends, interlocutors, and familiar strangers who had grown accustomed to Slo 'Mo's social contract. At the end of that night's memorial, many of Slo 'Mo's most regular attendees transitioned, unwillingly, to the edges of the dance floor to head to the bar for drinks or to simply stand and talk while seemingly oblivious hipster bros took over the dance floor.

If at The Whistler black queers could find space to sit, dance, talk, and simply *be*, the space and the clientele of the Slippery Slope forced them to the physical margins of the bar. In other nights, Slo 'Mo attendees were edged off the dance floor because hipster bros were directing too much of the wrong kind of attention to them. One incident had four or five white hipster bros dancing in a circle around three Slo 'Mo regulars who were not, by any means, encouraging the attention. I watched as the men posed questions to a woman with long locs dressed in all-black like "so, what's this all about?" as they danced. The questions were meant to simultaneously query why these women were at the bar and meant to interrogate out their sexual orientations. Exasperated but in good humor, the women weaseled their way out of the virtual corral that had been placed around them and retreated to the bar near where I stood. Rolling their eyes, they exclaimed to one another that the men were too clueless to even entertain the possibility that the women weren't interested in them, let alone that the two of them might be gay. Ultimately, the possibilities for intimate black queerness that The Whistler lent to Slo 'Mo were fully disrupted at the Slippery Slope where the party was largely reduced to disparate clusters of black queer people struggling to navigate the white heterosexuality of the bros who pervade the bar. Slo 'Mo's black queer partygoers were rarely if ever verbally told they weren't welcome at the Slippery Slope, but moments such as these enforced a more insidious claim that their racial, sexual, and gendered identities were illegible or unwanted within the party and, the women would come to believe, by extension, the neighborhood and larger city.

As Slo 'Mo experimented with new venues and formats, Sarah was among a growing collection of people who were increasingly suspicious of the party's mobilization of blackness and black music in particular. In Sarah's view, the party turned toward radio-friendly slow jams "made for white people's consumption, so they don't have to recognize and honor where that production comes from, or what that means for people who relate to it in more intimate ways." For her, there was a gulf between the party's aesthetics and the party's actual commitments to black people. Slo 'Mo, she argues, "doesn't articulate an intention around people who have an appreciation for slow jams *and also* the specific space of cultural production coming from black folk. Like, that is something that is important even though they don't articulate that. It's curious that they don't." Sarah felt a sudden rupture in her relationship to the party when it moved to the Slippery Slope, arguing that simply playing slow jams insufficiently signaled one's attunement to the social and political contexts from which the music emerges and the scenes of cultural innovation it continually refers back to. In not "articulating an intention" around blackness, Sarah argues Slo 'Mo both co-signs the kinds of aggressive white sociality found in the Slippery Slope and actively diminishes the historical roots the party has in the city's black queer communities. "Why should I *still* feel out of place in this setting?" she explained of the party's move. "Because I *still* feel out of place. And I *still* don't see anyone like me. And I *still* feel wrong, you know? It's just like when I feel like that I have to leave." The party's shift from The Whistler to the Slippery Slope framed the sense that belonging in and ownership over the party were not ensured by one's mere presence there. Black queer women visibly inhabiting the party did little to enforce the sonic or temporal practices of the party. Their feelings of ownership and belonging were instead registered in whether they could physically and psychically inhabit that space on their own terms—or whether they should just leave.

Black queer women's connections in and to the party were further exacerbated when the party expanded to host a handful of events at venues such as SoHo House, which opened in Chicago's trendy West Loop area in August 2014. SoHo forms part of the large network of bars and restaurants that, with the support of the Kinzie Industrial Corridor TIF designation, have sprung up in this neighborhood directly west of downtown.[21] The area's clientele is largely made up of affluent suburbanites who can easily access the neighborhoods on the expressway and city-dwellers who have transformed themselves from hipster bros to creatives and tech bros who work in the lofts and coworking spaces that line the sometimes-still-cobblestoned streets of this former industrial and meatpacking district. SoHo House offers people in creative industries exclusive access to a restaurant, gym, bar space, hotel rooms, movie theater, rooftop pool, and more for thousands of dollars in annual fees. When hosting parties there, Slo 'Mo was given a handful of invitations to disperse to regular attendees, as few of them are club members.[22] But while the party potentially served as an opportunity for a black queer contingent to "take over" a historically white space, claiming it as its own, the traditional practices of inhabiting a given Slo 'Mo party were overwhelmed by the embodied norms of SoHo's regulars, who were overwhelmingly white middle-class and wealthy people. In sites such as this, slowness took on ever-new contours as people like Sarah deployed a range of movements from slowing down, often to register confusion at the musical choices, to fully refraining from dancing altogether in order to palpably chart their resistance to the party's instantiation at SoHo and the SoHo crowd the party ultimately served. "See," she told me as Sister Nancy's classic "Bam" came on at a Slo 'Mo at the SoHo House, "this music is, like, from my childhood but I'm not going to dance to it right now with them here." She gestured dismissively to a group of very drunk white men lumbering to the music, remaining seated to visibly contest the practices of white sociality she saw the party underwriting. As she sat back in the plush chairs surrounding the small dance floor, she was like the handful of other black queer women in attendance that night for whom stillness had become a highly visible way of contesting their literal and figurative movement off the dance floor. This was apparently not lost on Kristen. While many white SoHo members were already dancing with gusto, she worked hard to circulate throughout the room and encourage the handful of Slo 'Mo regulars there to enjoy the event, and repeatedly got onto the microphone to enjoin "everyone" to dance—summoning, in vain, the smattering of black queers watching from the sidelines.

At Slo 'Mo at The Whistler, slowness provided a critical space, soundtrack, *and* movement vocabulary to the style of queer communion that attendees believed was grounded in and continually gestured to an ethical relationship to black queer life. The pace of the party, which fostered particularly black communion for black queer woman attendees, combatted the imperatives for movement-cum-whiteness that structured the city and social relations beyond it. At venues such as the Slippery Slope and SoHo House, however, the expected arrangements of black queer sociality that had long been tuned to the slow build of FKA Twigs, Sade, and Anthony Hamilton became subsumed under an aural-temporal rhetoric that catered to the white, heteromasculine sociality of Chicago's broader gentrifying landscape.[23] To be sure, black queer women often have the capacity to take time in nightlife scenes and gentrifying milieus that depend upon the time debt of others, yet their sonic and embodied battles at Slo 'Mo reveal the enduring potential of slowness as a racialized queer aesthetic and practice that provides them the theoretical language, surrounding, and scaffolding for embodied interventions into the normalizing spatiotemporalities of the neoliberal city. Where slowness was a measure of comfort at The Whistler, it dragged into a strategy of stillness that black queer women utilized at the Slippery Slope and SoHo in the hopes that, as Sarah sighs, "next time it will be different."

Next Time It Will Be Different

The Slo 'Mo organization responded to black queer women's mobilizations of slowness as a method of critique, and the party returned to The Whistler in February 2015. The party's tenure at the Slippery Slope was a difficult time for attendees and organizers alike. That party, Kristen explains, "is just like the Dark Ages, a black spot in the trajectory of Slo 'Mo, a slippery slope, which there isn't even one photo from. It has literally been erased from our history. We don't even reference it." Opting to scale back and return to the slow intimacy fostered at The Whistler catered to the needs of those who long supported the party, certainly to the detriment of a growth model that might have generated more people (and perhaps profit) to the Slo 'Mo organization. But "we really needed that [experience] to understand what was important to people," Kristen reflects. "I will sometimes feel really guilty of, 'Oh, I could have grown and brought this party to a bigger space,' but I think the intimacy is very integral to what makes that party so special."

Following its return to The Whistler, the organization soon welcomed the black queer woman DJ Audio Jack (Erin Jackson) on as resident and coorganizer, DJ Tess moved on to other endeavors, and the party quickly found its groove again. Erin's incorporation felt like a natural extension of Slo 'Mo's original goals, in no small part due to the fact that she herself "had been going from the beginning. I think I was the first person Kristen told about wanting to do this party. So, it made sense that it would be me. In my younger days, I was a standout on the dance floor! I feel like I was very much one of the many faces, regular faces, of the party anyway." Though back at The Whistler and helmed by familiars, Slo 'Mo did see fewer black people attending and fewer of the party's original regulars—but there were simply fewer people over the age of thirty in attendance. These demographic facts cause Kristen and Erin a certain amount of anxiety. They are acutely aware of how nightlife communities often skew young, and that the evolution of Slo 'Mo necessarily means that the pre–Slippery Slope audience has simply gotten older. "I think that there are many people who have been coming, like you, since the beginning and started going in their twenties, and now they're in their thirties," Kristen observes, "or people that were probably in their thirties and going into their forties, and they're just more selective about when they come." The demographic changes are encouraging to her, however, and she is "really happy that Slo 'Mo can be a space where younger queers are coming into an environment that feels welcoming, that feels affirming, where they feel seen there, where they don't feel ostracized." For Erin, the "reality is, everybody's dancing, everybody's having a good time. New people are still coming to the party. There's still a line. . . . It's still a fresh crowd, which is kind of cool."

At the same time, as people who are themselves over thirty and who are themselves seeking certain kinds of communion within their queer night-lives, Kristen and Erin sometimes experience an isolation at their own party. The twinge of nostalgia for the party's early years, mixed with plain difficulty in hosting a party every month, and inflected with what Erin describes as loneliness, "to look out and not see as many people [that] I recognize," has at times verged on a desire to stop the party altogether. "Last year I had very mixed feelings, and I was thinking about ending it," notes Kristen.

I can't believe I said that out loud because I've never really been like "I'm going to end it" but I was like I don't know how much I want to keep doing this. And then this year I felt really great because something about eight (just like [turning] thirty-four) felt really different for me, where I was like, "*Bitch*, you been doing it every fucking year. Eight years?!

In forging a commitment to going at least two years more, hitting the decade mark, Kristen had to reconfigure her own relationships to the pace of the party. In summer 2018, she started an all-vinyl, midtempo R&B party, Old Gold: Grown Music for Grown People at the Ace Hotel's rooftop bar, the Waydown. This free, monthly day party saw the return of DJ Tess into the fold and reintroduced slowness into the organization's soundscape, both the relative slowness of DJs working only with vinyl and not digital music, and the slow-jams content of the sets themselves. Like Slo 'Mo of yore, Old Gold brought a diverse crowd and saw an abundance of black queer women—and older black queer women—come through its doors. The party does not have the same kind of physical intimacy forged in The Whistler's small space (nor does it have those lines) where black queer women could "take over" the space. The very spacious Waydown has three bars, a vast interior lounge, and plenty of seating on its large rooftop area. It doesn't have quite the same social intimacy, either, as Old Gold attendees share space with people stopping by the Waydown in their larger wanderings through Fulton Market's very robust service industry. The bar-hotel sits across the street from a new Google building, not too far from SoHo House, and draws a wide-ranging crowd of people staying at the hotel, weeknight and weekend bar hoppers, and tech and business administration workers who come to the space after work. Old Gold nonetheless fills a great need for the party organizers and for people whose relationships to Slo 'Mo changed, whether as a result of the racialized dynamics of its aesthetics, as was the case for Sarah, or because people "aged out" of the scenes of their youth and want other, slower forms of communion.

Old Gold marks Slo 'Mo's long-standing efforts to incubate a kind of slowness that generates intimacy among partygoers and at the same time reflects questions of age and sustainability that Slo 'Mo organizers and attendees alike have been facing since the party's time at the Slippery Slope some three years earlier, and over the course of the nearly ten years that Slo

'Mo has been throwing parties (making it one of the longest-running queer parties in the city by the time this book is published). "Anyone that has been observing the party for a long time will know I basically re-created Slo 'Mo with [Old Gold]," Kristen explains. This meant re-creating a sense of play for her and the DJs, where they could inhabit a sense of lightness and joy in making their song selections, and "mak[ing] sure we were still having a moment where that midtempo accessible vibe was still happening. Where you could still have a drink and sit down and chill and have a conversation." Slowness, here, is simply critical to the sustainability of partying. On one hand, the pace of Old Gold reinjected the Slo 'Mo organization with a renewed vigor that allowed them to imagine themselves throwing parties at least until they turn ten. On the other hand, its slow jams allow for an economy of movement that is manageable for attendees who feel their bodies tightening up and who don't recover as quickly as they did after a night of dancing; for people who want to talk and catch up, and to reminisce about and sing along to music from their youth.

Across its iterations in the rapidly Logan Square and Fulton Market neighborhoods, Slo 'Mo reveals slowness is not a detriment to productivity but a mechanism of sustainability. It is necessary to remain viable in a landscape where economies of feeling are linked to the pace of the exchange of capital. It is important to remember here that slowness is not a full stop; it is not an outright refusal or wholesale dismissal of neoliberalism's grip on urban space, on a party, nor on the social choreographies that either circumscribe. Black queer women like Sarah continually returned to Slo 'Mo in its multiple locations knowing they may have to elbow their way onto the dance floor, to deflect intrusive stares with combative glares, or protectively surround themselves with their black queer peers in order to dance relatively freely. They went knowing they would stand still when a hipster or tech bro tried to engage them in dancing or refuse to speak when one tried to engage them in talking. They went knowing they might sit the whole night, either out of pleasure, or in visible and palpable resistance.

These enactments of slowness weren't meant to overhaul or utterly dismantle the black queer common sense Slo 'Mo cultivated, nor did they signal refusals to attend in an effort to shut the party down. Such stopping would argue that wresting control, be it of a city or a party, requires wholesale divestment in, and disentanglement from, the ways capitalism structures goods, services, cultures, spaces, and the communities that they are enmeshed with. As the black queer women who call Slo 'Mo home continually return to the party but insist on slowness as a critical rubric of belonging therein, they agitate for a semblance of an ideal black queer space that does not exist *outside* of the gentrifying districts that they circulate through, nor operate beyond the controlling regimes of whiteness and heterosexuality (and, to be sure, whiteness and homosexuality) that drive neoliberal urbanization. Black queer women's inhabitations of slowness at Slo 'Mo are more like moments of presence and pause that comprise strategies of endurance and subsistence that, in the words of Saidiya Hartman, "do not yield easily to the grand narrative of revolution."[24] For many of Slo 'Mo's attendees, grand revolution, the general strike, is just short of impossible. This is in no small part because the historical, material conditions of existing within bodies marked as black and as woman and as queer demand vigilant attention to the reality of the moment: that one of the very few opportunities you will have to connect with other black queer women may be done in a neighborhood, in a venue, or through an organization that might not meet all of your needs. Their strategies of remaining but at a different, slower pace instead articulate ways of knowing and becoming known within the gentrifying landscape that reimagine rights to the city as necessarily negotiated along ephemeral axes: not only via economic capital, but through the embodied and affective capital of pleasure that makes one intelligible within spaces like Slo 'Mo, gentrifying neighborhoods, and neoliberal cities. They don't return to the party hoping to escape the many kinds of violence that structure Chicago city space. They return knowing that, when all is right, they might find a space on the dance floor and hit their groove just as the melisma of Luther's voice falls up and down the scale and over their bodies.

TWO
WHERE'S THE JOY IN ACCOUNTABILITY?
BLACK JOY AT ITS LIMITS

NICK: Let others tell it: 2018 could've been a year that Party Noire dissolved.

RAE: That we stopped.

NICK: But we felt that we had a responsibility to this space and community that we created, that: fuck y'all, really [*laughs*].

RAE: Fuck y'all. But I'm so responsible to it that I am going to say: fuck y'all!

Nick and DJ Rae Chardonnay's complex intonations of "fuck y'all" capture the dynamics of responsibility and accountability that bring queer party organizers and attendees together—and at times threaten to tear them apart. On one hand, "fuck y'all" indexes the exhaustion the two were feeling after many years of hosting events as Party Noire. They cofounded Party Noire with Lauren Ash in 2015 with the intention to hold space for black queer women and femmes, and black queer people across the gender spectrum, all under the banner of "Black Joy." Party Noire began in "a loaded year," Nick explains. "And it was a year that was surrounding a lot of Black death. Black Joy doesn't exist in this vacuum that's just, like, an idealistic space. It exists in connection to us being oppressed *and* living." They hosted a day party every few months in the Hyde Park neighborhood and would soon unseat Slo 'Mo as "Best Dance Party" in Chicago. They expanded to include night parties and rounded out their practice of Black Joy with wellness activities that happen beyond the bar space, such as yoga sessions and bike rides. For Party Noire, then, Black Joy is not a passive affect, but "a practice that is resistance to these uglier things that happen," Nick explains. Black Joy is, for Rae, a practice of "how we respond to those things."[1] Black Joy—a critical language, affective orientation, and embodied practice—brings Party Noire's black queer organizers and attendees together in their shared desires to feel good on the dance floor, but also to experience black queer community as a response to and in the midst of the violence that can shape it.

But 2018 brought challenges to the practice of Black Joy, and tested Nick and Rae's drive to continue the hard work of nightlife organizing. That year, sexual assault allegations were lodged against the party's photographer, a cisgender heterosexual black man. Around the same time there was a surprising and high-profile leadership change as Lauren left the organization for other pursuits. The year also saw a lot of gossip surrounding one of the organizer's romantic breakups, which became very public on social media. These three events caused much conversation and speculation among the many black queer women and gender expansive people who attend Party Noire, and who worried that Black Joy was feeling less like a practice of collectivizing and more like a marketable brand without a political focus. Black queer women like Candace, a former Party Noire regular, are quite clear about the relationship between organizers and the image and practices of the events they throw. "I feel like now a lot of people have entered the queer nightlife-making space who aren't necessarily interested in just creating a space for queer people to be able to get free. People have created these spaces in order for them to boost their own clout, you know what I'm saying?" In her own "fuck y'all," Candace highlights the ways that securing a party's brand can come at the expense of the community that parties can incubate.

Nick and Rae's "fuck y'all" expresses their exhaustion as it was exacerbated by what they felt was a lack of support and patience as the organization figured out how to navigate difficult terrain that many, if not all, queer nightlife organizers face at some point. This includes how to respond to attendees' diverse needs, how to cultivate pleasure *and* safety within each party, and how to define the scope of what a nightlife organization can or should do when pleasure or safety is threatened. Threaded through each of these elements of nightlife organizing is how to understand the relationships between what happens within an event and what happens beyond it, and how to understand the relationships between organizers' private lives and their public organizational work. Nick and Rae experienced "fuck y'all" levels of exhaustion given how, often, there is little separation between party organizers' private lives and the politics of the organizations that they run.

At the same time, their "fuck y'all" indexes their insistence that critics can fuck off, that they will continue to feel their way through this work because they know how important the party is to themselves and to the people they bring together. This version of "fuck y'all" doubles down on the hard work of nightlife organizing as community building—an endeavor that, as they see it, is necessarily collective. As Nick explains, "I do feel like I do have a responsibility but again want to create this idea of collective responsibility. 'Cause it can't—literally you have two of us." Rae echoes this in explaining, "We feel an immense responsibility for the work that we do. But we do try to make the responsibility a *shared* responsibility. And we do ask community members to take ownership of the space in the same way that we have some ownership of the space." For Nick and Rae, Black Joy brings people together in their mutual desires to dance, to experience black queer community, and to ultimately feel good, and this entails a mutual responsibility to uphold the feelings and politics of the party.

Party Noire stakeholders' relationships to the scandals of 2018 say much about the antagonisms that can surface between party organizers and attendees as they negotiate responsibility and accountability within and beyond the queer party space. This chapter is specifically interested in how competing accounts of responsibility and accountability ("fuck y'all") sketch the complexities of galvanizing around a single feeling (Black Joy) in a neighborhood and city where feeling is a deeply racialized and classed commodity that is differentially mapped across distinct territories of the city. As the Party Noire community grappled with organizational upheaval, interpersonal conflict, and the violence of heterosexual masculinity, they wondered about the potentially limited capacities of Black Joy to consolidate Black queer community within the gentrifying, downtown Hyde Park area where the party is hosted. Their negotiations of the embodied possibilities of Black Joy at the party are shot through with critiques of how the neighborhood's redevelopment, underwritten by the University of Chicago, is conditioned by a racist geographic imagination that scripts the rest of the South Side as a physically violent space and an affectively threatening environment. The chapter examines how black queer women theorize the political economy of Black Joy as a product of the (re)investment in Hyde Park's downtown commercial district, where good feelings are the by-products of good investments, and where it seems Black Joy can only ever be rented from white profiteers. The Party Noire community's difficult navigations of accountability amid 2018's scandals—and, specifically in the ways that they remain at an impasse as to whether accountability has been sufficiently achieved—reveal the limits of crafting Black Joy as an ethically black queer arrangement within a neighborhood (and city) that is organized around the violent, heteropatriarchal, and capitalist control of black space in all of its spatial, affective, and choreographic coordinates.

Black Joy's Choreographies of Support

At Party Noire, as in other dance scenes, black queer women quite simply teach one another to move their bodies and feel their feelings, and how to do so toward specifically queer ends. Through choreographies of support that facilitate black queer women's individuality on the dance floor, they also produce senses of collectivity that, in turn, help black queer women realize the potentials of Black Joy, to be sure, but also a specifically Black *Queer* Joy. The party's Black Joy brand emerged around the same time that images and narratives of Black Joy, Black Girl Magic, Carefree Black Child, and Black Boy Joy were circulating in popular culture, especially online. The images and narratives these terms captured spotlighted black people looking and feeling good: dressed up, dancing together, laughing and goofing off, seeming unbothered, posing alone or with family, at special events, and the like. Using hashtags and captions to frame these materials as Black Joy serves to contradict images of black criminality and black death, and to contradict narrow stereotypes of black people as always producing or being on the receiving end of violence. The visual production of Black Joy "allows us," Javon Johnson writes, "to theorize a world in which white supremacy does not dictate our everyday lives."[2] Black Joy documents both the condition and the resulting feeling-good-while-black, which can be extremely hard work given the force of white supremacy.

The Party Noire organization distributes such Black Joy in the high-quality photographic documentation of their events, which feature prominently on their social media channels and on their website. These images focus on sharply dressed twenty- and thirtysomething black people across the gender spectrum posing for the camera, conversing with one another, and deep in the process of dancing. Where these images document joyous black people, the accompanying captions and hashtags typically explicitly frame them through the language of Black Joy (e.g., #HereForBlackJoy"). This visual circulation of Black Joy serves an important pedagogical function: images, sounds, videos, and texts framed as Black Joy model the forms, functions, and results of what Black Joy can look and feel like when you attend Party Noire.

Party Noire's vibrant dance floor reveals the reciprocal relationship between the image-idea of Black Joy and the choreographies of support through which Black Joy is produced. Choreographies of support describe the physical and affective ways that black queer women support one another on the dance floor: how they subtly and explicitly instruct one another in how to move their bodies alone and in concert with one another and, in the process, how to inhabit a Black Joy that is expressly queer. David Román's description of the conjoined process of coming into dance, gay community, and political activism in the 1970s and '80s is useful for an understanding of choreographies of support, as he describes how learning to dance alone and alongside other gay men was inextricable from his learning how to "do" politics. As Román learned how to ease onto the dance floor, he found that

> dance signaled not the promise of gay liberation but its *practice*. I knew that the first time I stepped into a gay bar and saw gay people dancing. I just didn't know how I was supposed to step into that dance, and I didn't quite know what were the necessary moves to get there. But there was no question that these people had figured it out and created something for themselves and for others like me.[3]

"These people" were instrumental in teaching Román the physical steps to sync himself up with other gays (and some lesbians) who'd already found their physical but also their political groove. Through their choreographies of support, Román was pulled onto the dance floor and taught how to hold on to the beat while also being taught how to move in step with them as they moved into the streets to create awareness around, and support to ameliorate, the devastations of HIV/AIDS.

Fiona Buckland echoes Román as she describes her own experiences of how the pedagogical functions of social dance in New York's queer clubs of the 1990s instructed her in how to move on *and* off the dance floor in expressly queer ways:

> Through going to queer clubs, I learned the rules of a lifeworld: how to dress, how to interact, and the in-jokes, argot, values, and issues. . . .

I also learned to incorporate and embody a way of being that allowed me to interpret any environment through a worldview informed by queerness. A queer lifeworld is not only a stage outside of the body, but a state of consciousness and a way of deportment. Movement is central to understanding this.[4]

As Román and Buckland describe, dancing is a highly individualized trajectory of learning how to absorb, process, and physically respond to audiovisual stimuli in ways that make you legible as a particularly sexualized body and politics. It is also a deeply social process, and how we dance reflects where we were raised, the extent to which our families and friends dance, the kinds of media we consume, and other factors. Román and Buckland describe how dance is thus a mechanism through which we can quite literally learn to inhabit and project identities, practices, and politics that reflect our relationships to sexuality and a politics of sexuality—and this is a decidedly collective project.

Black queer women's choreographies of support are made possible in large part by Party Noire's frank emphasis on dancing. Rae explains that "folks just really wanna dance. Folks are tired of going in clubs, paying money to be in a space and stand around looking at each other. It's the worst." So, musically, Party Noire strives to make it virtually impossible to *not* dance. Rae DJs each event and programs two or three guest DJs who bring together juke music, afrobeat, and trap mixes that emphasize giving dancers time to catch the beat. "The way I play is a very House-oriented style, even if it's not House music," Rae explains. "So, I'm letting the track breathe. . . . I generally am seeking out other DJs that have no problem letting a track ride." These DJs include Chicago staples like Bonita Appleblunt, Professor-wrecks, BoneReader, All The Way Kay, and Ca$h Era. While DJs largely get free reign to play whatever they want, the organization has "a very soft, 'please don't play white artists'" rule and a very hard "No R. Kelly" rule. Nick explains that the goal is for guest DJs to "pull from your blackest library, and really don't feel like you have to play Top 40, 'cause this is not a Top 40 party." For Rae, building in nontraditional club sounds is a process of honoring what she wants to hear, but also of acclimating dancers to new sounds and new ways of connecting with their bodies: "And so even if I'm not dropping Beyoncé, they know that when I drop this Kaytranada, you know, they're gonna like that. Or even if I drop a more kind of electronic remix it's gonna be in a way that's around some things that they can comfortably move to." For Nick, this makes Party Noire's sound "very visionary. We want you to come in, whatever you think that you can't actually play at your other gigs, you can play that shit in here."

DJs appreciate the opportunity to experiment with their sets and to also play their own original mixes, and a Black Joy manifests in the freedom they feel at Party Noire. As Professor-wrecks explains, "I have DJed *a lot* of different venues, and I will say that consistently Party Noire is probably the most versatile party that I've been able to DJ at where they're like: do your thing, play whatever the fuck you want, go for it." Key to producing Black Joy on the dance floor, in other words, is allowing DJs to themselves have a bit of fun. Ca$h Era feels like she can be playful and experimental when she DJs Party Noire, where she finds there's a particularly generative feedback loop between her and the dancers:

> I can get it ratchet and then I can slow it down in the same second and they will move to anything I put on. . . . For the Party Noire party, you can play any genre and somebody on the dance floor will kick off the dancing. And at Party Noire if you have one person dancing the entire room will dance with them.

As Ca$h suggests, much of the party's Black Joy is produced in the affective and choreographic relationship between one person dancing and the entire room jumping up to dance with them. This is especially important for Tess, who moved to Chicago from Atlanta and was feeling frustrated with people not dancing at the bars and parties she was attending to get a feel for the city. "Sometimes we go to parties, people don't want to dance or they don't want to dance with people they don't know," she explains. At Party Noire, however, things are different: "There it's like, 'I don't care if I don't know you, let's dance.'" The large space of Party Noire allows people like Tess, but also Taylor, to feel comfortable in arriving alone—if they wait until the party is a couple of hours underway, there will surely be enough people there where they can slip in and move around anonymously until they find people to link up with (if they want).

This is perfect for Taylor, who wants to be left alone to simply dance just as much as they want to feel part of a larger community. They explain, "If I go to Party Noire, it is just to dance. I've gone to Party Noire by myself. And I'm like, 'I'm just gonna put something on because I'm only going here to dance. I'm not going to talk to people or interact.' I might interact with them on the dance floor, but I'm really just going to dance." Party Noire cultivates their ability to focus on dancing alone while also providing points of connection to other attendees at the party, which they feel most of all when people are engaged in various forms of line dancing. "Man, at Party Noire, when the Swag Surf's on, it is *lit*," Taylor exclaims, referencing the 2009 song and accompanying dance. Unlike other line dances like the Cupid Shuffle where people stand apart yet move in unison, Swag Surfin' requires dancers to plant their feet and drape their arms over one another, physically holding on to one another as they collectively sway left and right to the beat. The physicality of the Swag Surf's choreography of support—the communality of everyone knowing the same dance, and gripping one another the minute it comes on—enters Taylor into a particular kind of Black Joy high: "And it's now [like] we're connected because now everyone's going to do this move, and it's like we're homies now."

Swag Surfin' is also a touchpoint for LJ as they link dancing at Party Noire with the possibilities of black queer community within and beyond it. LJ moved to Chicago from the South and, like many of the transplants in this book, were still working to find a sense of community three years later. "I feel like I *know* a lot of people here, but it's always so separate; it's not close and personal. There's not many folks I can just have over to my house. It's always like, 'Oh, I'll see you at the club.'" While they have many opportunities to simply see and be around friends (and strangers) in club settings, the collectivity of Party Noire's clublife was a particularly bright spot where they felt an immediate sense of deeper connection to the party and to black queer women. Of their first time at the party, they remember

> seeing all these black folks, all these black queer women around me, and it being so special. And everyone immediately was dancing. I remember just sitting down at the bar with my friend and being like pulled onto the dance floor, like, "We're going to dance," and Swag Surfing in a room with all these black queer folks and just having it be so great. And I remember hugging so many people that day and just talking to so many folks and telling them that, like, "Oh, I just moved here." And they're asking how they can be of support, asking if they can show me around, asking if I had been to downtown Hyde Park. Just really just trying to get to know me, and that was such a special day. I think in that moment was when I finally felt home in Chicago.

As LJ's language demonstrates, there is a very close relationship between dancing and community building at Party Noire, where the choreographies of support that Taylor finds in Swag Surfin' are part of cultivating a dense network of affiliation beyond the dance floor. The experience of being pulled onto the dance floor, seemingly immediately upon entry, is mirrored by the experience of being pulled into community within and beyond it. Party Noire was key to creating temporary and lasting connections with black queer people with whom LJ could forge connections through affective and material support that helped them become more grounded in the city.[5]

Party Noire can feel especially important to people who have never felt black queer collectivity in a party space or, sometimes, anywhere. "I had never been in a space where it was so many just queer people just dancing and moving," Ca$h tells me of her first time at Party Noire. Throughout and after college she was DJing and attending college parties and eighteen-and-up events, but she was often the only woman DJ and/or queer person in the room.[6] When she turned twenty-one, a friend took her to her first Party Noire party—which was also her first time ever attending a queer party. "It was freeing. I felt empowered. Yeah, that's a good word for it. I felt like I belong, and that was something that I think I had never felt at a party before." Like LJ, the music and dance drew Ca$h in as much as the sense of community built through them. She continues,

> And the party was just great. I was like, "Yo, I want to DJ one of these one day. This is what I want to constantly come to." And after that first one, any party they did, I went to. And it was just like, I became I guess almost like a regular, but it was like, I didn't know people's names, I just knew people's faces. But I felt welcome. It was like, "Oh, hey, how are you? Good to see you." It was constantly compliments. And it was, like, in those faces, it felt like a home that I knew I could dance and not be judged.

The party's Black Joy is sensed in these affective bonds that Ca$h and LJ forged when first entering the Party Noire space, where they felt welcomed by people who not only looked like them but who actively welcomed them in by pulling them onto a judgment-free dance floor. The warmth and affirmations that they describe underscore the affective elements of Black Joy that consolidate community as something that can be deeply intuited and felt even as it may not result in, for example, knowing someone's name. This Black Joy materializes in the drive to, like Erica, simply "be around people and just that revelry, like, 'Yeah! We out and all dancing!' . . . I just like to go out and have a good time because we need joy sometimes!" Erica's delight at the feeling of "We out and all dancing!" expresses the pleasure of being amid the sheer density of black queer people assembling together, moments when, as Romi Crawford suggests, black "collectivity is not supra-inscribed and codified but undoubtedly happening."[7] This practice of assembling is key to imagining and theorizing other ways of being, and our choreographies of support help us to translate our individual histories into collectively expressed being and shared futures. Such transformational exchanges of "embodied truths" happen when hundreds of black people Swag Surf, but also in smaller-scale moments where black queer women watch and discuss one another's dancing in the many cyphers that break out over the duration of any given Party Noire.[8]

THE CYPHER

In a cypher, Ayana explains, "a nice song come on, a nice beat where you throw it in the circle; 'yes, I'm about to do that shit.'" Dancers do that shit for a crowd that circles around them, watching, cheering, and often filming them, their cellphone flashlights providing supportive spotlights. Cyphers have deep roots in the history of black movement traditions that utilize improvised social dance and the shape of the circle to produce and consolidate group identity while honoring individuality, from the call-and-response formation of the ring shout to the competitive trading in movement and attitude that characterizes the hip-hop dance battle.[9] At Party Noire, cyphers can indeed be quite intense and full of the pressure that comes with jumping into the middle of a circle of people watching you dance. This does not mean, though, that cyphers are particularly competitive, or that they are only sites for technically skilled dancers to show off their dance moves. People like Austin often jump into the circle simply because the spirit catches them and/or because they want to feel the generous attention of their community. Austin is a self-described "bad dancer" yet they feed off of the attention they receive when they're in the middle of the cypher; they also feed off of the energy they feel when supporting other people dancing. For them, the cypher is about this balance, where "you get to be a part of that, be in the circle, or [if] you want to [you] can step back and watch and hype them up." Because the cypher allows people to participate as dancers and as onlookers, it is an ideal formation for understanding how choreographies of support physically and affectively bind people together at Party Noire.

There are many cyphers that spontaneously break out over the course of any given Party Noire, in part because the large, open layout of The Promontory effectively decentralizes the dance floor. When entering the space in the early hours of the party, attendees stand around a rectangular, four-sided bar with most of its barstools removed to make way for more people. If weather allows, they spill onto the adjacent rooftop deck where people socialize through conversation more than dance. The DJ booth is tightly nestled into a corner of this relatively small space that is cut off from the rest of the space by a heavy curtain. As the night progresses, the curtain is eventually drawn back and people rush to secure space among the movable tables and chairs that frame either side of the large dance floor, and that mostly serve to hold dancers' things and provide brief moments of rest. The DJs seamlessly transfer from the bar-side booth to the eighteen-by-eighteen-foot stage that heads the dance floor. As the Party Noire space effectively triples in size and the DJs move locations, attendees variously orient to the stage, to one another on the dance floor, and to the bar that lies opposite it. In other words, there is no one place where the larger dancing collective is compelled to orient toward for the duration of a Party Noire party. Instead, dancers themselves become the focus points, and cyphers serve as a constant yet temporary site around which dancers and onlookers coalesce.

The cypher's choreographies of support instruct Party Noire attendees in Black Joy as a collective endeavor. This is in large part because cyphers train people to "be aware of your space," Austin notes. In cyphers, people take turns dancing, watching, and waiting for a lull or change in another dancer's movements that signals a break where they can themselves enter in. A dancer in the middle of the cypher has to make a rapid decision when another dancer enters the fray: cede the floor or assess whether the new dancer wants to dance *with* them. The new dancer has, in turn, to manage their energy and attitude to signal whether they want to dance alone or together. These cyphers are highly intuitive, responsive sites where black queers learn to interpret and respond to energy as a communal networking force. Austin explains,

> I think there's just an unwritten rule of these social norms of knowing when to back out or sometimes an exchange can happen where you get up and somebody else is like, "OK, my turn." I personally try to find that balance between getting out of a cypher before you get pushed out of one, you just have to be respectful.

Even when lost in the pleasures of dancing, one must remain attentive to the needs of those surrounding and wanting to jump into the cypher. The practices of paying attention in a Party Noire cypher foster a sense of cohesion among black queers that Austin takes great relief in. "There can be a sense of being watched, or realizing that you are a show while in a cypher," Austin notes.

And that's why it's so important that communities of color have a space of our own to dance freely. For example, I went to . . . a predominately white school and there's a whole different feeling when it's a whole bunch of white people circling around you in a cypher, watching you, or literally saying, "I like the way y'all dance." I'm like, "No, bitch. It's time to *go*." I'm like, "I don't want to dance anymore." Being in a space like Party Noire, to have that kind of experience around other people of color, it's like, "OK, I feel validated and accepted."

Here, Austin gestures toward how the dynamics of respect within and around the cypher are grounded in the constitutive gaze of the cypher at Party Noire: you are either there to watch or be watched, and the dancer must also be responsive to when this gaze feels exploitative and when it feels validating. At Party Noire, where there are very few nonblack people, Austin can trust that the affirmation that surrounds the cypher is not rooted in racial stereotypes but black queer affirmation.

Cyphers moreover illuminate the expressly queer possibility of and within Party Noire's Black Joy as they normalize and train attendees to see and engage with the black queer choreographies of support that crop up on the dance floor. This happens in sometimes direct ways, as when people call upon repertoires like voguing, and in the general visibility of black queer bodies moving together within and around the cypher. Bri is very much an onlooker more than a dancer, and she rarely if ever jumps into the cypher herself. She nonetheless loves the space of a cypher because she wants to be a part of the feedback loop through which black queer life and energies are affirmed. "I also love seeing us enjoy music," she explains. "I don't mind seeing some girl that's getting it, and I'm like, 'Girl, you are *killing* it. I'ma hype you up.'" The choreographies of support fostered at Party Noire allow black queer women like Ayana a window into what a black queer lifeworld can look like. While her queerness is an unwelcome topic of conversation with her family and at work, "I tell someone at Party Noire and it's just like a regular thing. I don't need to have a conversation, I don't need to say anything. It's just a nod and, like, 'Oh OK, I got you,' and then no judgment." She is generatively overwhelmed by the access to the sheer diversity of black queerness on display, "because it's like you see so many different people, so many styles, so much fashion, and so it's just like, brah, I'm not limited to this one thing."

The choreographies of support at Party Noire also structure physical opportunities for people to experiment with their bodies in a supportive space where the networks of looking and feeling are not exploitative or threatening but affirming of their developing understandings of what gives them pleasure. In other words, the cypher's choreographies of support can more explicitly instruct people to inhabit the queer coordinates of Black Joy. This is the case for Alexandra, who attended her first Party Noire parties alone, when she wasn't entirely out to her community or family. She frequently saw black queer women dancing together in cyphers and felt they were powerfully enacting their confidence and pleasure, even as watching them pressed the limits of her slowly expanding notions of comfort and propriety: "There was extreme moments where two people was on the dance floor: damn, they're having sex! You know what I mean? Those moments. They were really getting into the dancing. I think that's a cool energy. You just in it. 'You sexy. I'm about to get it.'"[10] Bearing witness to the party's myriad cyphers quite literally taught Alexandra in the choreographic ways of black lesbian and queer identities and dynamics, which was extremely important for her own understandings of her own gender and sexuality. One party in particular helped her calibrate her relationships to black queerness as a fluid, flexible, dynamic, and adaptable practice.

She attended the party alone, as she often did because she was still very early in building an intentional queer community. Going to parties alone is easy for her because she has that rare skill of comfortably introducing herself and making genuine friends out of strangers, if only for the span of one night. Sometimes, of course, mutual attention-sharing was as much about finding new friends as it was about scoping potential romantic interests. This night she was getting a heavy dose of the latter, which gently forced her to take some risks in her budding queer identity:

> The attention I was getting that night at Party Noire was, *damn girl!* I was like, "OK, let me try this thing out." In my head: "OK, this is part of my experimentation, part of my phase, part of my body journey," whatever the hell. "Maybe I like being a femme role. That's what I'm used to, so it should be easy." It's interesting because this one moment I had with this chick, dressed masc; that's her thing. I wasn't attracted to her.

Alexandra wasn't particularly attracted to "this chick" but she spit good enough game for Alexandra to dance with her. "She really did a good job. Complimented me. Just keep it coming. . . . She called me beautiful like eight times. I said, '*Oh*.'" On the dance floor, Alexandra found herself assuming the "feminine" role of a traditional dance partnership, guided by the "masculine" lead who directs the body and movements of the duo. In this arrangement, Alexandra learned:

> What I more wasn't attracted to was being in that role with her. I thought that was surprising because I'm like, "Oh, I'm used to doing this with guys." Even if I'm not attracted to a guy, I'll still do that and dance with them if I'm cool and I like it. I didn't like it, in this case. I was like, "OK, lesson learned." Probably my cap with attraction is going to be andro, stemme—I learned that word—it's probably gonna be that. They gotta be a little bit of both. You can't be just all masculine.

In this exchange, dance becomes the physical and affective material through which she reconfigures her relationship to gender expression and desire. She was familiar with heterosexual dynamics of partner dancing that break down along binary gendered lines (man-woman) and that were for her not necessarily tethered to romantic attraction. Party Noire, however, was part of her larger and longer introduction to different relations of gender and desire in black LGBTQ communities. She was learning new descriptive terms like andro and stemme that chart nuanced expressions of gendered sexuality and given access to a rather open and amiable space where she could flirt, be flirted with, dance, and learn about her queer boundaries, needs, and desires.

The kinds of balance that make a cypher successful are largely energetic and nonverbal. People enter and leave the cypher through nuanced negotiations of sense and anticipation. A cypher is successful when there is equal participation in the (unwritten) rules of the social norms of the gathering and the exchanges it fosters. A cypher is successful when individual dancers are accountable to one another as well as to the larger group; at the same time, the larger group is accountable to the dancers, providing support and encouragement. Such a cypher translates the pleasure of moving one's individual body into a collective endeavor, translates individual investment in feeling into a more communal choreography of support. Through choreographies of support, black queer women move their bodies in concert with one another "in a community of movement in which the individual's own movement [is] essential and valued."[11] In the process, they are elevated, ever so slightly, out of the present moment. That is, their choreographies of support sync them together in a deep presentness that can engender a utopian optimism that, maybe, there is another world beyond this one—one where black queer life can feel like this all of the time.

Such utopian inclinations are only ever temporary, though, and are always grounded by the material stressors that can come with inhabiting black queer lifeworlds. "Addressing utopia in this context," Ramón Rivera-Servera writes, "requires not only an engagement with the cultures of pleasure that characterize the club, but with cultures of struggle that mark the multiple trajectories and negotiations undertaken by dancers on their way to and as preconditions for the utopian experiences of the dance floor."[12] In other words, we cannot isolate the space and practices of the dance floor, the production of Black (Queer) Joy, as somehow distinct and disconnected from the world that conditions their emergence. The dance floor can feel utopian precisely because black queers provide one another relief from the everyday struggles beyond it. Yet you engage in these choreographies of support knowing full well that, when the party's over, you've got to leave the dance floor, go back outside, and keep on enduring the rest of the world. The intrusions of this real world began to chip away at the utopian possibilities of Black Joy at Party Noire as the party grew in popularity and unsettled the choreographies of support that drew black queer women to the party in the first place. Black Joy at Party Noire came to feel less like a queer utopia and more, people worried, like a sanitized, generic Black feeling consonant with the redevelopment of the surrounding Hyde Park neighborhood.

BLACK JOY BREAKS DOWN

Serena left the East Coast for a job in Chicago, and "I told myself when I moved to Chicago, I was going to date women. So, I wasn't very much a connoisseur of queer spaces—I wasn't analyzing it, or I didn't necessarily see myself as part of the community." When Party Noire began, though, she started to attend regularly, and grew her network of black queers in the city. She was drawn to the party by "all the pictures that they put on social media, like beautiful black people having a good time. That seemed great to me, why wouldn't it be great?" The small footprint of the day party, in particular, afforded her the chance to actually talk to other black queers at the bar and on the rooftop deck. The sense of genuine connection and communality lost ground to the party's growing image-focused popularity, however. She explains, "I think as they got more popular and they really tried to pop on social media, it became a lot about being seen, too. I feel like a lot of folks are in it for the picture or who they're going to be seen with." Voters in the annual *Chicago Reader* "Best of Chicago" poll awarded Party Noire "Best Dance Party" in 2017 and 2018, as the party was also hosting more night parties and a growing roster of non-dance-party related events such as bike rides and other wellness activities. As the party shifted and expanded, Serena and others worried Party Noire was moving toward a generic rendering of Black Joy that was not specifically tied to any politics of black queer sexuality—and that, in some cases, seemed to excise the diversity of black queer life from its image altogether.

Diamond felt this shift in the rhetorical and visual language the party used on social media, where she saw that Black Joy was increasingly uncoupled from the actual black queer bodies, expressions, and feelings that she felt were present and valued in the party's early years. "I feel like every time I go on their Instagram or something it's always thin-bodied, able, brown to light skin folks doing it," she tells me. "But when I get to Party Noire I see fat girls dropping it down low, you know? . . . I feel like there are black, fat, butch—like, every type of gender expression you can think of at that place, but somehow it's not being portrayed all in your social media?" For Diamond, visual representations of the party should align more closely with how Party Noire textually frames itself: "You can't say all genders and all bodies, and you only have a certain type of body [represented online], you know? Don't say inclusive if it's not." For Diamond, as for Serena, the accolades shifted the organization's attention away from the diverse black queerness at the party: "I feel like it just started changing once it's like 'Oh, this is like, Chicago's Best Dance Party in 2017 and now that we're getting bigger we have to include other folks that we didn't start off for.'"

What was most concerning to her about the turn toward a generic dance party was a growing presence of cisgender, heterosexual men in attendance:

I feel like they were kind of like "OK, we're no longer a black queer dance party, we're going to be the black Chicago dance party." So, you kind of saw more dudes. More straight, more cis dudes in there. . . . I was kind of shocked to know that these white frat boys were at the party! And it's kind of sad because it started off geared towards queer folks and now it's become . . .

For Diamond, the party pivoted to be "a great dance party" seemingly stripped of its previous commitments to black queer sociality, and the entrance of cisgender, heterosexual men fundamentally and negatively affected the possibilities of the party's specifically Black Queer Joy. While I never saw anyone who could be described as a white frat boy, the space is large, the party is long, and there is only so much the individual ethnographer can see. By 2018, there was certainly a growing presence of cishet men at any given party and they definitely changed the networks of looking and dancing therein, disrupting long-established choreographies of support and creating a sense of unease among black queer women partygoers, especially at night parties.

"There was a lot of men there and just the vibe was different there," Serena laments. "And men can bring a certain level of disrespect. These same women who go to the day party who can't be themselves because they're policing themselves so that they don't get unwanted attention from men." Spaces that foster queer modes of moving and connecting can be grossly disrespected by straight people, whether they be straight men ogling queer women at Party Noire or bachelorette parties swarming gay bars. For Taylor, the sheer presence of people who are not queer raises suspicions about their intentions. They explain,

> Sometimes when I go to Party Noire, it's almost like, OK, I know there are queer people here. But there's also non-queer people. And that's the part where I'm just like, I don't know how much I trust the outside community. OK, you came to this party but you do see how many [queer] people are in here? It's just like, I don't know what people are thinking—and that could just be me as an over-thinker. It doesn't always make me feel comfortable.

Austin is pointed when they say "Well, the sense of safety [has changed]" at Party Noire:

> I know they've gotten a lot of good reviews and things like that, which I'm very proud of, but I think that also attracts folks that are not part of that community who just are like "I want to go to a nice party and have a good time." It's like, you didn't know what you were getting into, did you? So, the more popular it becomes, it almost feels like it's less and less for me.

Part of the sense of disrespect that comes with straight people encroaching on otherwise queer space is rooted in what Serena, Taylor, and Austin suggest is a kind of willful ignorance on the part of straight people. They are suspicious of people who enter the Party Noire space and either don't recognize its queerness or refuse to see it; this becomes even more suspicious if they assume that straight people *do* recognize the party's queerness yet do little, if anything at all, to honor it, whether that be by changing their behaviors or leaving the party altogether.

Bri and Serena were, on the other hand, equally suspicious of the Party Noire organization's own discursive framing of the party—that a lack of rhetorical intentionality opens space for heterosexual men to enter the space. As Serena explains,

I remember that their language at first was not intentional, it was never intentional. It was Party Noire and they were trying to make it a black space. . . . I never think that they were intentional about what the space was supposed to be, in that it was for women or queer women or whatever. So then the night party came, and because they weren't intentional, there was a lot of men there and just the vibe was different there.

Bri also highlights a certain lack of intentionality in her own reflections on Party Noire. She had been attending the party every now and then when a friend warned her that there seemed to be more men in the space and the next party she attended, sure enough, "it was hella straight people in there." On one hand, this didn't necessarily bother or surprise her because, "whatever, they don't necessarily advertise themselves to being exactly gay, but they're fully a safe space for everybody." But over the course of the party "it was just super weird in there. It was way too many guys, and it was way too many disrespectful shit." For black queer women, intentional, representational branding is of utmost concern when selecting where to party. What some saw as shifting visual branding, and others tracked to potentially unintentional language, led to growing numbers of straight men in the space. The shifting demographics of the party, intentional or not, made attendees worry about limits of the organization's expressly queer orientation and politics. And in their worry, they spotlighted the ways that the party's location in Hyde Park may be partly to blame.

Territorializing Black Feeling

SITUATING HYDE PARK

As Party Noire came to feel less like a place *for* black queers, it felt, in turn, less and less accountable *to* them. "But I respect their hustle," Diamond sighs. "They have become *the* party of Chicago. Can't hate on that." Diamond's reluctant admiration of Party Noire's hustle—their abilities to surreptitiously extract resources from the very systems, structures, and institutions that violently regulate resources—underscores the bind the Party Noire community found itself in by 2018. On one hand, Party Noire's successful mobilization of Black Joy creates space for black people, queer and otherwise, to simply feel good in violent times. On the other hand, the very marketability of black feeling, and of Black Joy in particular, entangles Party Noire with the machinations of neoliberal capitalism that strips neighborhoods and cities of demographic complexity. What does Black Joy mean in a party that seems to attend to queer life but where queer people's safety and security within the party feel threatened, just as their lives feel threatened in the neighborhood and city that surround it? Black queer women's developing criticisms of Party Noire's mobilization of Black Joy illuminate how racialized affects can become commodities in and of themselves that can be traded upon in order to gain ground in neighborhoods and cities where feeling good is powerful currency—and how a politics of and around queer sexuality can get lost in the process.

For some, the ways that Black Joy started to feel like it lost its queer way were inextricable from the ongoing development of Hyde Park, especially the neighborhood's "downtown" core, a small stretch of commercial, retail, housing, and service options on 53rd Street, where The Promontory is located. For Austin, the party's production of Black Joy is inextricable from the neighborhood, as they explain:

> I feel like I have to prepare myself for Party Noire, you know? Like the bouginess of Party Noire, especially because there's high-profile photography and I don't want to go anywhere not looking my best. . . . At Party Noire, there's a different sense of bouginess—and it's also the space itself, being at The Promontory in Hyde Park and having to buy tickets before they sell out. There's so much more that comes with attending a Party Noire event.

Here, Austin points to the dynamics of class and culture that shape the party and the Hyde Park neighborhood alike. Party Noire is a ticketed event, and day-of tickets for the party can be upward of twenty dollars. They have sliding-scale price options, and cheaper tickets can be purchased in advance of each event; all attendees are asked to reach out to organizers directly if cost would prohibit them from attending. The fact of ticket prices, though, mixed with the high production values of the event and its documentation underscore the perceived bouginess of the party.

This sense of bouginess Austin feels is further grounded in the economic and cultural economy that Diamond observes as shaping the Party Noire space. "I feel like it's becoming more like this is the party to be at if you're black," she explains. "If you're queer that's cool too, but 'if you're black and you're living in Hyde Park intelligentsia,' that's what Party Noire has become." Her assessment of Party Noire's attendees reflects the longer cultural history, and broader social imaginary, of the South Side as a longtime home to black artists, businesspeople, and activists who helped fuel the Chicago

Renaissance in the early and mid-twentieth century.[13] The Promontory draws on this history as part of its branding. The venue is owned by the restaurant conglomerate 16" on Center, helmed by the feared and revered Bruce Finkelman as well as Craig Golden, two white men. The collective owns bars and restaurants throughout the city, several of which use the racial and ethnic history of the surrounding neighborhood to brand its offerings. The Promontory, for example, "is dedicated to celebrating the eras when spacious ballrooms and jumping jazz clubs made Chicago's South Side the capital of American music."[14] Brandi Summers describes this site-specific method of branding as "black aesthetic emplacement," a mode of using the coded language of cultural preservation to retain *some* aspects of an area's Black history without providing any material infrastructure that would allow, let alone entice, actual living Black people to access the area's economic or cultural resources.[15] Highly selective elements of the region's Black history in turn become revalued as representative of the area's "diversity," broadly construed. Summers argues this deployment of diversity uses but ultimately acts as the *antidote* to blackness.[16]

Indeed, the University of Chicago has long positioned its Hyde Park holdings as feeding the intellectual and cultural curiosities of a diverse university community in a multicultural city, but without people ever having to leave university territory; they never have to enter the surrounding black neighborhoods, and the surrounding black populations will be heavily surveilled should they enter university territory. For example, David Greene, a university executive vice president, rationalizes the redevelopment of 53rd Street as "enlightened self-interest for us. . . . We've always been very competitive when it comes to providing a great intellectual community. But we found there was something missing when we looked at the quality of life for students and faculty who are used to the kinds of amenities you find in places like New York, Boston and Palo Alto."[17] The university's "quality of life" initiatives to provide "the kinds of amenities" that are characteristic of many university-funded gentrification plans: corporate retail and service options, upscale apartments and condominium buildings, and selective branding of neighborhood and community heritage. These initiatives are an outgrowth of what Teona Williams describes as "the legacy of urban renewal in Hyde Park and the university's construction of the South Side as an uninhabitable environment [which has] played (and continues to play) a major role in the political ecology of police brutality" on and off campus.[18] In short, the university's image of itself as a world-class, cosmopolitan institution has proceeded to render the region's black population as environmentally, culturally, and financially toxic to the cultivation of intellectual community.

Williams's work builds upon Davarian Baldwin's detailing of how the university has historically used the language of "perseveration" and "slum prevention," and the tactics of eminent domain, to displace black residents and further entrench the area's white population, and it rezoned its commercial districts to "diminish the possibilities for interracial sociability."[19] In 1892, the university was founded in then-suburban Hyde Park through a series of financial donations, and from land deeds that brought public transportation from the city and guaranteed the neighborhood would be free of manufacturing and industry. Hyde Park's property values increased as the result of legislation that developed the distinctive South Park system, where the Midway Plaisance connects Washington and Jackson Parks.[20] Across the early and mid-twentieth century, the university worked with its own faculty and staff, with neighborhood organizations such as the Hyde Park and Kenwood Property Owner's Association, and with the South East Chicago Commission to maintain and increase land values by fighting and clearing "encroaching" black settlement. UChicago selectively sat on the land that it forcibly acquired, waiting for it to accrue value, and/or redeveloped it for university use (e.g., student housing and administrative buildings). The university's successful urban takeover paved the way for local, state, and federal zoning and tax policies that would help universities nationwide buy and redevelop land for a profit, devastating low-income and black and brown neighborhoods in the process.[21]

The university's early segregationist, isolationist strategies continue to inform its twenty-first-century initiatives to manage land and power in Hyde Park, and in neighboring Woodlawn and Washington Park. The contemporary University of Chicago is like most universities in that it weaponizes its nonprofit status to hoard wealth; it operates as a real estate corporation to create ever more territory for itself; and, importantly, the university wields one of the largest private police forces in the country in order to maintain its separation from the nonuniversity (especially black and working class) community.[22] The University of Chicago Police Department works with the Chicago Police Department to overpolice black people, university students and not, on campus and in the surrounding neighborhood. The police are meant to protect the university community *and* the university grounds in the larger effort to maintain and increase the property values of the larger region. Williams writes that "UChicago converges with militant racial and environmental management practices in order to produce a 'college town' (mainly white and formally educated) environment in the Hyde Park area."[23] The college town environment of the twenty-first-century University of Chicago is produced through physical violence, to be sure, but also through a discourse of neoliberal multiculturalism that balances and entices corporate development projects with "heritage" and "cultural" sites that selectively extract and wield the region's black cultural capital—all for the greater good of the university.[24]

This process is built into the 53rd Street corridor that has been redeveloped using Tax Increment Financing (TIF) funds, meaning that a certain percentage of property tax dollars go toward developing infrastructure and beautification efforts, and providing incentives to private investors to develop retail, service, and housing (often in the form of mixed-capacity buildings) options.[25] The funds from this TIF subsidized the development of City Hyde Park across the street from The Promontory, a large block of residential, commercial, service offerings that includes corporate endeavors like Whole Foods as well as small, independent businesses such as The Silver Room, bars, restaurants, and convenience stores. The University of Chicago purchased Harper Court, around the corner from City Hyde Park, in 2008 for $6.5 million. With TIF support, it redeveloped the property to include a Hyatt Hotel, and commercial spaces like LA Fitness, Starbucks, and Chipotle—selling many of these holdings six years later for $114 million. These redevelopment initiatives that are meant to revitalize city areas are often linked with the negative impact gentrification has on small businesses; long-standing outposts Dixie Kitchen (a Barack Obama favorite) and Calypsó Café were closed down to make way for the chain restaurants that now call Harper Court home. The university-propelled development of Hyde Park's commercial core has gone hand in hand with its attempts to develop the Washington Park neighborhood, which forms the western border of the university, into an arts and culture district.

Nick and Rae are clear-eyed about how the region's gentrification intersects with the creative industries Party Noire engages in. Rae situates the party within the idea of "Hyde Park kind of being the cool Black neighborhood to go," and explains, "I think that Hyde Park was undergoing a shift that in some way shape or form Party Noire contributed to, you know, in terms of [the neighborhood] kind of being this hub for damn near all things. You know: education, arts with things like the Stony Island Arts Bank being minutes up the street, and Arts + Public Life doing all these very black-centric arts things." Here, Rae points to the 300 block of East Garfield Boulevard that the university's Arts + Public Life initiative calls the

"Arts Block," where they operate and manage commercial outposts and arts programming in the effort to bring the university community together with South Side creative enterprises. The Arts Block is one component of arts-based redevelopment initiatives happening in the neighborhoods surrounding Hyde Park. Millions of dollars of TIF funding were put toward building much-needed affordable housing for artists (KLEO Artist Residencies) in Washington Park. Urban planner and artist Theaster Gates, long affiliated with the university, has been developing a conglomerate of buildings to fashion the area's black history into vibrant black arts and cultural institutions, including the Stony Island Arts Bank that Rae mentioned, as well as Dorchester Projects, Bing Art Books, and the Currency Exchange Café.

Party Noire's Black Joy is settled in Hyde Park amid urban development initiatives that meant to create access for and to ensure a quality of life, a good life, that is commensurate with an elite university and a global city. Where early twentieth-century redevelopment efforts were made possible through the forcible removal of black populations, contemporary redevelopment plans strategically incorporate *particular* black people and cultural forms as part of their efforts to (re)brand themselves as demographically and socially integrated with the surrounding black neighborhoods. As Party Noire attendees point out, the materiality of such (re)development moves in step with symbolic practices that shape the racialized and classed social imaginary of Party Noire and of Hyde Park and the South Side in general.[26]

"WHEN YOU SEE ORANGE THEORY,
YOU KNOW SHIT IS CHANGING, BOY!"

Austin suggests that Party Noire's Black Joy is inextricable from the efforts to brand Hyde Park as distinct from the "rest" of the Black South Side. They argue the dynamics of Black Joy at the party and Hyde Park are specifically marketed in contrast to the racialized affects of terror that are used to stereotype the black neighborhoods that surround Hyde Park:

> Even the language around Hyde Park has changed: 53rd Street has become "Downtown Hyde Park" and I'm like when did this happen!? It's become its own world. By just saying that you live on the South Side, people assume that you live in a dangerous neighborhood. First of all, when we say we live in Chicago, period, people become concerned, especially outsiders. For example, my dad lives in Mississippi, and when he talks about Chicago, he's like, "I heard y'all had thirty shootings this weekend." I'm

like, "Dad, I didn't even hear that and I live here." So, the portrayal of being in Chicago and being on the South Side where the demographic is predominately black, it automatically means we're unsafe, right? But you can escape that stigma by saying, "Well, I live in Hyde Park. I don't live in Englewood or South Shore." The fact that Hyde Park now has a Whole Foods and an Orange Theory and shit! When you see Orange Theory, you know shit is changing, boy!

Here, Austin unpacks the stereotypes that link blackness, violence, and space together. They describe how "good" consumer habits like shopping at Whole Foods and exercising at Orange Theory seemingly result in "good" feelings that are meant to renarrate the force of blackness in Chicago's South Side neighborhoods. They suggest that the possibilities of generating good *black* feelings in Hyde Park are seen as proportional to the stereotype of "bad" feelings seemingly indexed in and by the surrounding black neighborhoods. If Black Joy is generated in Hyde Park, its violent opposite is located somewhere closer to Englewood or South Shore.

The belief that Chicago's southern (and western) black neighborhoods are particularly violent is pervasive. "People think that the whole city of Chicago is just like you walk outside, you about to get shot," Tess scoffs. "That's not true." Tess recently moved to Chicago from Atlanta and settled in a near suburb, close to her work. Upon arrival, she was nervous about traveling to some parts of the city, like South Shore, where Ayana lives, because of stereotypes of violence. "Ayana, first time I went to her house, I was like, 'You don't like me, do you. You're trying to get me shot!' She was just like, 'What!? Nothing happens over here.'" There is indeed very real violence in Chicago's black territories, which deeply affects people throughout this book and reflects how black geographies can be scripted by seemingly commonsensical narratives of safety or the lack thereof. Ayana was in fact quite rattled by the July 2018 murder of Harith Augustus, who was killed by police in broad daylight in her South Shore neighborhood. Since then, she tries not to be in the streets too much. "I don't hang around my neighborhood and that's really sad to say, but no I don't. I don't even casually walk." She continues,

If I'm walking I'm going to Walgreens and I'm coming back. I have a mission. If I'm leaving this apartment to be in this neighborhood, I have a mission that I'm trying to accomplish and I'm trying to get home safely. That's the only two points, but as [far as] "I'm just walking around" all that? Nah. Nah, it's not happening.

Ayana stays on alert in her neighborhood, largely in response to police presence, as is the case with Austin, who moved from South Shore to Washington Park, "mostly because it was unsafe for me, I got harassed by cops too fucking much. I'm still surrounded by cops in Washington Park, but they don't bother me as much." The two of them are like other black queers who share a frustration with how hyperlocal criminal statistics (e.g., shootings that are concentrated in just a handful of blocks) are flattened and over-represented as characteristic of the city as a whole. Negative stories about Chicago's violent blackness rarely provide nuanced accounts of the social fabric of the city. "From my experiences," Tess explains, "it's been hella chill, quiet. I haven't seen nothing too crazy. I was surprised because I expected the worst, honestly."

Across these people we find deft readings of the racialized territorialization of feeling, where some black territories are scripted by fear and violence while others, such as Hyde Park, accrue value as havens of good feeling. Often, the scripting of some black sites as violent is a concerted effort by public-private partnerships to contain and manage certain black territories, rendering them as backward, violent, deteriorating slums to be policed, poisoned, razed, or all three—these are sites where you certainly cannot feel good. Such spatialization of the distinctly racialized affective structures of terror in Chicago is rooted in the city's long history of violent segregation, and is continually rehearsed with every denied mortgage loan, every video of police brutality, every closed school, and every drop of leaded water in black neighborhoods. If "black" is always linked with terror in hegemonic, racist renderings of Chicago's racialized spatiality, the affective horizons of blackness are also rendered as incommensurable with normative regimes of political economic success therein. Building Whole Foods and Orange Theory becomes an important step in reconfiguring the *affective* expectations of a neighborhood, while having an impact on things like property values that also impact who is able and expected to circulate through the neighborhoods. As Hyde Park orients toward the kinds of corporate investment endeavors that traffic in economic profit—that raise rents, property values, and encourage the influx of money laundered through service and creative industries—the production of "good" feelings is good business, and vice versa.

By 2018, some Party Noire attendees were growing suspicious that Black Joy was feeling more like a marketing initiative consonant with the redevelopment of Hyde Park's 53rd Street corridor than a reflection of the forms and possibilities of diverse black queer community at the party. They worried that Party Noire's operationalization of Black Joy was capitalizing on what we might think of as a particularly narrow image-ideal of productive *black* neoliberal citizenship: through the individual agency of our purchasing power we are tasked with the responsibility of securing good feelings because, under the free-market rationale of neoliberalism, we are "the most qualified at understanding [our] needs and wants, so society should be structured around lowering barriers to the individual realization of this pleasure."[27] In other words, under neoliberalism, we are ultimately trained to govern ourselves, which includes the "cultivation and optimization of [our] own emotional potentials."[28] It is the specific burden of the individual to reorganize their racialized affective alignment in and to the gentrifying neighborhood and neoliberal city through practices like shopping at Whole Foods and exercising at Orange Theory—and cultivating Black Joy.[29]

Diamond sees this chain of expectations playing out in the rhetoric of Black Joy that pushes regimes of self-care that are themselves highly individualized. Black Joy's good feelings, in other words, are constructed as the individual black person's responsibility to attain in spite of and to spite the violence of white supremacy:

> I feel like for me Black Joy is more complicated than just like, "Stepped outside, Black Joy!" I mean, I'm not going to lie, I fell for the Kool-Aid when it first happened. For me Black Joy is: even though we are living in this white supremacist world, I'm also doing actual work of self-care and not just face masks and talking about "Oh, I have to take my anti-depressants today and my anti-anxiety meds"; [or] "Diamond! You spent the whole weekend on your bed, let's just get something to eat, it'll be fun."

Practices of getting fresh air, staying on top of medications, and maintaining one's glow are certainly important to one's well-being, Diamond qualifies. "Of course, this is not to knock anybody who thinks Black Joy is stepping outside. I'm not trying to say that. I'm just saying, take a little more steps, let's have more nuance." Her desire for nuance connects to critiques of how capitalism atomizes feelings such that good feelings become commodities that we can own and possess.[30] Something like Black Joy, to call upon Sara Ahmed's analysis of compulsory happiness, "becomes an instrument, as a means to an end, as well as an end. We make ourselves happy, as an acquisition of capital that allows us to be or to do this or that, or even to get this or that."[31] Diamond's desire for more nuance underscores how the pursuit, acquisition, and instrumentalization of Good Black Feelings can actually delink racialized feeling from the structures of racial violence that they are conditioned by. Black Joy becomes an object among other objects in Hyde Park that an individual is tasked with attaining as a specific remedy to structural violence. This violence is in turn rescripted as something that can be overcome if the black individual or community responsibly consumes and produces good feelings at, say, Party Noire.

Here, Diamond is in conversation with Rinaldo Walcott, who is critical of how representations of Black Joy can lack a critical analysis of how feeling, good or bad, is shaped in conversation with our highly toxic relationships to capitalism. "Indeed, what gets posted onto these monikers [like #BlackJoy and #BlackGirlMagic, and #BlackBoyJoy]," Walcott claims, "is anything but magic and joy, and instead [are] celebrations of access to the crumbs of imperial capital. Again, participation on the edges of capital becomes a celebration of Black life. But for me, it is a kind of perversity in which capital is still devouring blackness."[32] Walcott explains that the catch of Black Joy is that it is a product of capitalism and cannot thus be its undoing. Galvanizing around Black Joy, for him, celebrates moments "when we seem to be inside capital. And the irony is black people are always inside capital: either as its commodity or as its problem. *So, to celebrate when we notice ourselves inside of it is a particular kind of political trouble for me.*"[33] For Walcott, representations of Black Joy are too often representations of the seeming triumph of Good Black Feelings that direct our attention away from his desire for "radical politics that's about undoing capital. I want a radical politics that's about a particular kind of black self-authorizing that can be about something more than capital."[34] For Walcott as for Diamond, Black Joy, as both a product of capitalism and evidence of its enduring violence, provides shaky grounds for organizing political solidarity against the ways that capitalism (dis)organizes black queer life.

Their reflections provide framing language for the trajectory of people's changings attachments to Black Joy at Party Noire. The configurations of Black Joy in the party's first couple of years joined people together in an emotional potential that suggested resistance to the violence of antiblackness, and in solidarity with queer lifeworlds. As Black Joy felt increasingly bound to the mechanics of neoliberal urban development initiatives, though, it felt like an increasingly insufficient remedy to the manipulation and exploitation of racialized feeling within and across the South Side. The prerogatives of neoliberal governance seemed to seep into the production of Party Noire and threatened to dismantle its long-standing *queer* choreographies of support. As Party Noire became ever more established in Hyde Park, organizers and attendees questioned what, exactly, brought them together and who, exactly, was responsible for maintaining the Black Joy within and beyond the party.

Owning a Politics of Feeling

It's not so easy, however, to assign responsibility when the cypher's systems of accountability require a lot of direct and indirect communication between individual dancers and between individual dancers and the crowd that surrounds and watches them. The cypher breaks down when a dancer takes up too much time and loses the crowd's interest, when someone jumps in too quickly and interrupts another's flow, when two dancers in the circle become overtly competitive rather than complementary. Cyphers can suffer from the wrong kinds of looking, the wrong kinds of touching, the wrong kinds of taking up space. These impositions at times put people in danger or create powerful waves of discomfort. Energy can become antagonistic, the crowd can dissolve, and what was once a mutual endeavor turns toward other modes of moving, feeling, and relating that can feel quite disconnected from the dance floor's capacity to foster collectivity.

The failures of the cypher to incubate a Black Joy oriented around accountability to black queer life came to a head in 2018, when a person took to social media with allegations that the party's primary photographer, a black man whose images of Party Noire events were central to imaging the organization's Black Joy brand, was a sexually abusive person. The social media callout of the photographer alleged abuse that did not necessarily happen at Party Noire. By virtue of having the photographer in its employ, though, the Party Noire organization became framed as complicit to the allegations and was positioned as an arbiter of restorative justice in the process. Around the same time, Lauren, one of the founders of the party, abruptly left the organization. In that same year, an unrelated narrative detailing the climactic dissolution of one of the organizers' romantic relationships circulated on social media and drew direct and indirect input from diverse Party Noire stakeholders. These moments and the conversations around them blurred the boundaries between party organizers' personal lives and their professional labor.

This turn toward the end of this chapter is not an investigation of these events, nor an attempt to piece together the "truth" of these moments of crisis. This is valid and important work, especially when it comes to documenting the important and difficult labor of queer communities implementing restorative justice protocols. This conclusion is instead interested in what the Party Noire community's debates around, and efforts toward, accountability in the wake of 2018 can tell us about the practice of, and constraints around, governing black queer feeling(s) in the midst of the neoliberal city. Party organizers and attendees wrestle with the extent to which a party's Black Joy brand should be consonant with the lives and relationships of the organizers beyond the work they do in the club. In the process, they examine the spatial boundaries around Party Noire's responsibility to and for the physical and psychic well-being of its black queer attendees, asking just how big is the cypher? Just how durable are our choreographies of support once we leave the dance floor?

Partygoers and party organizers' reflections on the mechanics of accountability shed light on problems and antagonisms that many queer nightlife networks experience, and which are further explored in the conclusion to this book. At the core of these reflections are different perspectives on who carries the burden of responsibility and accountability within queer nightlife spaces. Candace was a longtime Party Noire attendee and is representative of people for whom the events of 2018 sparked an intense reflection on the relationship between queer party organizations and their constituents. For her, individual party organizers as well as party organizations are responsible for quickly addressing matters that concern them, even if only seemingly tangentially:

> [Accountability] looks like acknowledging when harm has been done in your space, in the space that you're making, whether you were directly a cause for that harm or if that harm was reported to you or if that harm is being spread on the internet. You have to address it. You have to sit down with folks and make sure that you are directly communicating with people about what happened, what is presently happening, and what you're gonna do in the future to keep this from happening again or to change something. Let people know. Let people in the community know how you are working to make the space better after that situation.

Candace believes that the dynamics of responsibility and accountability are weighted toward the organization, arguing they have an *extra* responsibility to accountability given how they make cultural and financial capital off of their work and, by extension, off of the communities that they throw events for. "I think the community definitely makes the space," Candace explains, "but the community isn't the people taking the interviews or getting the awards. It's the people who organize it." Following this, Black Joy is not only produced within any given Party Noire event but is carried by Nick and Rae wherever they go. The scope of the organization's Black Joy brand thus extends beyond the physical space of the Party Noire event, and so party organizers bear the burden of responsibility for people and behaviors they are broadly affiliated with.

For party attendees like Candace, accountability necessitates modes of direct and lasting communication where party organizations are self-aware and take on the responsibility of outlining expectations, managing community safety, and shouldering the burden—and it is often quite a burden—of representing the community. Yet when it came to their photographer and his behaviors beyond the Party Noire event, Party Noire felt undue pressure to "rectify a situation," Nick starts, "that literally had nothing to do with us," Rae finishes. They certainly recognize their role in creating a sense of safety and community among partygoers and severed ties with the photographer. But at the time they felt ill-equipped to do direct, restorative justice work with and around him, as community members were asking them to do. As Nick explains, "This is literally not in the wheelhouse of the work that I can personally do. And even when it is, 'cause some of it is in this instance, again we'll do all we can and should do for our community. But leading a whole process for this person is just something that we—" Rae picks up: "Yeah, I'm not a restorative justice professional. I've never done that process."[35] Nick and Rae's experiences show how party organizers can possess limited experiential and administrative tools to manage breakdowns in safety and communication in and around the spaces they organize, which can make it especially challenging to rise to the expectations of party attendees and community members like Candace.

At one level, the breakdowns in communication and mismatched expectations between party organizers and attendees highlight the challenges of consolidating group identity; there is always dissent and discontent within the (potential) collective. At another related level, partygoers and organizers' debates about the parameters of responsibility and accountability highlight a larger debate about how black queer life can, if at all, take place in neighborhoods like Hyde Park. The crises of 2018 pushed the Party Noire community to reconsider Black Joy's choreographies of support as inextricable from the neoliberal development of Hyde Park and the related racialized territorialization of feeling throughout the South Side. In Hyde Park, hundreds of millions of dollars are used to subsidize the production of good black feelings, and of Black Joy in particular. This happens in a city and neighborhood that effectively restrict how and where black people take place. The challenges of maintaining Black Joy at Party Noire describe the fragile incorporation of black queer sexualities into university-driven, neoliberal capitalist urban development projects that produce (and demand?) flattened, easily consumable images and expressions of black life. Party organizers and attendees' attempts to understand the complicated contours of accountability in the face of multiple modes of crisis thus trace the difficulties of crafting an ethical black queer politics and community through the language of Black Joy and trace the difficulties of doing so from within the territories of neoliberal urban governance.

It is perhaps no surprise that Party Noire organizers and attendees alike wonder whether responsibility to one another, and shared accountability for Black Joy, would be easier if they simply *owned* the spaces wherein black queer life can flourish. Indeed, for Serena, any attempt at accountability within Party Noire is hampered by the fact that the organization rents space from The Promontory, which controls management of the bar staff and the security. "I think what that boils down to is a lack of space. Even them choosing The Promontory: it's the closest thing that you're going to get when you have black people at a certain income level who are going to feel safe and show up and be able to pay for everything; that's the best space, and that's white-owned." Serena applauds Party Noire for hustling in any environment where venue management can antagonize black queer people. "So, they're doing the best that they can in getting the space that feels most accessible, but we have literally not many other options." Concurring with Serena, DJ Professor-wrecks explains that there are myriad problems that can arise when you're "putting on a party in the space that you just *fundamentally have no control over*." For her, the lack of ownership directly hampers the possibilities for Black Joy. "I feel like I'm not really sure that a party can be revolutionary," she explains. "I feel like you really have to own this space top to bottom, whether that's the bar, the security, the everything."

The Party Noire organization (same as Slo 'Mo and E N E R G Y) does indeed see building ownership as necessary to producing sustainable Black Joy, in large part because ownership is seen as allowing organizers to shape the dynamics of the cypher and choreographies of support that they incubate from the ground up. "So, we've been definitely conversing and trying to ideate on ways to literally have ownership of all the whole operation," Nick explains. "The *whole* operation," Rae emphasizes. "I will train and hire my own security team." Until they have the resources to surmount the immense barriers to purchasing property, though, Nick and Rae are incubating alternative practices of ownership rooted in shared accountability among organizers and attendees. These are practices that might institutionalize the choreographies of support that have been so instrumental to building the Party Noire community. As the two of them were initially overwhelmed by whether they had the skills to undertake the kinds of labor that accountability structures would entail, they spent a lot of time simply gathering resources. "So, there were lots of conversations," Nick explains. "Individual conversations, conversations with our immediate team. Conversations with the person that we employed [the photographer] that the allegations were against. Conversations with the person who created the allegations and then lots of conversations with different community partners." They ultimately enlisted the help of two black women who work with the University of Illinois Women's Leadership and Resource Center to help strategize around responding to their community's needs and to help develop transparent mechanisms for producing and fostering safety and inclusion at the parties.

Using this information, and honoring their emotional and administrative limitations, Nick and Rae worked to build a distributed responsibility at Party Noire, where the organization may set the framework for convening—providing space for black queer women, femmes, and others to produce and experience Black Joy—but it is also the partygoers' responsibility to help care for everyone within and beyond it. "When making space for people," Rae explains, "you're bringing traumas and dramas into the space that you know nothing about. And then you bring them into a space where alcohol and drugs and things are involved. You don't know how they respond to them, you don't know what makes people irate. You don't know—" "what triggers individuals," Nick finishes. To this end, Rae explains,

> If something is happening in the space that is ill it needs to be addressed, and it just shouldn't have to be addressed by us. We're all in here together, we all need to be addressing it in ways that are effective and impactful and meaningful and thoughtful so that people can leave here and go home safe.

For Rae, party organizers and community members have a *shared* responsibility to craft the Party Noire space. To foster this mutuality, they held a community accountability session before a July 2018 night party. From this and other informal conversations with community members, Party Noire implemented several strategies for ensuring the safety, security, and continual practices of Black Joy at their events. The organization developed a community support team that remains sober for the duration of a Party Noire event, and who can be identified by shared clothing, tags, and/or signage. These folks assist Nick and Rae, who is often unavailable to monitor the party because she's DJing, in maintaining a safe and secure atmosphere for patrons. The organization also set up a phone number that patrons can text if they need support, which all Party Noire organizers receive. As Nick explains, they've also created cards that encourage community feedback and support: "You come into the party, you receive this card, it has our phone number on it. Any issues, questions, comments, feedback, love, whatever the fuck you got for us you can text us." Where people can feel free to communicate with the Party Noire team via text, they can also retreat to a green room, staffed by sober community team members, that Party Noire instituted for people who may need to remove themselves from the party for a time.

The community support team evidences Party Noire's beliefs that accountability is a community-based effort that depends upon direct communication. Instituting the community support team and creating direct lines of communication between party organizers and attendees represents, Rae explains,

> this evolution of moving beyond systems that don't work anyways. Like you end up calling a security guard over, and we've seen it happen time and time again, where the security guard might restrain a person or commit more violence on this person who might be going through a thing and need support.

Establishing new and different, clear and direct communication lines between the organization and the community is important for the safety and security of the patrons and for the peace of mind for the organizers. "Someone that chose to come to our party, I wanna know what's happening," Rae notes.

> Because the thing that I hate the most is waking up to an email from somebody saying, "This is something that happened and security did blah, blah, blah, blah" and I'm ill-informed on the situation! So now I'm expected to respond to this patron, this guest that spent money to come to my party, with zero information on what happened. And that's why I'm like, "tell us first" because it comes back down on us anyway.

Nick and Rae are firm believers that accountability is a community process, not a unidirectional one whereby Party Noire alone is answerable to the multiple kinds of conflicts that can happen at any given event. Their community accountability strategy aims to distribute the massive amount of work that accountability actually entails, and it is an explicit effort to *not* reproduce nor rely upon institutions that often violently govern black and black queer lives. Rae says, "I want to see us secure each other in ways that look beyond these systems that don't necessarily always work in our favor."

The struggles of 2018 pushed Party Noire organizers and attendees to the limits of *fuck y'all*. Their interrogations of the mechanics of Party Noire revealed how Black Joy may not be all that pleasurable in Hyde Park and vis-à-vis the racialized territorialization of feeling on the South Side more broadly. Their desires to use the dance floor to come together in black queer community were routinely shaped by the ways that, Cornel West suggests, "pleasure, under commodified conditions, tends to be inward. You take it with you, and it's a highly individuated unit."[36] But "the Party Noire space is way bigger than personal issues," Rae explains. "While there are these sides [to party organizing] that might be ugly," Nick reflects, "there's still so much more to me that is beautiful and transformative and healing." Nick and Rae's subsequent efforts to foster transformative healing prioritize direct, IRL communication streams over internet ones, and instrumentalize sobriety to create a reciprocal system of accountability where patrons are responsible for communicating conflicts as they happen, and where organizers can in turn work toward collective redress. The choreographies of support they're working to build move Black Joy out of the individuated pleasure that defines the larger neighborhood. The collective and cooperative joy they work toward is a material practice of developing modes of ownership that refuse the proprietary accumulation of pleasure that defines Hyde Park's racialized urban development and that has at times infused Party Noire functions. They work toward a black joy that is built in and through the cypher's generous demands of felt responsibility: a shared acknowledgment of the risks and demands of vulnerability that come with dancing with one another. Party Noire's efforts to build a distributed system of accountability thus "try to get at those nonmarket values—love, care, kindness, service, solidarity, the struggle for justice—values that provide the possibility of bringing people together."[37] What might emerge is a cooperative black joy reflecting Rae's hope and aspiration that, ultimately, "we are our own security, we can secure each other. We can keep each other safe."

THREE
ORDINARY
ENERGY

Gay can be normal. Like, you know, like we can enjoy a normal life in a way that hetero people get to. Like we can just get out of ourselves and not have to feel what it's like to be queer because that's what we feel everywhere.

What do you think when you read that?

At first glance, Tori's turn toward the normal could be read as "bad" queer politics. Critics of the language of and aspiration for "normal" life worry it sanitizes radical politics from lesbian, gay, trans, and queer political movements, and that it romanticizes the legal rights and protections that the state seemingly guarantees through things like marriage licenses. They argue that we should not strive to be part of a racist, homophobic, misogynist, transphobic legislative-cultural system, and that securing legal rights cannot guarantee physical or ontological safety in the eyes of the state nor among family, coworkers, familiars, and/or strangers.[1] Tori speaks of the normal as someone who is nominally afforded some protections of the state given that they and their partner Jae married when they were both just nineteen, traveling from their Illinois college campus to Iowa to do so. Yet, as a black, queer married couple that is also polyamorous, they are well aware of the constraints around "normal," especially as "normal" is typically configured through and as monogamous romantic relationships between two people with financial stability and upward mobility. Moreover, their status as black queer people who work multiple jobs in order to afford life in an increasingly perilous economy is intimately entangled with the multiple forms of violence they continually face as visibly black and queer people.

Tori's quest for normal isn't a refusal of the radical possibilities of queerness nor is it an unthinking embrace of homonormativity, assuming heterosexual ideals and ideologies in ways that depoliticize LGBTQ life, history, and culture.[2] Normal isn't an unwavering allegiance to the supposed securities of legally adjudicated rights. Their turn toward the normal is instead a complex and nuanced desire to shed the sensorial forces that accompany being and inhabiting extraordinary black queer bodies and relationship(s) in a violent hetero- and homonormative, transphobic society. Such a desire to inhabit the normal is a refusal of the rhetorical and haptic resonances of "queer" in a world where black queer bodies and lives are presumed to exert a particular and particularly extraordinary force. This normal aligns neatly with the ability to do ordinary things like be out in the world and have nobody pay attention to you, or to be in a world where you are ignored because everything and everyone around you is just as ordinary as you are.

Such "taken-for-grantedness of everyday life is unequally distributed, more easily accessible to some than others," writes Andre Cavalcante. The stakes of ordinariness are thus high for people like Tori who are hypervisible and who are surveilled in a variety of mundane and spectacular ways. For black queer people who do not often, if ever, have access to a sense of ordinariness, especially in the public and semipublic sphere, ordinariness is not merely a normative striving but a "hard-won, practical accomplishmen[t]."[3] This chapter is interested in how we might pay a different kind of attention to the register of the normal as a quest for ordinariness, and how thinking with the ordinary may help us pay a different kind of attention to black queer life. It does so through an experimental reading of the weekly party that Tori and Jae throw, E N E R G Y: A Party for Women + Their Buddies. Every Sunday from 8:00 p.m. to 2:00 a.m., they create space to converge around some "black as fuck music," Jae explains. "Especially if Tori's DJing: it's going to be trap, it's going to be hood as fuck." The party's extraordinary power lies in its ability to produce a sense of ordinariness among its black queer attendees; as Austin explains, "there are bougie people that come, but then there's also the really down-to-earth people, or folks that don't give a fuck about any of that." At E N E R G Y, "the dress code can be casual, I don't feel the pressure to have to stunt." DJ Professor-wrecks explains, "I could show up to E N E R G Y as I am and just be cool and kicking it. . . . It's uncomplicated and you could go, you can kick it, you can post up at a bar, you can listen to the music that you know and chill."

For all of its chill, there are certainly momentary spectacles, events, that are produced within the party, like any party. Every week E N E R G Y hosts rappers, singers, and poets who are scheduled to perform for a short period of time each party, and there are of course the spontaneous raucous sounds and shifts in attention that happen any time people gather to party. As much as these moments draw everyone's attention, they just as quickly dissolve back into ordinary activities of kicking it, posting up at the bar, listening to familiar music, and chilling. Coming together every week removes the heightened expectations that can surround monthly or quarterly events, when expectations are high that this party will be *the one*. There isn't an urgency to maintain the high of the party because it will happen again next week or the week after—the party becomes an extension of people's weeks rather than an irruption into them, and they often feel less pressure to cut a figure, to hook up, or to see and be seen when they do go out. "At E N E R G Y," Austin shrugs, "it's kind of like, who gives a fuck; it's a lot more casual and relaxed." In its frequent repetition, E N E R G Y is emblematic of how queer nightlife is often uneventful, boring, only OK, or "hit-or-miss," as Bri says; how, as DJ Ca$h Era explains, "The vibe at E N E R G Y varies every time. You either get a very lit crowd or a really chill crowd." This chapter is curious about how we might apprehend the forms of the ordinary that are crafted in the interstice of a very lit crowd and a really chill crowd. It is interested in the information that can be gleaned from a shrug, or in the experience of "hit-or-miss"; that which can be interpreted in the routine of partying: mustering the energy to get out of the house, heading to the party, getting a drink, chatting, dancing, sitting down, maybe getting another drink, maybe chatting, wanting to flirt, trying to flirt, failing to flirt, hittin' it when your song comes on, getting another drink, maybe dancing more, thinking about going home, maybe one more dance or one more flirt, going home, and so on. In the ordinariness that is borne of such regularity and as this regularity crafts a sense of normalcy—in the uneventfulness of the event—black queers experience a time-space where we can, as Tori said, "just get out of ourselves and not have to feel what it's like to be queer because that's what we feel everywhere."

Building a vocabulary for sensing the ordinary energy of E N E R G Y requires us to reconsider some of the methodologies of Black, Queer, and Performance studies. In these fields, our analyses often depend upon the palpability of the *event* as a rupture in time and space that helps us see and assess differences between then and now and, critically, to imagine a more just future.[4] Thinking with the event is useful in minoritarian studies that delineate the material effects that shocks to the system, cultures, and nations have on personal and collective identity, especially as these events can galvanize political thought and movements.[5] We hinge our studies of social, cultural, and political fields on events where the sensoria of everyday life become heightened and thus more available for interpretation. This has been a methodologically rich course to follow for queer and queer nightlife studies, in particular, where wild parties and the appearance of club kids and majestic drag performers, as well as the appearance of interlopers like the police and city officials, constitute events within events within events that jolt our research into being. We take up startling moments when the punctum pricks us or when the performative *does* something to how we see and feel, because these events *as* events help us to see how the implicit and explicit rules of society, culture, and politics are shaped, governed, and at times broken. Moreover, especially catastrophic events can attune us to the violence of the world and clue us into (or at least help us imagine) ways of living otherwise. The event, then, is attached to the potential transformations it can engender.

This "event-potentiality matrix" is baked into fields where deployments of the event can secure the status of minoritarian scholars and departments in institutions that assess value based on perceived usefulness. To be sure, the framework of the event has important worldmaking consequences for the study of minoritarian life and for minoritarian scholars: the force of the event helps us validate and valorize minoritarian experience as *doing* something, as having an effect, as being of consequence. The framework of the event can in turn validate and valorize minoritarian scholars and departments as generating important and consequential scholarly and political insights, especially in institutions that value new and pathbreaking scholarship. The project of making discipline, however, is too often dependent on our abilities to render a single, consistent, rather uncomplicated problem—an event—that our study can be organized around solving. Moreover, our work to train others in learning about (if not necessarily solving) such event-problems often serves to justify the existence of our individual and departmental work in and for the institution.[6] Through the event-potentiality matrix we render minoritarian subjects legible within institutions and systems of thought that depend upon our abilities to make our subject-objects of analysis transparently available, knowable, and thus relevant.[7]

The event-potentiality matrix can overdetermine studies of black queer life, as black queer people and black queerness as a broader field are rendered as events in and of themselves and put to work in the academy. Writing against the event-oriented logic of Anthropology and Black Queer Studies, Shaka McGlotten argues an overcommitment to the framework of the event streamlines black queer life into and as a teleological summation of (often traumatic) events, such that black queerness becomes configured as the effect of an "accumulated series of injured effects of structural forces like racism or homophobia."[8] The supposed eventfulness in and of black queer life is constructed within a broader politics of representation where, Kevin Quashie writes, "black subjectivity exists for its social and political meaningfulness rather than as a marker of the human individuality of the person who is black."[9] This supposed meaningfulness is linked to the expectations of visible, triumphant struggle over catastrophic events that surround (the study of) black life and politics. "As an identity," then, "blackness is always supposed to tell us something about race or racism, or about America, or violence and struggle and triumph or poverty and hopefulness."[10] The sign "black queer" has been increasingly folded into this expectation. As black queers instantiate the transformative and informative event and/or are mere products of it, they plot the trajectory from past to the future. They thus continuously signal the next, if not the new; they are always about to be, or about to do. And in progressive politics and critical theory alike, we invest them with hopeful potential that, as they institute or *are* the future, they will model how to be better, more radical, or more ethical in it.

Read through and as the event, black queer people—and the black queer people who are presumed if not expected to study them—are burdened as analytical categories that are supposed to reveal something about the world around us. We reproduce this event-potentiality matrix in the mechanics of our research, writing, and reading, where we put a lot of pressure on our minoritarian interlocutors, field sites, and objects of study: there is undue expectation that black queerness be productive, that it *works*, that it makes our research *go*, that it makes our learning *productive* and *valuable*. The issue is not whether the events that make up a life or that facilitate critical thought are important or not. Rather, the question is about the ethical contours of our commitment to the event-potentiality matrix and how it shapes the scope and possibilities of thinking about black queer life. In our fixation on thinking with the event-potentiality matrix, we risk abandoning the material now of minoritarian life, losing track of the actual continuum between eventful events and the mundane, ordinary violences that are distributed across all aspects of everyday black queer life. We lose track of the prevailing conditions of minoritarian life: (barely) enduring the accumulation of minor or nonevents that wear us down in seemingly untrackable ways.[11] Subtle, quieter, less public, often invisible, and entirely ordinary modes of living black life are devalued as seemingly carrying less political force and have been thus devalued as sites of critical analysis.

A methodology of the black queer ordinary works to complicate the timeline and force of the event in order to situate our interlocutors' lives more carefully, as events overlap with, and are sometimes indistinct from, the ordinary conditions of life under neoliberalism when, "sadly, hardship, we're used to it," Tori states matter-of-factly. "We've been through things." Tori doesn't specify what, exactly, these "things" are because "things," with the shake of a head and a sigh, point to all that Jae and I already know during our interview: that things only ever lead to more things, and that a crisis can never really be a crisis when there are always other crises on the horizon that will need to be endured. "Things" simply suggests an abundance of what Elizabeth Povinelli describes as non- or quasi-events that do not accumulate into a single spectacular, catastrophic, or sublime event but simply point to other non- or quasi-events: to the rough doing of life itself.[12]

Tori and Jae had in fact been throwing E N E R G Y for around seventy straight weeks when "I had a nine-pound tumor taken out of me," Jae says, looking sideways at me on their couch, eyebrows raised. A much-delayed doctor's visit regarding abdominal pain turned into an ER visit which turned into a life-threatening infection that had to be managed before the surgical removal could take place. "I could not come to E N E R G Y for, what? What were we at? Like a month and a half?"

TORI: Yeah, like a month and a half.

JAE: Yeah, I definitely came back too soon. But, yeah, a month and a half, I did not come back to E N E R G Y at all, actually. Could not get out the bed. It was a lot. I mean, we had an event the day of my surgery.

TORI: Yeah, yeah.

JAE: So they saw me get out of surgery and went right to an event.

While Jae was out, Tori took over the entirety of operations, from social media promotions, to coordinating food vendors and the party photographer, to scheduling the occasional performers they host. Where Tori had occasionally DJed portions of E N E R G Y parties, perfecting their craft, they began DJing in earnest to fill Jae's absence. Each week the party continued uninterrupted until Jae returned.

JAE: I came back on my birthday like, "No, I'm DJ'ing my birthday. Fuck that." . . . I'm like, "Shit, I'm coming back off of surgery. I'm still in pain, but fuck it, we're going to do this because it's necessary," not only for our income but it's necessary for the cultural equity in Chicago, especially in our community. I don't know what a lot of people would do without E N E R G Y, I don't know what *I* would do without E N E R G Y sometimes.

E N E R G Y didn't take a hiatus or stop altogether, Tori explained, "partly because people needed it, and partly because this is one of our forms of income as well. It's not much, but it's something. And I think that the moment you take a break, people, they'll forget." "Attention spans are short," quipped Jae. Their persistence in working through Jae's medical incapacitation was related to their drive to provide people uninterrupted access to E N E R G Y. It was also related to the simple demands of operating in an economy that demands constant labor—and different *kinds* of labor—from black queer people. Tori and Jae had to continue to show up, set up, host, and DJ events just to be able to maintain an unbroken revenue stream, which demands consistent image management to maintain the unbroken visibility of their brand. Jae explains, "We have faith in our audience and we have the utmost faith in our people that come to E N E R G Y but, I mean, in the world of social media and in 2019, if you not steadily going, then your brand is going to collapse. And we didn't have room for our brand to collapse."

Tori and Jae are clear in how the endeavor of crafting nightlife, black queer or otherwise, is a mission of establishing a strong brand identity and pushing it on multiple platforms in order to remain competitive in a broader cultural field. The two of them must simply hustle on a variety of fronts in order to ensure sustained visibility and viability. "It's nonstop. It's nonstop," explains Jae.

And it has to be nonstop when you don't have any parental money, or any connections in that way. It has to be nonstop because you have to make your own money and make your own connection. In Chicago, you better be out, you better be talking, you better be going and have drinks with somebody, you better be smoking a blunt with somebody. Something to get into these spaces and the places that you need to be. So, it has to be nonstop, or we got to give it up and get nine-to-fives—and that's not an option for me.

Here, Jae peels back the fantasies of neoliberal capitalism's startup culture that often obscure how generational wealth typically underwrites people's abilities to secure the capital to work for themselves. They at the same time describe just how much freelance work is spent simply forging connections that may or may not result in more freelance opportunities. Working freelance or working in the gig economy means working across many different fields at once and bouncing between multiple gigs in order to ensure a survivable income. In fact, Tori and Jae host E N E R G Y under the umbrella of their larger events promotion organization, smallWORLD Collective, which contains their individual DJ businesses, DJ Dapper and TORi, as well as their joint DJ endeavor, Fiat Lux. They also contract out Tori Photography + Design through smallWORLD, and are increasingly marketing themselves as speakers and panelists interested in talking about queer sexualities and kinships, especially polyamory. Through smallWORLD, Tori and Jae can canvas broad parts of the city and cross-promote themselves and other organizations that they partner with, like the party Swoon, with whom they host kink-friendly dance parties that draw large numbers of younger queers of color. smallWORLD's larger revenue stream makes it possible for them to host E N E R G Y for free but, as they say, the hustle is nonstop—through sickness and in health—in order to ensure that they generate enough income for themselves to provide this accessible black queer space for other people. "And if we are not doing this nonstop," explains Jae, "we're not able to do that. Our quality of our cultural equity goes down if we're not working nonstop." Tori and Jae's freelance and contract work to sustain E N E R G Y is completely ordinary under neoliberalism, when undue burden is placed on individuals to support themselves amid waning structural support that should be provided by employers, the state, and the medical industry. (It is no surprise that they set up a GoFundMe to collect individual donations from people in their community in order to defray the costs of Jae's medical care and related loss of income.)

Their work is emblematic of the completely ordinary conditions of life for black queer people under neoliberalism, where near-death is a quasi-event that is intimately entangled with the joys of release at a weekly party like E N E R G Y. But in critical frameworks where black queer life grasped through the event is often of the past (trauma) or of the future (liberation), this present where events and the ordinary continually overlap seems impossible to imagine or inhabit. Writing E N E R G Y into history demands a rethinking of the tools of black, queer, performance, and nightlife studies that have operationalized the event-potentiality matrix to draw out the spectacular event in the service of a theoretically better future. People's experiences of E N E R G Y remind us that sometimes the elements of black, queer, and black queer life are only extraordinary when we are removed from them, when we return home to write our field notes and then turn them into talks, articles, chapters, and books; sometimes the events we write about were completely uneventful in the scene of their occurrence. Sometimes the eventfulness that we map onto black queer life or onto the black queer party is simply ordinary among black queer people. Sometimes black queer women go out and party at E N E R G Y *because* doing so feels so ordinary. So, what does it mean to constantly escalate our observations into the realm of the event? How does the expectation of and around the event do a disservice to the lived materiality of black queer life and to histories of black queer women's nightlife, in particular, where elevation into event-status has historically been risky and not in a sexy way?

In fact, the very small body of work we have on black queer women's material (night)lives demonstrates the event can be a dangerous site to inhabit and ill-fitting analytical framework to mobilize. Black queer women are largely absent and illegible within existing queer nightlife scholarship that is overwhelmingly centered on people who identify as men and where the very phrase "queer nightlife" has become a kind of metonym for the scenes and spaces that they have historically attached to, such as gay bars and drag scenes.[13] The other nightlife genre that queer scholarship centers, but which we should continue to pay more attention to, is the ball, which has historically cultivated diverse trans femme subjectivities. However, we have yet to illuminate how, if at all, the language surrounding, and experiences of, black queer and lesbian women may shape ball scenes. This does not mean, of course, that black queer women do not go out and party. The limited archive of black queer women's (night)lives shows us that they are not folded into or are systematically policed out of public space and allegedly safe spaces like gay and lesbian bars and clubs—and these exclusions are almost always a joint effort of the state and ordinary LGBTQ people. The very appearance of black queer women on the street or in line at the club is seen as the result of our inappropriate publicness: we become events in and of ourselves and our presence is read as a punishable misplacement in and misuse of public and semipublic space. Our genders are suspect, our IDs are suspect, our motives are suspect, our music is suspect, our sexualities are suspect, our dancing is suspect, our leases are suspect. As a result of this policing, and as a way to avoid this policing, black queer women have long crafted their nightlives within ordinary spaces of the private home, the rented apartment, the ultra-secretive invite-only event, and in sites that are not explicitly queer or queer-friendly but that provide them cover for gathering, such as ordinary, corporate sites like sports stadiums and restaurant chains.[14]

The ordinary is a site that black queer women have been *pushed* into because of cultural and legislative practices intent on limiting our ways of thinking, moving, and feeling in public. Black queer women are also pushed into the realm of the ordinary by knowledge systems that traffic in and depend on the event and its attendant publicness for coherence: black queer women's modes of being out in the night are not legible within systems of thought that depend upon the highly gendered framework of the event, which directs us to sites full of people who can afford to appear in public in particular ways (i.e., men). When I'm feeling especially pessimistic about the work we do in the academy, I think that black queer women are not of interest to academic thought because of these ways we have been pushed into the ordinary, deemed uneventful and thus uninteresting and unprofitable. Scholars invested in black queer women's lives have to compete for attention—attention brings us accolades that bring us resources that buy us time to pay more attention to black queer women—but how to compete with entire academic (and popular culture) industries built through producing queer and gay men's nightlives as extraordinarily eventful? As deeply consequential? As highly productive to think with?

Black Queer Ordinary Methodology

Maybe we can pay a different kind of attention to black queer women's lives when we divest from the terminologies of the event-potentiality matrix—including "new," "different," "progress," "liberation," "healing," and "freedom"—and get wrapped up in the ordinary's terminologies of endurance, persistence, expectation, regularity, normalcy, and even boredom or disaffection. Thinking with the ordinary might help us attend to the ways that black queer lives are sometimes deliberately staged out of view or at a vibration that is only barely felt, certainly by those who aren't supposed to be seeing or feeling the energy in the first place. The ordinary can be a racialized and gendered space-time that we can historicize and contextualize in order to illuminate black queer and lesbian women's modes of coming together.

An interdisciplinary cohort of people committed to black, feminist, and queer life have been deploying creative methods for rethinking the timeline of and relation between the event and the ordinary in order to sense black and black queer life in more generative ways. In the process of thinking through the ordinary, they demand more from the practice of academic writing but also critical inquiry writ large: detailing the black queer ordinary requires a particular analytical and ethical attention that can reshape how we read and write about black queer life while also reshaping the ways we tend toward the black queer and lesbian women we work with in the academy. Excavating the black queer ordinary might tell us a lot about what we expect from black queer life and from the *study* of black queer life. Our work is to illuminate possibilities of expansive black queer feeling while also paying more acute attention to how our hopes, desires, and expectations of the pleasures of black queer (night)life might be grounded in an event-potentiality matrix that can actually flatten black queer life and overdetermine the physical and temporal conditions in which we think such life is lived. Maybe we can write ourselves into more generative and just practices of tending to our interlocutors in the process.

First and foremost, a methodology capable of rendering the black queer ordinary sidesteps the analytical sway of the event and draws out the non- and quasi-events that black queer women sink into and that make them feel ordinary. This can be achieved through modes of writing that experiment with and press the boundaries of traditional academic prose, writing that embraces lyricism and that uses non- or seminarrative short scenes.[15] This writing may not stitch together complete narrative plotlines organized around distinct narrators or clear beginnings and endings. It thus matches how "ordinary experiences do not always 'signify' larger meanings," as Lisel Olson explains, "nor do they have Aristotelian beginnings, middles, and ends. Rather, the ordinariness of life is omnipresent and diffuse, so that to embrace the everyday is to embrace our inability to envision life as a narrative, for we cannot know the structure of how it will end."[16] Capturing the omnipresent, diffuseness of the ordinary can be achieved via scenes of zoomed-in and/or slowed-down moments that leave us with impressions of what living in the ordinary looks and feels like.

This method of rendering the ordinary aims, as Kathleen Stewart richly demonstrates in *Ordinary Affects*, to "fashion some form of address that is adequate to their form; to find something to say about ordinary affects by performing some of the intensity and texture that makes them habitable and animate."[17] The work is to stretch out the quasi-event as an invaluable site and mechanism through which we might, following Stewart, momentarily sense the slippery "modes of attention, attachment, and agency that catch people up in something that feels like *some*thing."[18] As McGlotten writes, developing a methodology capable of rendering the black queer ordinary is "an initial, tentative, and partial effort toward tracking the ways Blackness and queerness are experienced as meaningful through the ways they are *felt*."[19] While refusing narrative expectation, and siting us in the intensity and texture of what the ordinary feels like, a methodology of the black queer ordinary nonetheless acknowledges that the violent specter of homophobic, transphobic, misogynoiristic anti-blackness *always* foreshadows "how it will end," and the myriad of feelings that such foreshadowing incurs.[20] But we shouldn't look to the ordinary as an escape from the (often-violent) eventfulness of black queer life. As anthropologist Veena Das explains, "our theoretical impulse is often to think of agency in terms of escaping the ordinary rather than as a descent into it."[21] Racialized, gendered, and sexualized violence in fact scaffolds the ordinary's possibilities, so attending to the ordinary requires a different scale and duration of attention—a commitment to sit amid the minor notes of pain, for example, rather than escape to the utopian potentiality of the elsewhere and the otherwise. Drawing on Aliyyah Abdur-Rahman's language, this is a methodology "that is not temporal—that is, not future directed—but that reaches in and reckons with the ruinous now as the site of regenerative capacity and of renewed political agency."[22]

There are certainly people who have been reaching into the ruinous now to shed light on the black (queer) ordinary, and their methods are instructive. In *Don't Let Me Be Lonely: An American Lyric* and *Citizen: An American Lyric*, poet and essayist Claudia Rankine wends the first- and second-person voice through nonlinear scenes of everyday life—watching TV, lying in bed, walking in a parking lot, calling one's siblings—to produce the experience of living amid the miasma of anti-black violence. She illustrates late twentieth-century modes of black ordinariness that surface in daily negotiations of the banal cruelties of neoliberal governance, where the fantasy of the good life buckles given the diminishing returns of capitalism *and* in response to the failed promises of racial justice.[23] Rankine details the modes of isolation and loneliness generated in a neoliberal economy that demands individual solutions to structural racism. In turn, neoliberal discourses of well-being that push pharmacological remedies to insomnia, boredom, overworking, and grief are no salve for the routine police violence, rampant misogynoir, accidental and intentional death, and sheer trauma that shape everyday black life, and that generate black affects including exhausted apathy, dignified resignation, and barely stifled rage that become ordinary in their enduring presence.

Rankine reads well alongside black feminist investigations into the ordinary that operate by unsettling the narrative authority of the event, and that experiment with tense and grammar in the process.[24] Saidiya Hartman, for example, draws out the possibilities of the ordinary by using a method of "critical fabulation" to imagine the possibilities of a black girl's life lived amid the violence of the Middle Passage, a method that undoes narrative expectations and works to "jeopardize the status of the event, to displace the received or authorized account, and to imagine what might have happened or might have been said or might have been done."[25] Hartman later puts such narrative reconfiguring to work in *Wayward Lives, Beautiful Experiments: Intimate Histories of Social Upheaval*, a book that notably begins with "A Note on Method" that speaks to the challenges of sensing the ordinary in historical archives where black women and girls, if they appear at all, are logged through and as often-disastrous events. Hartman works to document their "waywardness" as practices of refusing such event-status, and she does so through a writing method that displaces any assumption of her own narrative authority. She operates through "a mode of close narration, a style which places the voice of narrator and character in inseparable relation, so that the vision, language, and rhythms of the wayward shape and arrange the text."[26] This results in a text whose polyvocality is conceptually and visually evident in the italicized passages that serve as "utterances from The Chorus": "all the unnamed young women of the city trying to find a way to live and in search of beauty."[27] By calling upon the chorus, Hartman's writing displaces the status of the scholar-writer as "entitled to experience" by virtue of having revealed the event (in Hartman's case, the archive).[28]

Experiments in method demonstrate how writing the ordinary can be an ethical endeavor to not only think *about* our interlocutors but think *beside* them, such that rendering the ordinary might be considered a form of ethical commitment to black queer life.[29] Key to this is how an ordinary methodology is plotted through description instead of, say, explanation—but does not wield this description in the service of transparency. "Description," Katherine McKittrick writes, "is not liberation."[30] A methodology of the black queer ordinary might instead operate from the vantage point of what she calls an ethical distance: "I found her picture. I hope to write an ethical distance and grieve what I, we, cannot know without industry-of-objecthood enveloping her. I kept your secret."[31] In a passage of her essay on the black ordinary, Savannah Shange practices this ethical distance as she reflects upon the descriptive demands that ethnography, as a discipline and a method, places upon her black girl interlocutors like Tarika who cannot or will not appear. Shange explains,

> Built into the genre of ethnography is an expectation of narrative thickness, a rich tapestry of voices that leaves the reader satiated by the elegant rhythm of *I saw, she said, I saw, she said.* The "right" way to end this essay is with a pithy quote from Tarika, an emic insight that could stand in for twenty-odd pages of academic grandstanding and simultaneously give me cred as a community-accountable ethnographer who gives her research participants the last word. But to reach out to Tarika with the intent of hearing her perspective, even in the interests of a putatively liberatory ethnographic project, still demands access to Black girl interiority as the price to ride on the freedom train. If both the carceral and the decolonial engagement with young Black women rely on the same remedy—her performative transparency—then both political projects prioritize their pre-authored frameworks over Black girl self-determination. Perhaps here I fail as an anthropologist, and the petticoat of my disciplinary drag is showing. But I sense there is more explanatory power in Tarika's agentic absence, in the opacity of not-knowing, than I would find tracking her down (*like a runaway*) and feigning a complete circle of analysis.[32]

The power differentials built into the ethnographic process can demand too much from minoritarian life. The expectation if not demand that our interlocutors be wholly known to us can produce modes of surveillance, control, and maybe, at worse, *lies.* Shange's practice of ethical distance embraces opacity as a historically grounded protection for black people who have long been mistreated in and by institutional study.[33] As Shange suggests, though, the problem, as it were, is not necessarily or only borne by the researcher: the expectation of eventful transparency is rooted in the reciprocal relationship between the academic and the academic's audience. Our commitments to the event and to the event-potentiality matrix are rooted in our desires, or the need, to satiate *the reader* (the student, the committee, the review board, the funder) above all else.

This is all to say that people committed to black, feminist, and queer life are devising creative methods for rethinking the timeline of and relation between the event and the ordinary in order to sense black and black queer life in more generative ways. In doing so, they demand more from the practice of academic research and the consumption of it. The rest of this chapter subsequently breaches the presumed stability of the event-potentiality matrix in order to open other ways of seeing, feeling, experiencing, and (only ever partially) knowing black queer life—and to reconfigure how we read and understand it. My rendering of E N E R G Y drops us into conversations in progress and swells of feeling that never quite land. It never gives us a full picture of the party but offers speculations on interior selves and wonders about other people's motivations and intentions in attending. In so doing, I attempt to emulate the quality and force of black queer feeling(s) and relation(s) that are forged at E N E R G Y, and which underscore its ordinariness. This ordinariness is as palpable in the sensations that surround Tori and Jae's hustling as it is palpable in how E N E R G Y's black queer and lesbian attendees pay attention to one another: their ways of moving together, grabbing onto one another, clapping for one another, egging one another on; how black queer women talk to one another in the space and how they think about one another when they're gone; and how they speculate on missed connections and would-be scenarios. Ordinariness is felt in these forms of recognition and attention that can't quite be named, in eye contact made and lost, in the surges that surround the possibility of touch, conversations that seemingly go nowhere, or in their missed opportunity.

What emerges can only ever be a partial glimpse of the modes of physical and affective attention that compel black queer people toward one another at E N E R G Y, and that ground the expressly black queer milieu of the party. The following scenes bring you in closer to E N E R G Y's ordinary energy in ways that underscore how the ordinary is inextricable from ethical questions about the relations of intimacy and proximity between us researchers and readers and the people, places, and subjects that we engage and depend on for our critical insights. My attempts to capture E N E R G Y's ordinariness subsequently and directly prompt you, dear reader, to reflect upon the networks of interest, desire, and proximity (and lack thereof) that govern your practice of critical inquiry.

A Question to Ask Yourself: Why Am I Reading This? (For Real. Ask Yourself.)

The party instantly pops off when "Back Dat Ass Up" comes on and everyone dutifully takes position: a thicc woman with a long weave jumps up from the low-slung lounge in front of the raised DJ booth to twerk, hands on her knees and smiling with tongue out on the middle of the dance floor, while her friend, a masculine-of-center person in an oversized white T-shirt and joggers, hair tightly braided, walks a slow circle around her. She's dialed in as she walks this circle, brows furrowed, mouth screwed into an approving smirk as she claps loudly and intently in support of her friend's dexterous twerking. She pauses only to smack her friend's ass while the black women around them shout *aaaaaaaay* and record with their phones. She keeps twerking as the energy swells around the two of them as people crowd onto the cramped dance floor. DJ Dapper is hyping everyone up. They stand on the small DJ stage wearing only their chest binder, swinging their T-shirt above their head while yelling into the blown-out mic for people to dance, shouting out people who they know in the room, and reminding everyone to tip the two bartenders. I don't think Jasmine is here tonight, but she gets it:

> I'm really just here because I have this tension built up from the week. I had a rough one. There's family stuff going on, maybe relationship stuff, work was hard. Whatever it is, paying bills, I just need to move my body to release this tension. People will just gas you up, like, "Ayyyyy!" You know? That community feeling of, "You look like you are having a really good time out there. Let's hype her up real quick."

You can basically hype anyone up because you can basically see everyone at the bar: the capacity is only sixty-five (a number that is frequently, grossly overshot) and it's up for debate whether the ten-by-ten space where people dance is an actual dance floor or just part of the walkway between the front door and the rest of the bar. Regardless, deep movement happens throughout every inch of the bar; you simply dance wherever you are and with whomever is next to you, puzzle-piecing to find space in, on, and in between one another's bodies.

Bri would actually hate this if she were here. She's lowkey laughing when she tells me, "When I want to dance, I don't want to be like, 'Damn, this seat is right here, I can't.' . . . So when the music is hitting you, you're like, 'Damn, I'ma have to elbow ole girl who's just sitting here minding her business!'" She usually can't resist dancing, though.

> I'm a sucker for a big booty, so, if I see somebody who can actually dance—or I see them dancing with somebody else, the way their rhythm is—I definitely will be like, "OK." If something good comes on again, I make my way over there. There's definitely times I'm like, "I want that, don't she look good? Let me see if she can throw it back real quick."

Someone is throwing it back for her two friends with extra-long bundles. They had up to that point been posted up at the bar, alternating between talking and using social media. When their song came on, though, they took to their positions: one turned and grabbed hold of the bar, chest close to the bar and arms bent at the elbow giving her the leverage to twerk, the other two recorded her, flashlights on, solemn in their BFF duties. They catch her as she alternates between playfully looking back at it while her friends record, and ducking her head down between her outstretched arms, elongating her back and straightening her legs to make it really pop. Her friends shout quite literal descriptions of how well she is working it—"there she go, there she *go*"—that double as encouragements to keep working it. They take turns smacking her ass to demonstrate its shake and bouncing it up and down with her rhythm to enhance the depth of her twerk. A black ass practice of honoring the black ass.[34] We watch, here for it. They finish when the song finishes, smoothing their hair and checking their nails.

A Series of Questions to Ask Yourself: What Was I Expecting? How Much Did I Hope to Learn? About What, Exactly?

A very handsome, very young-looking stud sits on one of the three, single lounge chairs at the entrance of the bar, feigning a casualness that belies an undercurrent of giddy delight at their good fortune: their femme boo has been intermittently grinding on their lap and standing up to dance for them for the past hour. The stud hasn't seemed to quite grow into their gangly body which becomes even more visible when they eventually stand up to partner-dance and they are entirely uncoordinated, unsure of what the relation of the top half of their body is to their lower half. They don't know where to put their hands on their boo, when to move with her or how.

What I had been ready to see (and, admittedly, assess) as a "traditional" masc-femme gender dynamic simply looks sweetly awkward, self-conscious, and uncomfortable. "There's still these heteronormatives that it is still, I guess, more acceptable for a more masculine person to dance with a more feminine person," Austin explains. I watch the stud's stoic coolness belying the moments where they break into a furtive glance around, to see if anyone is watching—maybe hoping nobody is watching. Within these heteronormatives are expectations of kinesthetic skill—which this stud does *not* possess—and I have a flash of anxiety on behalf of every dyke, stud, MOC, butch, aggressive, and so on, who has ever had to dance in public, in part because Erica is in my ear groaning that she's

> like, terrible at grinding! I'm really like, "I'm sorry, I'm very terrible at it." And, like, so, a lot of times people will come up and they're like *ready* and I'm like, *OK!* And then they like turn around and then I'm like, *Oooop. OK, I gotta, like, hold on.* And then I feel embarrassed because I'm like, *Goddamn, I feel like this is something I should know how to do.*

I've seen her dancing, there in the middle of the floor, if maybe a little to the side of it, drink in hand, expertly executing the rhythm from the tops of her shoulders, through her neck and chin and resulting in an effortlessly cool head bob. That's kind of where she leaves it because for her there's an expectation in black queer spaces that dancing will "have that romantic kind of connotation to it" and, as a result, being a "bad" dancer like her, well, she tries to avoid visible dancing altogether because "it's like I don't wanna disappoint you, in a way, because I feel like there is that: when people have that expectation and if you can't even master that, people don't think you can master them, in a way." If you can't dance you can't flex in the bedroom— but if you *do* dance, you can't hang. Austin took their crew of studs to Party Noire, a place where dancing is foregrounded, and dancing

> felt good and safe for me but I looked around and I noticed that someone else who was also masculine-identified was looking at us with a stank face! This is like the two-stepping nigga, the one that stays on the wall, like, you know, "I can't dance" and shit. I'm like: Nigga, move your *body*. I'm like, you sitting here judging me! And so it made me hyper aware of what I might look like. I felt myself combating that, trying to resist it, but it was already there.

Sometimes studs do dance. Well, they mostly sit with their bois, chatting and/or dialed in watching the dance floor. Always looking like they're busy or maybe just about to leave. Sometimes when their song hits, though, they stand up or move off the wall, one hand moving with the beat or punctuating their linguistic recall as they rap along. Sometimes they catch one another's eye as they do this, excitement in mutual recognition intensified by their devotion to performing their knowledge of the music, competitive play that makes the femmes around them sweat. If they are alone, a good number of them will pull their phones out as they bounce to the beat, looking busy as they flip between apps while rapping along to themselves; the bolder ones, or the ones for whom solitude is tempered by social media excess, will mug for IG Live. The studs really do dance at E N E R G Y though, especially when they host the thematic Boi E N E R G Y every last Sunday of the month. "We had to incorporate Boi E N E R G Y just because, you know, as a masculine-of-center, *I* felt left out of the conversation," Jae explains. "In every space, in every queer space, whether it's black or white, I felt left out. . . . So we also know this, that we do have a high concentration of bois, and MOCs and studs and butches—whatever you want to call yourself—that is what we try to center every last Sunday of the month." They dance with one another, they sing along, they find dance partners, they drop it low. A MOC drops it low in the in-between space between the bar and the lounges, changing this tight thoroughfare into a runway as they twerk in front of their femme partner—a new boo—who playfully holds on for dear life as people call out *aaaaaaaayyyyyyy* before they continue their path to the bathroom. "I definitely have been behind the stud from time to time," Bri tells me conspiratorially, "because they like to twerk."

How Did It Feel to Read That? Do I Know More about _____?
About _____? Am I Supposed To?

Ari first attended E N E R G Y with a friend, bringing along a companion to an unfamiliar space and an unfamiliar party. She was immediately struck by the number of people who approached them to chat and shoot the shit, and that it was easy for her to strike up conversation with the strangers around her. She found an ease simply by following Jae and Tori's lead. "The organizers of the party would talk to *every single person* that came in the door." They also introduced people to one another, and struck up conversations between strangers to facilitate a larger atmosphere of connectedness. She started coming to the party alone. Going alone "was more fun by myself, sometimes, because I would just talk to everyone there." I actually could never go to E N E R G Y alone, I always roped someone or a whole crew into going with me. Bringing my friends was reinforcement at the tail end of my research when I needed help mustering the energetic resources to go out late Sunday nights. But I also brought friends because the party was *too* friendly, too intimate. Taylor in my ear, "You can go to E N E R G Y and you'll leave with a new friend." I was feeling especially prickly in the years leading up to 2020 and if I went alone, knew I would be engaged by people, and *not* engaging in such a small space would give off bad vibes. I couldn't hide or slink away or stand on the corner when I needed to recharge, like I could at Slo 'Mo or Party Noire. My friends were at times my social lubricants and at other times a protective barrier and I was always jealous of the people who were there alone; who were so active (and brave) in crafting the community they wanted to see and be a part of.

There are a lot of folks who go E N E R G Y alone; you can always tell from the way that they look around from the corners, barstools, and lounges they sit on. They scan the room rather than stay focused on their phones. They make their whole bodies open and available for people to approach them. I tried to make my way to this stud at E N E R G Y all night, the one with the impeccably greased ponytail, their black-on-black shirt, tie, and vest, looking around the room, occupied in their mind but not in conversation. The way they looked around the room, chin up, shoulders back, giving a constant side eye to the room, just barely perceptible through their slim, square, silver glasses. I kept meaning to head over to them but I kept getting caught up in chats with Reese. We might be one of those E N E R G Y Best Friends that Jasmine told me about: "People that you know you're going to see consistently at E N E R G Y, and they don't necessarily talk outside of that space, or I literally have never thought of hanging out with you outside of this space, but when I see you on Sunday, I'm really genuinely happy to see you. . . . And you're looking forward to this conversation with me just like I'm looking forward to you." I know their whole astrological chart, and their family's very black migration throughout the South and southern Midwest, a skilled labor force following the trail of industrial jobs. Their drive from the suburbs is faster than my public transportation from within the city limits. I'm here with other folks but you came alone again tonight, come sit with us. I'm gone now but we're IG friends now, LOLing in the DMs. I understand their memes about introverts, puppies; their wanting to be a human dildo makes so much more sense now. I still got my eyes peeled for the perfect girl for you; she better love the fact that you know, like, every word to every early-2000s rap song ever played on the radio.

"People at E N E R G Y is just, like, a lot of times if I know you, I probably just met you at a party and it's kinda like that drunk, like, *Hey, like, let's chat* and we just constantly see each other," Erica tells me. "You build a friendship just by seeing each other over all these years." Ari

> didn't go to E N E R G Y for like two months and then I showed up like two weekends ago and everyone was like "where you been at? Are you good? How you been?" and everyone was super welcoming. It was like a "take your time if you don't wanna be here" but it was like a "we've missed you, we noticed that you were gone. How you been? If you don't wanna talk about it, let's dance." Or "Would you like me to buy you a drink?" or whatever the situation may be. It's like people that you don't even have to talk to all the time because they may not even be your homies like that, like on the daily, but they are in the same space as you often. . . . It makes an impact when you're there or not, just like I notice when people are there or not.

The regularity of E N E R G Y allows people to come into contact repeatedly for short periods of focused, intentional time and they have built a following of regulars for whom E N E R G Y feels, as Taylor notes, "almost like a family reunion. Everyone is just like, 'OK, we went to work this week. Now I'm going to go see my family.' It's just like a nice family hangout type of thing."

It's a different kind of family, to be sure. Not like the ones we sell drugs for; not like the ones we move cities and states for, to take care of parents, grandparents, siblings, nieces, nephews, and cousins; not like the families we learn how to adjust to when they finally get out of a lifetime in prison. It's not the same family that we move in with every now and then to get out of shitty landlords and abusive relationships, broke and in new shitty apartments and new shitty relationships. This family isn't the same one you fled the suburbs for the city for, or the ones who gently suggested you leave the South to join them in the city ("but maybe don't tell your uncles why"). This E N E R G Y family may only be felt in the same space once a week but, shit, that's more than I see some of my very best friends who live down the street, and way more often than when I see my blood family two states away anyway. This is the family that I bring my best friend to meet, and the family that introduced her, for better or for worse, to double Henny lemonades.

It's not family so much as a shared intention, if not an ethics of care, under-written by boundaries and consent and without expectations of reciprocation. An "I'm not pushy with her business or anything" intention, a "but, hey, I'm popping in your DMs like, *You coming out on Sunday*?" intention. An "*I've been looking for you, you haven't been here. You good?"* intention. A *"Yeah, I'll be there on Sunday, we'll talk about it.* And then she comes in and she does have a story, a reason why she wasn't there. But it's like, *yeah, thanks for checking in. I hadn't really felt like coming out, but I didn't think anyone missed me either"* intention. "No, you don't have to be at a bar and drinking to be OK. But someone recognizes that you haven't been here."

Sometimes the Questions We Ask Ourselves about Our Research Are the Same Ones We Ask Ourselves about Partying: How Much Longer Do I Need to Do This? How Does My Body Feel? What Am I Going to Remember and Tell People? Who Am I Gonna Look Up Later? What Am I Going to Ignore? What Am I Embarrassed About? What Do I Want to Forget? *Who* **Do I Want to Forget? Should I Twist the Knife? Why? Is It Because of Something Kemi Said, or Something about Myself?**

A methodology of the black queer ordinary has to be an extremely self-reflexive one where we deeply consider our investments in and expectations of and for the black queer subjects that we encounter in critical thought—if we encounter them at all. This self-reflexivity is key if we're going to approach black queer women in the first place, and if we're going to approach them differently within fields, disciplines, and politics that have been built on and through the bodies of black queer women but have continually undercited and underfunded them. It's pretty straightforward to state that the lack of scholarship documenting the complexity of black queer women's material lives certainly reflects how we are not doing enough to admit and financially, emotionally, and intellectually support people who might study the material lives of black queer communities. Racism, misogyny, homophobia, and transphobia are built into decisions about who we admit into institutions of higher education and how we support them. But the answer isn't only or necessarily more graduate students—we know full well that including minoritized subjects in violent institutions and discourses makes their work all but impossible. No matter how many graduate students there are, or how many articles and books and classes there are, we are continually confronted with the fact that, in the academy, black queer women are always someone else's object, someone else's work.[35] (That is, until we're talking about *using* black queer women to do the extraordinary work of upping the diversity of our institutions, curing racism, solving politics, cleaning up HR messes, redefining literary genres, appearing in that one throwaway sentence we use to make any given statement intersectional, and so on. We use black queer and lesbian women, and our chronic avoidance of them, in order to paradoxically justify the work that we are doing—we've got to do *this* work in order to get to *that* work later.)

Maybe we need to be trained to engage black queer women in a different way. I like to think that the constitutive forgetting and compulsory super-ficiality that surrounds the study of black queer women is rooted in our inabilities to reckon with the racialized and gendered relation of the event and the ordinary, especially given how this relation structures our relation-ships to production within the academy. That's why I want a reckoning with the ordinary as something that might force us into a different relation with black queer women, where we are more than experimental, theoretical events on one hand or easily forgettable citational fodder on the other. Generat-ing a methodology of the black queer ordinary should be deployed to give texture to the lives of black queer women but also, just as importantly, as a practice of thinking with and beside them without engaging in an extractive reading practice that *uses* them.

Through the difficult process of breaking our critical attachments to the event we might be able, as Sharon Holland suggests, "to reach an epiphany of sorts—one that would allow us to see what happened to us collectively. This collectivity might restore just what we did and do to one another at the moment of our intimate interactions—erotic, racist, and otherwise."[36] I'm taking liberties with that "otherwise" when I read Holland as suggesting that the reinvention of critical tradition is about deep self-reflection in the service of reconfiguring our relationships to the racialized and gendered political economy of *production* in critical thought. That's why building a methodol-ogy of the black queer ordinary must also be a consideration of what kinds of critical thought come into being and gain value in the academy, and raise questions about who accrues value in the academy, how, and why.

These questions are very important because they are related to how and why we relate to one another, invest in one another, work with one another, depend on one another, and forge connections with one another in critical thought. I've tried to balance these dynamics in this chapter, wanting to contextualize a portrait of E N E R G Y but without exploiting its specialness in the service of extractive learning. The protective gestures of the ordinary methodology may always fail—no matter what, I have published this work and it will circulate beyond this book and into conversations that I and my interlocutors will not be able to participate in. But this chapter was never really *about* E N E R G Y. It is an attempt at a methodology of the black queer ordinary that is built through practices of description that open us up to speculation through, critically, self-interrogation. If we're committed to thinking in relation, we have to be able to take account of our own selves, drives, needs, and conditioning. So, a series of questions to ask yourself:

How Do I Need Black Queer Women to Do My Work? Do I Avoid Black Queer Women in Order to Do My Work? How Do I Need Them to Help Me Think? How Do I Need Them to Be Absent to Help Me Think? What Are the Keywords I Use to Describe Black Queer Women? Where, on the Spectrum from Ordinary to Extraordinary, Do My Keywords Position Black Queer Women? Is My Writing about Black Queer Women or Is It about My Ego? Am I Just Hoping that My Research Is about Badass Shit or Is It Really? Is My Research Radical or Am I Just Citing Black Queer Women? Are Black Queer Women Actually Doing This or Am I Just Assuming They Are? What Do I Need from Black Queer Women? What Do I Expect from Black Queer Women? What Do Black Queer Women Expect from Me? How Am I Listening to Black Queer Women? How Do I Know? How Do They Know? Do I Think about Myself More Than I Think about Black Queer Women? Be Honest.

CONCLUSION
AN ORAL HISTORY OF THE FUTURE OF BURNOUT

Each month and sometimes each week the black queers in this book weigh the odds that going to the queer dance party will make them feel good. As any given Slo 'Mo, Party Noire, or E N E R G Y event approaches, they work through the basic algorithm of black queer (night)life—calculating the relations among energy, intention, endurance, and outcome—to determine whether or not they should go to the function. Sometimes the relations can be low stakes: Do I have the energy to party tonight, and for how long? How much am I invested in the feeling of community that may result from going? Is going out more or less important than watching TV for the rest of the night? If I *do* watch TV the rest of the night, how much energy will I spend with FOMO? The stakes can be much higher in the derivatives that emanate outward from these questions, as the calculus of black queer life is always done in plain view of the specter of physical and psychological violence/harm that may come in the daily navigation of the city. Do I have the energy to take my black queer ass out in the world today? Can I endure walking on the street and riding public transportation to get to the function? Will I feel safe in the Uber? Can I make it safely inside the bar from where I parked my car? What will be the outcome of my going out: will I be unbothered, will I be harmed, will I even make it back home?

If the outcomes are favorable, black queers work through an entirely different set of decisions to ensure they'll attend the function. They secure a wealth of administrative, financial, and temporal resources to be able to get to the function: they manage home and family arrangements, negotiate work schedules and labor loads, and (re)apportion spending money. Then there's the routine of mustering the emotional and energetic resources required to actually *get* to the event: you've got to get motivated to go out even when you don't feel great in your body, and distribute your emotional expectations when you don't feel great about a party or its organizers, or suspect the music won't be great. Energy has to be stored, reserved, and properly distributed when you think your ex might be there and so going might not be a great idea—or when you think that your ex might be there so going might be a *great* idea.

There's a whole routine of talking yourself up so that you can be dressed and ready to leave the house at 10:00 p.m. (or, if you're a pro, you make sure you're out having dinner or something around 8:00 p.m. so that by the time dinner is over it's party time and you just ride the wave). To say nothing of the routines of people who prefer parties that start at 1:00, 2:00, and 3:00 a.m. Regardless of when the party starts, a not insignificant amount of rationalizing, self-bartering, and bargaining goes into preparing for long public transportation trips or expensive cabs and rideshares or securing a coveted seat in the designated driver's car. Last but not least, there are the mental gymnastics that are sometimes required to convince yourself to chill, relax, and have a good time if and when you do arrive.

Then there are myriad of frustrations that happen once you do arrive at the event: there is a long line to get in in the first place, the DJ isn't playing anything you like, dancers are taking up too much of the wrong kind of personal space, people keep interrupting the music to make announcements, the bartenders are taking *forever*, the bathroom line is too long and once you do get in the bathroom is filthy, and not in a sexy way.

The labors of getting to and being at the function are only ever amplified by the energy that it takes to wake up the next day and endure whatever hangover you might have and to recuperate from your physical exhaustion, "especially when you go hard one night," Bri sighs.

Oh no. My knees be like, "*Yo*. You tried it! You tried a little too much, little too much." I need a bath the next day with some Epsom salt if I didn't sit down. I guess it's my bad for going in, but at the same time, I'm like, I actually do want to dance—but my body's like, "girl you tried."

Jasmine, also in her midtwenties, tells me "I'm starting to get older," as I playfully roll my eyes. "I just turned twenty-six so I know that I'm not very old, but I'm definitely starting to feel it!" She's not only starting to feel the weight of a body that doesn't move as smoothly as it may have in previous years, but also starting to feel the exhaustion of simply going out night after night.

> Being able to have the energy to go out sometimes; I love it but it's not something that I want to do three times a week anymore. Once or twice is fine, or like every other week. I just see there's not as much longevity in nightlife when you get into the older crowd and trying to figure out how to maintain that. Like, am I going to be able to keep dancing like this? 'Cause the body don't roll the same.

As they look forward to their thirties, Bri and Jasmine are reassessing their physical capacities to go out at night and querying their own longevity, not only in terms of how many years they may or may not have left in them to party but, as Bri exclaims, their very abilities to simply stay up late. "Oh man, it's a celebration getting home before 10! I'm like, *What!!* But that's how I know that I've gotten older. I ain't got time." Tracy is around a decade older than the two of them and has lived many different kinds of party lives, from the after-party rave scenes that moved her through her early twenties to the slowness of Slo 'Mo that suits her energy in her late thirties. For her, assessing the value of black queer nightlife entails changing considerations of physical and social exhaustion, and she's in a space of reprioritizing what her body needs (to sleep, namely). In her younger years, she explains, "I loved being able to know that I could go somewhere at three o'clock in the morning and party until whenever I wanted. Now? Hell no. Hell to the *no*. Absolutely not. Don't even call me. My phone does not even ring, and if it does after nine o'clock I'm like, who the fuck is this?"

Party organizers balance the same pleasures and pains of going out that attendees do—they make the same calculations of energy, endurance, and outcome—but they are doubly weighted by the sheer responsibilities of event organizing that are further intensified by the expectation if not assumption that such organizing provides the structure for black queer community. This organizational work, which is indeed the work of community building, is simply a lot and there's not much room to ditch last minute and stay on the couch. The organizers of Slo 'Mo, Party Noire, and E N E R G Y host their regularly scheduled flagship events and they also host auxiliary events at other venues throughout the city. Some have launched additional events altogether, as Kristen of Slo 'Mo did with Old Gold, the all-vinyl party hosted at the Ace Hotel. Twice a month Nick and Rae, organizers of

Party Noire, host a "Black Queer Joy Ride" cycling club, building upon the organization's investment in broad-based self-care and wellness initiatives that extend beyond the club space. On top of that, the organizations regularly partner with other parties and organizations to cohost events, and on top of *that* DJs Audio Jack (Slo 'Mo), Rae Chardonnay (Party Noire, and 2019 winner of "Best DJ in Chicago"), and DJ Dapper are regularly hired out to play different events throughout the city. Pride season may likely be the most taxing time of the year, as they must continue to host their own flagship event(s), work as freelance DJs, *and* host Pride-specific event(s), oftentimes in tandem with other organizations, which adds considerable amount of administrative labor to their already busy schedules.

They do this work in a growing, productively crowded queer nightlife landscape that has grown to provide people so many sites, soundscapes, and choreographic opportunities to stake their claims to the Chicago landscape. Over the course of this book's research, the Chances Dances collective retired after ten years of throwing three parties a month while FKA, catering to a young, relatively diverse crowd, continued steadily on the north side. Events like Jai Ho built themselves up around an audience of South Asian queers and allies while black-run The Lesbifriends Cartel lost steam and LGBTQ+ women and femme Peach Party picked up, while parties like Swoon, Duro, and Molasses built space for black and Latinx queer and trans people. Former Chances organizer-DJs developed their own endeavors: DJ CQQCHIFRUIT began to cohost TROPITECA with La Spacer in Pilsen and Hijo Pródigo continued to establish themselves as a queer club kid icon throughout the city. All the while, black club promoters like K-star and AllGirlsChi continued to host events throughout the city that blur the line between explicitly queer lesbian functions and traditional "ladies' nights."

Slo 'Mo, Party Noire, and E N E R G Y organizers must always be mindful of working to remain relevant and to increase the visibility of their programming in this landscape. Nick notes "that we've had some people who have like been around from the very beginning and literally probably have missed, like, zero to two to three parties." At the same time, "Chicago is expansive and like every single time we do an event there are new people that I've never seen." Running Party Noire has subsequently entailed attending other queer, black, and black queer events to show support as members of overlapping communities and in acknowledgment that there are always people who could be attending Party Noire events; as she says, "there are always new grounds to cover." The future orientation of "new grounds to cover" encompasses the variety of people Party Noire could be serving and the need for a nightlife organization to be able to process and adapt to these new grounds. As Nick continues:

I think, in that, being mindful not to be complacent or stagnant in what we're doing and to always think about those people who have never been to a Party Noire or never, like, seen [a] Party Noire. It can be easy to jump into doing something like due process and just kinda repeating and doing the same shit over and over again. And I think for me, this last three years has taught me really to be just agile and able to adapt and be flexible, I guess, and also just continue to think about those people who have never experienced a Party Noire.

As organizations must meet the current *and* future needs of the current *and* future communities, they must be attuned to what these communities are currently engaging with and must speculate about what they might need or want in the future. Here, what Nick describes as the ethical drive to connect to the furthest reaches of a community, to reach all those people who have never heard of nor attended Party Noire and for whom that space might be vitally important, is undoubtedly bound up with the material pressures that accompany throwing nightlife events. An organization's impulse to grow and expand is always linked to its need to be at least fiscally and emotionally sustainable if not materially profitable.

Sustainability and profitability are interlaced here, as a profitable organization may not be sustainable, and a sustainable organization may not be profitable. Free parties may secure 15 percent of the bar sales, which is often just enough to pay the DJ or performer or just enough compensation to satisfy the organizers so that they don't totally burn out. Ticketed parties often bring in more money and organizers often funnel profits toward DJs and performers, giving them better compensation for their labors. This 15 percent of the bar or the door sales is rarely enough to compensate the sheer amount of labor that goes into organizing, promoting, hosting, or DJing the events covered in this book. On top of the administrative labor required to throw these events, organizers are often formally and informally training bar staff and managers in best practices concerning the LGBTQ communities coming through their doors. There is no small amount of frustration among party organizers who, in their need to produce safer spaces, are tasked with, as Kristen describes, "procuring the right person that's going to come and do staff [training] and you're not even *on* fucking staff? Are you doing that? Are you doing that with your multiple jobs? You're doing that for fifteen percent of the bar that you can't even charge a cover for?" Doing unpaid work for venues in order to do the largely unpaid work of generating queer nightlife scenes is exacerbated by the fact that all of the organizers in this book throw parties on top of other work that they do to secure income. Some of them have a single full-time job; often they are working across multiple gigs in a larger freelance economy that provides little by way of job security, let alone benefits.

The work that organizers do to produce black queer nightlife is simply exhausting and they do this work on limited funds and, often, on limited sleep. Because their night shifts are always dependent upon their daytime hustling, "a lot of times, there won't be any sleep," Tori, who co-organizes E N E R G Y, explains. "We won't get home until 4:00 a.m., but no matter what, we're early risers. Eight o'clock is late." Their working conditions put them at great risk of burnout, and the threat of burnout is amplified by the kinds of energetic and emotional output that are expected of them within and beyond the parties they throw. As the faces of parties, which are equated with good feeling, organizers are themselves expected to be high energy, happy-looking people. This is a sometimes-impossible facade to maintain, especially when organizers face small- and large-scale challenges that have been touched on throughout this book. Organizing nightlife requires many different types of labor and the stakes feel especially high when it feels like the very possibility of black queer community is on the line. What feels like fun, release, play, and possibility for partygoers is made possible by the hard, draining, and often thankless labor of organizers who are also often the targets of partygoers' ire when things go wrong or when their expectations aren't met.

Rae's struggle with burnout peaked during the era described in chapter 2, when rifts between organizers and attendees threatened to end Party Noire. Since then, she explains,

> I'm really trying to find this happy medium of making sure that I still love what I do. That I still appreciate my community as a whole and not just these very isolated incidents that have shown me different things about the community and how they respond to certain stuff. So, I've been, like, also in conversation with myself about "OK, well where does responsibility"— and I don't even know if it stops, it's just like: what is my cut-off where I say "OK, well this is what I literally have the capacity to deal with."

Knowing one's capacities and cut-offs is incredibly important in a nightlife industry where a significant amount of an organizer's job is to simply care about the people they are throwing events for, and to make themselves available to them within and beyond the party. Organizers' thinking through burnout is always, then, thinking through ways to maintain senses of self *and* community, especially when the demands of the latter can feel like they overwhelm the former.

Finding a balance between doing valuable work for the community and ensuring that you can simply marshal the emotional resources to continue to do that work is subsequently a top priority for organizers. When someone asked in a Q&A session what Kristen does for self-care, she semi-jokingly responded, "'Not be around you.' And that was real. I intentionally stay home. I spend time with a very select few people because what I've realized is that I need to maintain a certain level of—what's the word? Diplomacy." Diplomacy, here, is the understanding that party organizers provide an incredible service to people who need it, and that they must toe a delicate line of providing that service despite the ways that their constituents may ask for things that they feel go above and beyond the party's scope. "Not that we can't have standards," Kristen notes, "but when I see . . . the impossible standards sometimes that party organizers have been held to it really bums me out. Because then you're operating from a place of fear when you're organizing, and you're operating from a place of defense. It can really hinder your creativity." Organizers work to build sustainable community that they feel responsible to and for while also, given the outsized expectations placed upon them, feeling quite alienated from it. For Kristen, it's important to have boundaries around her personal life. For Rae, even the smallest affirmation can create a sense of reciprocity that helps keep burnout at bay. She explains,

> I've been doing my best to not get burned out and to just constantly remind myself of the people that do genuinely care about the space that Nick and I have developed, and show that on a regular. And show that even just by showing up to a party or like genuinely liking and engaging with a post on social media—like, those things are helpful because they're like reminders and affirmations that this isn't in vain, you know? Whether it's fifty people or five hundred people, it's not in vain. So, I have to hold onto those reminders and do my best not to get burned out.

Physical and digital affirmations help Rae feel a sense of reciprocity that goes a long way in assuaging burnout. But no matter the boundaries organizers can create between themselves and their work-party lives, and no matter the amount and style of affirmations they might receive, it is rather difficult for nightlife organizers to *not* get burned out, in large part because providing space for other people is a job that requires immense amounts of different kinds of labor.

For Tori and Jae of E N E R G Y, then, organizing sustainable events is dependent on their abilities to make money. "That's always been our focus," Jae explains: "how do we do both? A lot of this community is like 'I'm just doing this for the love of art.' Hey, that's great but we have to *eat*. We gotta eat. So that's always been our focus. How do we generate this revenue, how do we build wealth, while building community at the same time, and putting wealth into the community?" Party organizers seeking forms of cultural and fiscal sustainability in this market are increasingly tapping into strategic brand partnerships, from explicitly partnering with entities like alcohol brands that sponsor events to having recurring gigs at corporate events. Given the realities of privatization, Tori argues,

> It's OK to make money off of artistry, and right now we're going through the biggest corporate exploration of art right now that I've ever, ever seen. I don't know any corporation that isn't having grassroot and local artistry going on right now. So, I'm trying to get in tune with that. I'm trynna have E N E R G Y and smallWORLD have some collaboration and sponsorship with corporations because they aren't going anywhere. A lot of people want to abolish capitalism, but I don't think we have the capabilities of doing that. What's next, you want to abolish capitalism, but you want to do it from your *iPhone*? That's not going to happen.
>
> **JAE:** Oh! Oh! Issa quote! You gotta put that on a shirt! "You can't abolish capitalism from your iPhone." Oh fuck!

Tori's comments speak to the latent and explicit expectations that queer parties have a particularly radical politics, especially one invested in anticapitalism. Their work is indeed often aligned with efforts to secure the health and safety of underserved black queer, trans, and polyamorous communities. They are at the same time strategizing around what they see as the contradictions that can face activism (or radical thought) under capitalism: organizers need to fund their lives if they're going to be able to provide space for other people to gather. So party organizers often look to grow the size and the number of the events they host in order to be attentive to the community's diverse needs, to avoid stagnancy, and in an attempt to secure the financial resources to continue to be sustainable. From organizers' perspectives, they must continually market themselves and their events, and must continually expand their brands, in order to remain visible and viable—and they see the sheer amount of their labor and their offerings as necessary to consolidating a broad-based black queer community.

In a kind of catch-22, however, party attendees can be skeptical of organizers' drive to offer more or larger events and/or to make money. On one hand, the presence of multiple parties serving black queer people signals a large and varied community that has diverse needs and desires that Slo 'Mo, Party Noire, and E N E R G Y cater to in different ways. So partygoers can be playfully critical of the sheer number of events that are held: there are too many events to attend, especially in the summer Pride season, and it is exhausting if not impossible to attend them all. On another, less playful, hand, attendees can interpret organizations' attunement to the demands of the market as actually *detrimental* to the formation of black queer community; that the growing number of black queer nightlife options will fracture black queer community at best and, at worst, signals organizers' unethical collusion with capitalism's greedy aims. Indeed, for Austin, the sheer number of events that are hosted during any given month is an outgrowth of a kind of explicit capitalist "selling out" and simultaneous moving beyond black queer community. "When I think about these organizers," they explain, "sometimes I'm not certain if they prioritize the community's goals, the goals of the people that are attending, or their own personal goals of 'My vision is to become the biggest queer party.'" Not speaking about any particular organization, they continue, "Yeah, I'm glad they're doing this work, but not once have I seen an organizer sit down with their attendees and say, 'What do y'all really want? What do y'all really need? How can I provide that for you?' It's always, 'I had a dream. I need y'all to buy in.'" For Austin, growth itself is a kind of unchecked manifestation of greed, one that has an inverse relationship to black queer community. "What is more important," they ask, "the needs of the community or the needs of the organizer?"

This question looms large for attendees who can become wary when individual parties grow in size or adjust how the event is thrown, and when organizations expand to host multiple convenings. "It's like, sometimes you got to just keep it simple," Bri explains. "Sometimes it's not necessary to ruin the recipe, sometimes you add too much stuff and you kind of start to get away from why you start to do these things in the first place." Austin echoes her in explaining, "A lot of times parties start to change over time. For example, a party might start off small, and then start to include a whole bunch of people and before you know it, it's somehow become this entirely different thing." They continue: "I want consistency. If you gon' be tiny and inclusive and only going to meet one need, well just do that. I feel like people keep trying to change with the times. I get it, everybody wants to grow, but then you lose sight of what your purpose was." As the two of them suggest, adhering to "what your purpose was" and "why you start to do these things in the first place" is central to producing and maintaining a sense of black queer community and solidarity. Deviating from this path creates competition between organizers and attendees, and also among attendees.

Professor-wrecks is a DJ and is grateful for the growing number of black queer nightlife offerings because they provide her more opportunities to work, and more opportunities to tap into an expanded sense of community that she gains from attending events as a partier. Yet she worries about how growth can lead into competition, a theory she develops by using the example of her own coming into queer nightlife in a relatively small city with few LGBTQ nightlife offerings. There, a tight-knit queer community was carved out at the one or two queer nights at local bars, and splitting off to form different forms of queer programming was a response to the barriers of access and safety in the region's nightlife offerings. In short, a diverse queer community emerged from the sense that "OK, well, these bars are all owned by these up-at-the-top motherfuckers who really aren't trying to share. Let's start our own party." These days she wonders whether that small-city model is "a little more revolutionary" than what she experiences in the comparatively saturated market of queer nightlife options in Chicago. Here, she worries that, faced with any manner of major or minor challenges, people are inclined to just go to a different party or start new ones altogether. She echoes Austin's anxieties about a kind of cliquishness that can form around different though related parties, suggesting that that very cliquishness puts people off and drives them to start their own events. The logic being "These black queer people are throwing a party, but I don't feel like I'm going to fit in, so I'm going to throw another black queer party on the same night and do these things that force people to pick and choose." She explains further that "part of me feels like the community has just been so split because the attitude is then, 'I'm just going to start my own.'" This sentiment—for Professor-wrecks as for Austin—can create competition that is devastating to their interpersonal experiences in queer nightlife spaces and in terms of the possibilities for broad-based community.

More events mean more opportunities to go out, which also means more opportunities to become overwhelmed with or burned out by going out; people will conserve energy and consolidate choices in ways that, some fear, undermine a sense of community. When parties are competing with one another for audiences, Austin worries, it "creates a sense of competition *within* the people that attend [it], and then it becomes 'Oh you don't go to this party, you go to that party?' I'm like, what is this *high school*? I don't like feeling that it's a competition or a cult or something." The heart of the problem for Professor-wrecks is that the existence of multiple, somewhat related parties undermines black queer people's abilities to effectively face issues *as* a community:

> I feel like if you have an issue with the space—especially in Chicago, the party culture, what goes from being one party where we can all converge on and possibly together do something to address what's happening there, whether it's issues of assault, issues of harassment, issues of just being welcoming, whatever it is—I feel like we could probably address those things a little bit better together in one party than a split of like ten and twenty parties where it's like, "Well, I can only go to one of them anyway. So, I don't care necessarily what's happening."

In this reflection, Professor-wrecks plots black queer nightlife along two poles: a community-building endeavor where people negotiate the rules that govern their coming together or a rather apolitical site where people simply pursue their individual needs and where there is a lack of interest or care for broader interests affecting everyone in the party or between parties. "Is there one thing that the community as a whole really needs that can be presented in the space?" she asks. "Or is it that we just all have such different needs in the function of a dance space that it's never going to be this one cohesive thing?" She is resolute in concluding, "Our community is so big but we are still all that we have. So, our inability to reconcile with each other and to just keep splitting off, eventually, it's going to have so many splits that it doesn't feel like a community anymore." As Professor-wrecks, Bri, and Austin suggest, partygoers' thinking about the various futures of Slo 'Mo, Party Noire, and E N E R G Y is often bound to their anxieties around market saturation (that there are perhaps too many parties and events), to competition that arises as a result of this saturation, and to fears of a fractured black queer community.

Across the different concerns organizers, DJs, and attendees have for black queer nightlife lies the question of what, exactly, makes a community feel like a community. What do the bonds of solidarity feel like in landscapes and parties that are scripted by capitalist logics of growth and competition, that push partygoers and organizers to the edge of burnout, and that create antagonisms between them? Throughout this book, we have seen how parties like Slo 'Mo, Party Noire, and E N E R G Y that variously cater to black queer people are often loaded, fraught spaces where the very idea of black queer community, as a notion and as a practice, is tested. We have encountered black queers in the midst of the deep labor of entering the queer dance floor and understood that this is always at the same time the practice of black queer community, and we have seen how the stressors that come with negotiating the myriad of bad feelings that surround and envelop it can also index the strains of producing and inhabiting such community. At Slo 'Mo, for example, black queer women's changing abilities to dance slowly to slow jams shaped their understandings of the limited extent to which the party could incubate specifically black queer community. Where slowness was a mechanism of fostering black queer community at The Whistler, it became a pointed method of refusal when the party moved to Slippery Slope. Black queer women came to deploy slowness as a refusal of the party's increasing incorporation into the broader neoliberal governance of the neighborhood and city which demand ever-faster movement. The choreographies of support at Party Noire incubated the rich sensoria of Black Joy, which was especially palpable in the many cyphers that break out at each party. But subtle yet rapid changes in organizational structure, demographics, and tense negotiations of accountability and responsibility created strife between organizers and black queer attendees. Black queer women narrated their changing relationships to Black Joy in their changing abilities to participate in the cypher's networks of looking, moving, and feeling, and in direct conversation with the gentrification of downtown Hyde Park. The first two chapters highlight how black queer women articulate the relationships among movement, feeling, and space as integral to the practice of politics in the neoliberal city; that the boundaries around "black queer community" are shaped and debated in direct conversation with their capacities to dance together in its midst.

The chapter on E N E R G Y thought about the possibilities of black queer community from another angle. It charted some ways that black queer community is sensed, how it is felt in the repetition of simply being together, caring for one another, and tending to one another. Taking the sensoria of community as its starting point, the chapter specifically questions our own investments as producers and consumers of queer nightlife studies. It was particularly interested in how we as critical thinkers place certain demands of transparency on the black queer nightlife space and the people who populate it. Throughout each chapter, we see that the queer dance floor is both an extremely vibrant but also a physically and emotionally taxing space to build black queer community. Part of the draw of E N E R G Y is that the party seemingly takes some of the decision-making of community building out of the picture. The party's weekly nature lessens the heightened expectations that can surround black queer nightlife, making the scene ordinary in otherwise extraordinary conditions of inhabiting black queer bodies.

Each chapter has drawn out the feelings that come with dancing together as a way to document the practice of politics, and we've seen that breakdowns in movement are intimately entangled with ideological struggles around the forms and function of black queer community. Party organizers and attendees' critiques of queer nightlife spaces observe the difficulties of consolidating "black queer community" in a city that is built on modes of ownership and consumption that rarely if ever sustainably benefit black queer women, and in nightlife structures that are not divorced from those modes either. They experience swells of exhaustion and burnout from weeks, months, and years of trying to dance together at night. They feel it in strained joints and strained intimacy alike, and party organizers and attendees can sometimes take it out on one another. In this book, we have seen, for example, that both party organizers and attendees wish that the other played a larger role in creating accountability and that the practice of creating and fostering black queer community be actually distributed across organizers and attendees alike. Attendees are critical of what they feel are organizers' inefficient and insufficient responses to accountability questions, whereas organizers lament the pressure that attendees place upon them to intuit and address their needs. There is a sometimes vast space between the two entities, and their antagonisms, subtle or explicit as they may be, are often rooted in their different understandings of this labor of community building *as* labor—and different expectations for how such labor should be recognized and compensated.

The process of black queer community can surely be a painful, exhausting one full of burnout, bad blood, and bad feelings, yet people continue to show up because the desired outcome—robust black queer community—demands it. Partygoers muster the energy to get up and get out the door even when they could be in bed because they *need* the people, conversations, dancing, and black queer communion that these events provide. Party organizers continue to choose to devote their time, money, and administrative powers to throwing events in venues they hate, among attendees they're beefin' with, and despite having to wake up in the morning for draining nine-to-fives or overwhelming freelance gigs. They too need the feeling of being with and among other black queers; they too want to hear the music, move their bodies, talk, be with, and survive and thrive, if only for a few hours a month.

Rather than theorize the (sometimes) gulf between organizers' and attendees' perceptions and experiences of the queer nightlife landscape, the conclusion to this conclusion instead puts their voices in conversation as they work their way *out* of it, as they imagine a future of black queer nightlife community. Their words are pulled from interviews I had with each of them; I've arranged them to appear as if they were in direct conversation with one another. Throughout my interviews, they often indirectly overlapped and built upon one another—they are usually thinking about and striving toward the same feelings as the person next to them on the dance floor. Together, they don't imagine a simplistic, utopian future completely divorced from the draining realities of life under neoliberalism and the endless precipice of burnout that it produces. They instead propose novel ways of producing black queer community in its midst. Their collection of voices describes a growing dissatisfaction with going out at night, and they muse on what the future of black queer nightlife could look like, where it could be hosted, how it would be governed, how it would feel to be there, what practices a revised black queer encounter might allow for, and more. They share a critique of the market's influence on party-life; namely, how emphases on selling and consuming alcohol and the lack of building ownership undermine black queer community. For many, coming together around modes of disorienting, intoxicated consumption in sites where resources are extracted to benefit white ownership can only ever generate a fleeting intimacy that simply cannot serve as the basis for sustainable community. Their prescriptions for the black queer nightlife space, one that may not even take place at night, often interrupt the logics of consumption and co-optation that govern the market. For example, if black queer women gather together without the imperative to purchase alcohol, their (oftentimes limited) financial capital cannot be directed toward white profiteers. If black queer women come together without the presence of party photographers, their images and aesthetics cannot be (re)directed to serve an unregulated profit cycle capitalizing on Black Joy, and black queer women might feel differently comfortable and rehearse different models of desiring one another in the process. If black queer women own the buildings they throw events in, they may consolidate and redistribute resources in more ethical ways. If black queer women gather together at all times of day and night and across generations and without the influence of intoxicants and in buildings that they own, they may form sustainable coalitions that are perhaps not grounded in capitalist exchange, but in intimacy itself.

JAE: It's actually sad what we have to go through: we're like, "OK, do we have to talk to security about not looking at people's IDs? Do we have to do this? What about the gendered bathrooms?" I would love for people to not have to go through that queer checklist before you go and venture off into an establishment, because it's tiring. It's tiring and it's an awkward conversation to have with venues. So that is another goal of ours, to eliminate that checklist that queer communities have to go through when they want to throw an event.

NICK: We've been definitely conversing and trying to ideate on ways to literally have ownership of all the whole operation.

JAE: Two years, tops, we should have our own shit.

TORI: Yeah, because we can't keep making a demographic that is not our specific community so much money.

RAE: I'm totally down with [scaling back in size]. Selling out five-hundred-plus-people parties is a lot of fucking fun.

NICK: It's also a lot of work.

RAE: But it's a lot of work.

NICK: It's *a lot* of work.

JAE: More of like multipurpose thing. Definitely a stationary bar, but maybe a venue that we can break up into two different things, and there's a music venue in the back with a dope stage and an adequate sound system type of deal. So, an establishment that yes, there is a bar, but you can also come if you don't want to drink.

AUSTIN: When it comes to partying there's this expectation of certain party elements that you must have in order to have a good time: you've got to have a DJ, you've got to have liquor, food preferably, or be near food. I don't know that I always *need* that. I would like to find spaces that really just want you to come and have a good time without necessarily all of these prerequisites of liquor, and fanciness, and all this other shit.

PROFESSOR-WRECKS: Not everybody thinks like that. Not everybody wants to be in a bar like that. Not everybody feels comfortable being in those spaces.

LJ: Have you seen how they pour these drinks at E N E R G Y? It's fucking sick! It's straight-up alcohol essenced with Coke!

TRACY: Then I start to notice that people's behaviors weren't the same, and I didn't like it when they were sober versus when they were partying with drugs. And then I didn't like my . . . behavior when I was partying with it after a while. At first it was fun, and then it became weird.

DJ AUDIO JACK: I'm trying to be realistic about, what about my particular profession triggers these mental things that I'm going through. I think about all these DJs that I hear about—that are on different levels than me—committing suicide and being addicted to drugs and pills and stuff. I'm not addicted to anything, I can say no to a drink most times, but the wear and tear it takes to do that every night.

TORI: I like a good drink, but I don't necessarily want every event that I want to throw have it depend on liquor only.

JASMINE: I don't even necessarily feel that drinking is a drawback. I feel the only thing that I would see as a negative is people feeling it as a necessity in the space. I don't like that burden of it. Some parties generally even have a two-drink minimum, or something of that sort. Rules to that effect, I feel, put too much pressure on people when it's like, no one should ever have to feel like alcohol has to be involved to be able to create community with like-minded people, is more so what my issue is with it. It's always optional, but if you go to these spaces, it's alcohol centered.

TRACY: No one's thinking with their clear mind, people have been up for days. People are doing all kinds of weird shit. And I just noticed that I had a lot of great moments, but I had a lot of moments that—you know what, thankfully I'm protected.

PROFESSOR-WRECKS: I'm not a practicing sober person, but I know a lot of people who are practicing sobriety. I have been in several situations as a DJ where drinks are offered as a compensation, which I'm just like, "That's a little bit hard." The assumption that everybody just wants to be plastered and be drunk versus just paying somebody is a little bit hard of an assumption because I've had friends who've shown up to sets and they're like, "Hey, they gave us ten drink tokens and there's no water." Like, "Yeah, there's no fucking water, what's up?"

TRACY: At my ideal place to go would be someplace that has just as much emphasis on soberness as it does drinks. Sober cocktails, stuff like that. That would be really nice, things to try.

JASMINE: Day parties are a nice in-between for that because you don't have to go out all night. You don't have to stay up all night. A day party is an easier way to be able to get out earlier and still be able to enjoy the day and have that community. Even with it being at a bar and things like that, a lot of the time these day parties there doesn't feel as much pressure as far as drinking and things like that. There's more people that you can see walking around, just enjoying the space, more so than feeling like they have to buy a drink. It's more optional during the day. I feel people have more of a comfort with that.

CA$H ERA: I did an 18+ party to create space for people who are under twenty-one, because I didn't get to have that. I feel like by doing that is how I'm combatting what doesn't exist in this city. I feel like 18+ queer parties are heavily missing. . . . That's what's missing, and that's *been* missing.

CANDACE: I think for me, the next step in my life is building a family. So, I want queer spaces that are family friendly, you know what I'm saying? Somewhere I can take my kid, somewhere I can have a good time during the day and not have a hangover. I feel like I'm not *that* old, I'm not about to be sore—I was sitting on the floor for a couple hours the other day and I'm still sore, so maybe I might be.

CA$H ERA: Most of my friends are like twenty-six to thirty so it's awesome seeing people who are above that age bracket and still seeing them occupy these streets and they're dancing and they're queer and they're out and they're happy.

LJ: You don't stop being queer when you turn thirty-five. It doesn't go away.

CA$H ERA: I love seeing the older studs or like the older dykes. I'm just like, "That's going to be me in a couple of years! Cool."

JASMINE: I feel like my ideal space would have to include amazing art, a performance of some sort, whether that be a visual, dance, or music performance, or something of that sort. Having a space for that included, as well as dance. There definitely has to be room for dance.

TESS: Somebody be selling crystals, somebody be selling their art, or painting live there. It's also a party.

BRI: I want to go see some art, I want to go have a conversation, I want to go watch a movie. And those are the things I think are a little bit harder to venture out and go find, because I think our nightlife, we always think of our nightlife as going out and being around loud-ass music. Sometimes you don't want to hear loud-ass music, sometimes I just want to be around good people and then maybe we all smoke.

JAYLA: Man, we got some video games, we got some blunts. Man, we got some snacks; we got some music, man.

CA$H ERA: The recipe for the perfect queer party is queer organizers, queer DJs, queer party promoters, understanding mindset, and easily accessible place to get to. . . . How can you easily make a space accessible to someone who might have lost their job or someone who's fallen on hardships, whatever the case may be? Because you have so many queer people who are disowned from their families, like funds are not always easily accessible. So, I feel like making sure the event is easily accessible, people can easily get there, always having queer people that they can look up to.

TAYLOR: I would love to see us doing more and being more active and intentional about welcoming new people, where they don't feel alone. . . . [When] you're an introvert it's hard to build that community.

CA$H ERA: I know that for me, I make sure people know they can DM me anytime and I'll respond. I act like that's crucial because if someone has a question about a party, or if they're afraid to come by themselves, if they can ask a question, it's going to make them more welcome to want to come. And I've had that plenty of times where someone will text me like, "I would come tonight but I don't have anybody to come with me." I'm like, "No, come. Come, hang out in the booth with me for a little bit. I spin this time and this time. I'll hang out with you when I'm done or before my set." . . . I feel like that's major. Just connecting so that someone feels included in the party, not like they're just coming just to fill the space but they feel like they're meant to be in the space.

NIKKI: No photographers. I know that when I go to Slo 'Mo, my face is gonna end up on the internet. And it has and that's fine but people need to not be afraid to come out, number one. . . . Because in these spaces, I want there to be a type of physical freedom that happens, and that privacy relies on that discretion.

AUSTIN: Oh my God, and especially because the community is so small, I got to run into my exes and shit! I'm like, you turn around and still see the bitch! Oh God, a little too much intimacy.

TAYLOR: Someone might be more willing to go to something more intimate than a party, and I think that's what we're missing: those spaces where you'll see queer people and queer people of color in this small setting, where instead of you having to go to something drastic and be like, "Can I talk to them?" It's not like you can build that out and create community from there.

NIKKI: When that privacy happens, the cliques aren't as there. Of course, there's gonna be talk. Of course, there's gonna be people gravitating toward each other, but people are out for their own. It needs to be OK to look. There needs to be something that teaches queer people to not be afraid of the gaze, and also not to be afraid to produce the gaze on each other, but also figure out a way to do that lovingly and consensually and vulnerably. Not like, "Oh my God. Who's that person with?" More like, "What is that person doing? Do I desire it? If I desire that, how can I replicate that?"

AUSTIN: It's been hard to find that here because there are cliques and that same competitive spirit of "I'm better than you" or "I got this many girls" or "this much money"; and I don't have time for all that. I just want to go out and have fun and make friends not enemies.

JAYLA: That's why I don't really like the nightlife because at the end of the day it's just a lot of people in my opinion celebrating nothing. And, I mean, I understand it's an escape, I just don't make a habit of going that often because at the end of the day I know I'm young but, like, priorities.

CANDACE: I think having meaningful relationships really means a lot to me right now, and nightlife does not. The dance floor is kind of associated with fleeting relationships, or seeking. I'm at a point where I'm not seeking.

JAYLA: At the end of the day, what are your emotional traumas? Do you have any generational trauma? Can we work through this together and grow as friends? That's what I'm trying to get to know. How do we get past you telling me about what shorty wore on the red carpet, because I don't really care in real life. (But she cute though.)

TAYLOR: [My roommates and I] were like, people could come here, and we can do something here. For people who E N E R G Y might be too much for them. Party Noire might be too much for them and they're like, "Oh, I just wanna meet people and talk to people in a more intimate setting and maybe not dance. Do this and talk about this."

TRACY: Last night, we had family dinner. . . . We're asking each other, "How can we help you this year?" Those are the questions that we're asking. Those are the things that I'm interested in now. I'm interested in movements. I'm interested in revolution. I'm interested in self-exploration and all of that.

CANDACE: I don't want people to just think they know me, type shit. I really want to build a legacy through the people that I love and build with, you know what I'm saying?

AYANA: I feel like club scenes are very sexualizing and it's like you're there to find someone to go home with and do all this stuff, and it's just like, brah, no. I just want to connect with new people and extend my friend group.

ERICA: See, my ideal, I've always said, more so than a partner, kind of to get corny: you know, an *L Word* or like a core group of friends. And I always liked that dynamic and I always really wanted that; like, to have like this kind of group where we can all like go get brunch together and talk about our crazy night, completely platonic.

ARI: I'm just really not interested in looking for anyone romantically or sexually at the moment. I just wanna be friends with people and I wanna make friends with new people, new types of people.

ERICA: I love platonic relationships! And it's really interesting that it's so hard to do. How do we have all these TV shows about core groups of friends who hang out, you know, all of this, and it's hard to make one friend—let alone four friends that all get along together and don't have any drama between?

LJ: You need these spaces! I don't know how to go about making friends. I'm not just going to go outside and just fucking yell. I have to go to these queer-centered events and just hope that they aren't only centering white queers, and cis bodies, and white folks in general.

TAYLOR: It's almost like, I have to bring the people to me. So, what can I do to bring them together? Because I'd like to see that. And I think that's the thing: it's almost like you can't wait for someone else to do it, you just have to do it yourself. And then if I do it, someone else might be more inclined to do something else. And it's not a competition—I'm not trying to take anything from anyone else or whatever. We can do this and then you have yours and it grows from there, so that it's more community, and more spaces.

AYANA: Let's do, like, a queer brunch or something, anything. Let's bike together, we're having a barbecue. I would love shit like that.

RAE: We need another community healing kind of space where we can just meet folks, talk, learn about each other, learn about different stuff. But also do a physical healing exercise practice. We started [a regular bike ride] in April and there were people that had never been to the actual party that came to the bike rides first.

NICK: We don't just throw these cool parties. There's conversation, healing space. Community space happening that's just, like, disconnected totally from a dance floor.

TAYLOR: Maybe we can have a cook night or something. Just anything that will attract people so that they feel safe in those spaces and create community.

ALEXANDRA: I'm not the best dancer but I love to dance. I love to just be out there, be in my zone. . . . Not that I don't like sitting at the bar talking to people and meet people [but] that's my favorite thing.

LJ: There have been many a times where I've had a terrible fucking week and I'll call my friend and I'm just like, "Bitch, let's go dance. We have to go dancing this weekend. We have to get it out." . . . When I go inside these spaces, even if it's for a moment, even if it's for a few hours, I feel so good, like I'm able to dance and experience that moment of joy in a world that doesn't offer many of those moments.

AYANA: I just have moments I'll text my group chat like, "I feel like shaking ass, let's just go out. Let's just go have fun." Because I do work five days out the week and I'm constantly through the motions of basically a corporate job. It's like this is my time to release, to be myself and just breathe instead of what I usually go through during the week.

TAYLOR: I move through my daily life holding in a lot of who I am, especially at work. I say that my queer side doesn't go to work. I mean, my whole body does and I go dressed as I am, but I'm very restricted. So, when I go out and when I'm in these spaces, I feel seen and I feel free. And it's nice to have that and to be around people that are doing the same.

AYANA: I just want more queer folk. I just want better music. I want better vibes. I just want new people all the time. . . . More dance, more everyone on the dance floor instead of cuddled up or talking or make-out sessions in the back. I want more of us connecting.

TRACY: I want everybody in there together, sweating, having a good time. Definitely some AC, but I'm just saying. You know what I mean? Really dancing it out.

CANDACE: I originally came here and found queer nightlife because I needed a genuine space where I could just be myself. I didn't feel like I needed to fit into a box, I didn't feel like I had to. . . . This was the only place that I could go and be myself.

CA$H ERA: I haven't felt like an outsider at other parties but it was just like at Party Noire, I felt like this party was geared towards me, like I'm supposed to be here. It's not like they're trying to get my money out of me. They actually want me to be here and be present.

AYANA: Definitely free. Definitely carefree. It's exactly how I wanted my club experience to go. I don't have to worry, because as you move through life you have to deal with [cishet white men] anyway and I don't want to have to worry about that when I'm supposed to be at a party.

DIAMOND: It was really bumping that night (maybe because I was super drunk and high). No, it was super fun because I wasn't harassed! I wasn't annoyed by men or vultures or stuff, we're just dancing with each other. "Knuck if You Buck," which is a Negro Spiritual, was playing.

CAROLINE: I gotta *sing*! I gotta let it all out on the dance floor. Do some like Motown steps or something. If I'm gonna go out, which I don't really do often, but if I'm gonna go that's the motive.

TAYLOR: It feels like being like a plastic bag in the wind and just blowing, and not having any direction or any point. There's no destination. It's just I'm just out here wherever the wind is going to take me, wherever this music is taking me, I'm just going with it. And that's what I mean by free.

DIAMOND: The sense of black space where I can see people like me, and it's really comforting to see queer people having fun on the dance floor and allowing themselves to do whatever they want to do.

JASMINE: I feel like half the time I probably still look awkward and clumsy, but it's like it feels good. It's not, genuinely, it's not about anybody else. It's not about what anybody else is going to feel if I rub up against them, it's not what anybody else is going to think when they see me. It just feels really good.

LJ: I just love being able to get together with other black queer folks, despite everything. We can always come to that space, and dance together, and that's powerful. Black folks dancing, there's power in that. There's so much power in that. . . . We still dance. We still dance and Pulse happened. We are still at the club and this happened. We are still going into these spaces.

NOTES

Introduction

Throughout this book, I use the given names of party organizers and party DJs, as they are public figures. I use pseudonyms for all party attendees.

1 The use of the phrase "N-word" here is reported speech: the DJ used this phrase in recounting the events that had just transpired.

2 While long home to a large number of black residents, the South Side has a complex racial and ethnic geography. The neighborhoods composing the South Side have long been home to successions of migrants, including African Americans, Polish, Irish, and Latin Americans. See Allan H. Spear, *Black Chicago*; and Mario Luis Small, "Is There Such a Thing as 'The Ghetto'?," 413–21.

3 Black women have been doing excellent work on the ways that blackness becomes an aesthetic in and of itself that is used to market the so-called revitalization of historically black neighborhoods. See, in particular, Brandi Thompson Summers, *Black in Place*. Allie Martin's doctoral work pays particular attention to the aestheticization of racialized sound. "Sonic Intersections: Listening to the Musical and Sonic Dimensions of Gentrification in Washington, D.C."

4 In Chicago, political ward maps are often the most specific indices of the racial makeup of neighborhood areas, despite the ways that the jagged boundaries of wards (meant to equalize the number of voting constituents) often encompass and cut across vastly different communities. The Logan Square neighborhood includes, roughly, a majority of the 35th ward and the top half of the 26th ward (the bottom half being the overwhelmingly Puerto Rican neighborhood, Humboldt Park). Of the 101,604 people counted in 2010, just 8,426 classified as "black." Emily Chow, Christopher Groskopf, Joe Germuska, Hal Dardick, and Brian Boyer, "Reshaping Chicago's Political Map: Race, Ward-By-Ward," *Chicago Tribune*, July 14, 2011, accessed March 5, 2018, http://media.apps.chicagotribune .com/ward-redistricting/index.html. For an introduction to the movements of Puerto Rican communities in the region, see John Betancur, "The Politics of Gentrification," 780–814; and Natalie P. Voorhees Center for Neighborhood and Community Improvement,

"Appendix: The Socioeconomic Change of Chicago's Community Areas (1970–2010),"
https://voorheescenter.red.uic.edu/wp-content/uploads/sites/122/2017/10/Appendix
-Oct-14.pdf.

5   The Target store is now part of the reigning visual hierarchy in this previously industrial
    landscape that is giving way to the signage of hypermodern consumer spaces. On the
    displacement of Chicago's industrial landscapes in this area, see Robert Giloth and
    John Betancur, "Where Downtown Meets Neighborhood," 279–90.

6   For some insights into the practice of, and resistance to, asset stripping, see Jodi Melamed,
    "Racial Capitalism," 76–85; Sara Safransky, "Rethinking Land Struggle in the Postindus-
    trial City," 1079–100; Clyde Woods, "Les Misérables of New Orleans," 769–96; Clyde
    Woods, "'A Cell Is Not a Home.'"

7   Neil Smith, *The New Urban Frontier.* Throughout this book I deploy "minoritarian"
    in the spirit of José Esteban Muñoz, who claimed the term to describe people who,
    despite their vast differences, are compelled to relate to the normative formations of
    racialized gender and sexuality anchoring national formations in similar ways. José Es-
    teban Muñoz, *Disidentifications.* Joshua Chambers-Letson elaborates that minoritarian
    "describes a place of (often uncomfortable) gathering, a cover, umbrella, expanse, or
    refuge under and in which subjects marked by racial, sexual, gender, class, and national
    minority might choose to come together in tactical struggle, both because of what we
    share (often domination in some form by the major, or dominant culture) and because
    of what makes us different" (*After the Party*, 15–16).

8   Neil Smith, "Giuliani Time," 1.

9   Martin F. Manalansan IV, "Race, Violence, and Neoliberal Spatial Politics in the Global
    City," 4n.

10 This gluing is not only to particular neighborhoods but also to spaces such as the
    kitchenette and the prison cell. See Rashad Shabazz, *Spatializing Blackness.*

11 On the development of Chicago's black neighborhoods in the twentieth century, begin
    with Arnold R. Hirsch, *Making the Second Ghetto*; and Davarian L. Baldwin, *Chicago's
    New Negroes.*

12 There are many studies on the racism that underwrote (and continues to underwrite)
    white flight, suburbanization, and a generalized fear of the city. Nathan Holmes charts
    how these sentiments play out in 1970s crime films, which reflected contemporaneous
    anxieties and had an indelible effect on how we engage contemporary cities *and* film. See
    Holmes, *Welcome to Fear City.* Steve Macek usefully loops in the question of right-wing
    moral politics. See Macek, *Urban Nightmares.* In *Race for Profit*, Keeanga-Yamahtta
    Taylor details the infrastructural mechanisms that have historically locked black people
    into underserved homes and communities.

13 Mary Pattillo's work on black, middle-class homeownership in Chicago demonstrates
    the fragile status of "ownership" for black families whose holdings have always been
    precarious in the face of the racist organization of the city. See *Black Picket Fences* and
    Black on the Block.

14 Here, this book contributes to a diverse collection of ethnographic work on queer social
    dance spaces as invaluable sites where individual and collective political identities are

forged; examining, in many ways, what Judith Hamera describes as "dancing communities" in *Dancing Communities*. See, for example, Fiona Buckland, *Impossible Dance*; Kareem Khubchandani, *Ishtyle*; Ramón Rivera-Servera, *Performing Queer Latinidad Dance, Sexuality, Politics*; Micah Salkind, *Do You Remember House?* Related work is being done on black and brown ball cultures. Marlon Bailey, *Butch Queens Up in Pumps*.

15 Rochella Thorpe did critical, foundational ethnographic work on midcentury black lesbian communities and, specifically, the tenuous relationships they had in and to lesbian bar spaces. Thorpe, "'A House Where Queers Go,'" 40–61. Thorpe's oral histories of lesbian Detroit are collected in the Division of Rare and Manuscript Collections at the Cornell University Library. The documentary on black lesbian activist Ruth Ellis also spotlights the importance of the private home to consolidating black queer sexualities. *Living with Pride: Ruth Ellis @ 100*, directed by Yvonne Welbon (1999).

16 There has been a lot of important writing on the role of the bar within lesbian communities, especially working-class lesbian bar culture in the twentieth century. Two good places to start are Marie Cartier, *Baby, You Are My Religion*; Elizabeth Lapovsky Kennedy and Madeline D. Davis, *Boots of Leather*; and Kelly Hankin, *The Girls in the Back Room*. The dismantling of what lesbian bars *have* existed is wrapped up in changing economic structures that make it harder for people to purchase buildings and/or to hold onto leases—political economic conditions often obscured in larger debates around the place of trans people and politics within lesbian (and feminist) spaces. See Clare Forstie, "After Closing Time," 130–42. Jack Gieseking has been hard at work collecting oral histories of multiracial, multigenerational lesbian people whose continuing search for community traverses these multiple sites, reading these narratives across diverse archives. See essays like "Dyked NY," 1–17; and their book *A Queer New York*.

17 That said, the sites that black life were removed to become important "interzones" where people of all races and sexualities congregated, and the linking of race, sexuality, and vice often had its own spatial protocols and profits. Kevin J. Mumford, *Interzones*.

18 On the particular (and particularly insidious) impact of zoning regulations on gay nightlife, see Laam Hae, *The Gentrification of Nightlife and the Right to the City*. Samuel Delaney's beautiful rendering of the transformation of what would become Times Square documents how zoning, policing, and public morality initiatives violently dismantled erotic theaters, video stores, corners, alleyways, and apartments in which gay men found communion and community. *Times Square Red, Times Square Blue*.

19 Grace Kyungwon Hong discusses such selective absorption of *some* kinds of difference in *Death beyond Disavowal*. On gayborhoods more broadly, and on Boystown and Andersonville in particular, see Amin Ghaziani, *There Goes the Gayborhood?*

20 In response to ongoing criticisms of the neighborhood's actual *lack* of inclusivity and many instances of overt racism, the Northalsted Business Alliance decided to rename Boystown to Northalsted in September 2020 and developed the slogan "Chicago's Proudest Neighborhood." It remains to be seen whether this rebranding will have any effect on how embedded whiteness is in the neighborhood.

21 Christina Hanhardt, *Safe Space*.

22 There has luckily been a lot of work done on how fucked up Boystown can be: Owen Daniel-McCarter, "Us vs. Them!," 5–17; Zachary Shane Kalish Blair, "Machine of Desire"; Rae Rosenberg, "The Whiteness of Gay Urban Belonging," 137–48; Theodore Greene, "Gay Neighborhoods and the Rights of the Vicarious Citizen," 99–118; and Jason Orne, *Boystown*.

23 Sa Whitley, "The Collective Come-Up," 13.

24 Katherine McKittrick, *Demonic Grounds*, xv. While McKittrick receives this particular citation, this book, and my entire way of thinking, wouldn't be possible without her entire body of work.

25 We could have a longer conversation that foregrounds how race and sexuality script the expectations of affective comportment as central to legibility within gayborhoods, and the ways in which the diversity of black queer woman's affective inhabitations continually provide a crisis of legibility for men, in particular. If that's a line of thought you're interested in, consider reading Ana Ramos-Zayas's detailed ethnography of black, brown, and immigrant life in Newark, New Jersey. In it, she demonstrates how one's status in the neoliberal city is very much regulated by one's ability to skillfully deploy the racialized codes of affective comportment that neoliberal governance demands. These codes conform to what José Esteban Muñoz described as the United States' "'official' national affect, a mode of being in the world primarily associated with white middle-class subjectivity" and which he wryly described as "flat and impoverished." Ramos-Zayas, *Street Therapists*; Muñoz, "Feeling Brown," 70.

26 LeiLani Dowell, "Wolf Packs."

27 Kafui Attoh, "What Kind of Right Is the Right to the City?," 10.

28 Here, I refer to Nikki Lane's doctoral work on black queer women's scene space in the Washington, DC, area. Charneka Lane, "In the Life on the Scene."

29 All three of these parties experienced massive shifts in the COVID-19 pandemic that wreaked havoc worldwide, beginning in winter 2020. Tantrum was among many locally owned venues that permanently closed during this time.

30 Jafari Sinclaire Allen, "For 'The Children' Dancing the Beloved Community," 319.

31 Allen, "For 'The Children,'" 318.

32 Here I am indebted to Sianne Ngai's *Ugly Feelings* as well as to the "affective turn" more broadly.

33 Henri Lefebvre, "The Right to the City," 147–60.

34 As a starting point, see Chris Butler, *Henri Lefebvre*. See also Peter Marcuse's and Mark Purcell's many writings on the right to the city.

35 See, for example, Kafui Attoh, *Rights in Transit*; Mustafa Dikeç, "Justice and the Spatial Imagination," 1785–1805; Tovi Fenster, "The Right to the Gendered City," 217–31; Kurt Iveson, "Social or Spatial Justice?," 250–59.

  These conversations indirectly converse and at times overlap with Hannah Arendt's examination of the right to have rights in *The Origins of Totalitarianism*, an examination that continues to spark conversation around the forms, functions, possibilities (and lack thereof) of citizenship, politics, and the ontological status of the human. To dip your toe into this vast field of conversation, start with Stephanie

DeGooyer, Alastair Hunt, Lida Maxwell, and Samuel Moyn, *The Right to Have Rights*; and Frank I. Michelman, "Parsing 'a Right to Have Rights,'" 200–208; before moving on to Jacques Rancière, "Who Is the Subject of the Rights of Man?," 168–86.

36 Of course, "black queer woman" is not a neat political category and it does not always signal the kinds of progressive, racial justice politics that the aforementioned organizations espouse. Chicago mayor Lori Lightfoot, elected in 2019, is the first openly gay black woman to serve as mayor of a major city in the United States but has spent a career working for, supporting, and protecting one of the most violent police forces in the nation.

37 Don Mitchell's work usefully ties together these two realms of rights to the city discourse, providing rich political-economic context for the production and regulation of public space alongside analyses of the social imaginary of public space that scripts who we believe "belongs" and not therein. Mitchell, *The Right to the City: Social Justice and the Fight for Public Space*.

38 David Harvey develops a conversation about the right to the city across multiple texts. See Harvey, "The Right to the City," 2003, 939–41; Harvey, "The Right to the City," 2008, 23–40; and Harvey, *Rebel Cities*.

39 Harvey, *Rebel Cities*, 5.

40 Harvey, "The Right to the City," 2008, 32. He elsewhere explains: "We live in a society in which the inalienable rights to private property and the profit rate trump any other conception of inalienable rights you can think of. This is so because our society is dominated by the accumulation of capital through market exchange. That social process depends upon a juridical construction of individual rights" ("The Right to the City," 2003, 940).

41 Harvey, *Rebel Cities*, 4. Emphasis added.

42 Important work has been done on the microgestures of dissent and reformation that black communities have long practiced, and they often reveal the fundamental ambivalences they have to formal politics and the systems of capital that structure them. James Scott's and Robin D. G. Kelley's work on "infrapolitics" is essential to analyses of the politics of quotidian black performance—as is Cathy Cohen's generous and generative critique of them, especially the ways that our understandings of black politics often assume intentionality where it may not be. Cohen, "Deviance as Resistance," 27–45; Kelley, *Race Rebels*; Scott, *Domination and the Arts of Resistance*.

43 Khubchandani, *Ishtyle*, 4.

44 Cameron Duff, "The Affective Right to the City," 516–29. Bibi Bakare-Yusuf connects the question of embodied rights amid waning juridical access in the essay "I Love Myself When I Am Dancing and Carrying On: Refiguring the Agency of Black Women's Creative Expression in Jamaican Dancehall Culture," 263–76.

45 Dwight Conquergood, "Performance Studies," 146.

46 Conquergood maps the risks of the ethnographic encounter in "Performing as a Moral Act."

47 Conquergood, "Performance Studies," 146.

48 Conquergood, "Performance Studies," 146.

49 Kai M. Green, "The Essential I/Eye in We," 195.

50 Zenzele Isoke, "Black Ethnography, Black(Female)Aesthetics," 153.

51 Conquergood, "Performing as a Moral Act," 10.

52 D. Soyini Madison, *Critical Ethnography*, 11.

53 A small collection of scholars has dutifully documented the diverse gender expressions that occur among black lesbian and queer communities. See, for example, Laura Lane-Steele, "Studs and Protest-Hypermasculinity," 480–92; Mignon R. Moore, "Lipstick or Timberlands?," 113–39.

54 Saidiya Hartman, *Scenes of Subjection*, 58.

55 Two foundational texts of this argument are Hortense Spillers, "Mama's Baby, Papa's Maybe," 65–81; and Evelynn Hammonds, "Black (W)holes and the Geometry of Black Female Sexuality," 126–45.

56 The construction of this sentence is indebted to Barnor Hesse's definition of black politics, which he defines, in part, as follows: "As an irrepressible symptom, the recurring incidence of black politics reveals and exposes a modern Western social order of things constitutively liberal-colonial and democratic-racial, whose discourses and institutions of representation are socially grounded in disavowing that creolized inheritance" (977). Black politics, in other words, points to the fact that black/blackness is central to yet continually erased from the very formation, definition, and expression of politics in the West. See Hesse, "Marked Unmarked," 974–84. On the white spatial imaginary, see George Lipsitz, *How Racism Takes Place*.

57 Sarah Haley, *No Mercy Here*, 200–201.

58 Kara Keeling, *The Witch's Flight*, 21–22. Previous iterations of this introduction have spent much more time reading This Black Girl through and as Keeling's "black femme function," which names a politics of racialized gender and sexuality as well as a mode of thinking and a mode of imagining radical politics.

59 On opacity, see Édouard Glissant, *Poetics of Relation*. On dissemblance, see Darlene Clark Hine, "Rape and the Inner Lives of Black Women in the Middle West," 912–20.

60 As a result of an expanding labor market in the Midwest, the 1950s brought an influx of Puerto Ricans to the Chicagoland area who, because of their status as US citizens, were able to easily remain even after their labor contracts expired. Logan Square, West Town, and Humboldt Park soon established themselves as areas with the largest Puerto Rican populations. See Ana Ramos-Zayas, *National Performances*.

61 For a discussion of Puerto Rican racial formation in Puerto Rico, see Isar P. Godreau's work, namely, *Scripts of Blackness*. For a discussion of how Puerto Rican identities are specifically shaped in musical conversation between US and Caribbean notions of blackness, see Ramón Rivera-Servera, "Musical (Trans)Actions," 1–13. For a discussion of the gendered dimensions of racial formation in Puerto Rico, see Maritza Quiñones Rivera, "From Trigueñita to Afro-Puerto Rican," 162–82.

62 Of Puerto Rican perceptions of African Americans in Chicago, Ramos-Zayas writes, "The vision of Puerto Rican culture as black gains value in the market of symbolic goods only insofar as it is assumed to be pure and representative of resistance. Hence, activists could frown upon rap as co-opted and as an expression of Puerto-Ricanness

that is identified with U.S. black people while celebrating [Puerto Rican mulatto nation-alist Pedro] Albizu along the lines of Afro-Puerto Rican Pride" (*National Performances*, 196). While activists might selectively take up blackness to articulate resistance to the state, and Puerto Rican youth might express hip-hop literacy to establish their cul-tural capital within a global city, Ramos-Zayas observes that Puerto Ricans throughout Chicago "categorized blackness as African American culture, a gendered and classed hyperculture capable of co-opting Puerto Rican youth, women, and ultimately, nation-alism. . . . African American blackness was hyperculturalized through a youth street culture embodied in gangs and in constructions of a threatening black professional elite" (*National Performances*, 230).

63 In this language of perceptibility, I am indebted to Kara Keeling and her thorough narration of the black femme function within the cinematic structures that govern how we see (and not) black women on film. This is, for Keeling, a deeply proprioceptive process—which lends her film studies analysis to a performance studies reading of everyday life. For Keeling, the appearance of the black femme on screen instigates a process whereby our common sense is shifted, reorganized, or adjusted to accommodate her; her appearance makes us think beyond the frame to a lifeworld where she makes (more) sense. The site of the dance floor, where music and movement coalesce across bodies in deeply physical ways, and beliefs about race, gender, and sexuality are phys-icalized in hyperpalpable ways, is a useful site to extend Keeling's theorizing. Keeling, *The Witch's Flight*.

Chapter 1: Slo 'Mo and the Pace of Black Queer Life

1 As briefly discussed in this book's introduction, the title of the Slo 'Mo party changed by the time of this book's publication. Where it was long described as a party for "Homos and Their Fans," it is now described as "Slow Jams for Queer Fam." By the time you're reading this, the party's name and intended community may have changed again.

2 Throughout this book I use the words "straight," "queer," and "heterosexual" knowing that these terms never contain the range of feelings and beliefs about sex, sexuality, and identity that the people I am describing experience. Here, I use "straight" to describe people who may very well identify otherwise, but whose dance floor performances of gender and sexual preference, among other things, contribute to a public persona of heterosexuality.

3 On the mechanics and politics of TIF programs, see Richard Briffault, "The Most Popular Tool," 65–95; Diane Gibson, "Neighborhood Characteristics and the Targeting of Tax Increment Financing in Chicago," 309–27; and Brent C. Smith, "The Impact of Tax Increment Finance Disticts on Localized Real Estate," 21–37. See also Ben Javorsky's many-years-long, devasting critiques of Chicago's use of TIF published in the free weekly alternative newspaper *Chicago Reader*.

4 Teska Associates, "Fullerton/Milwaukee Tax Increment Financing Redevel-opment Plan and Project Eligibility Study: Amendment No. 1," October 25,

1999, A-1, https://www.chicago.gov/content/dam/city/depts/dcd/tif/T_087
_FullertonMilwaukeeAmendment2.pdf.

5   Teska Associates, "Fullerton-Milwaukee Tax Increment Financing Redevelopment Plan
    and Project: Revision No. 2," December 21, 1999, 2, https://www.chicago.gov/content
    /dam/city/depts/dcd/tif/T_087_FullertonMilwaukeeAmendment2.pdf.

6   Teska Associates, "Fullerton-Milwaukee Tax Increment Financing Redevelopment Plan
    and Project: Revision No. 2," December 21, 1999, 16, https://www.chicago.gov/content
    /dam/city/depts/dcd/tif/T_087_FullertonMilwaukeeAmendment2.pdf.

7   For 2004 projections, see Teska Associates, "Fullerton/Milwaukee Tax Increment
    Financing Redevelopment Plan and Project: Amendment No. 1," December 30,
    2004, 17, https://www.chicago.gov/content/dam/city/depts/dcd/tif/T_087
    _FullertonMilwaukeeAmendment2.pdf; for 2011 projections, see Teska Associates,
    "Fullerton-Milwaukee Tax Increment Financing Redevelopment Plan and Project:
    Amendment No. 2," February 15, 2011, 2, https://www.chicago.gov/content/dam/city
    /depts/dcd/tif/T_087_FullertonMilwaukeeAmendment2.pdf.

8   Julia Thiel, "One Bourbon, One Scotch, and 20 New Hipster Bars," *Chicago Reader*,
    August 28, 2013, https://www.chicagoreader.com/chicago/logan-square-new-bars
    -analogue-robert-haynes-henry-prendergast/Content?oid=10746020.

9   The overall population of the neighborhood dipped slightly during this time, but
    saw a decrease of the majority-minority "Hispanic or Latino" population from nearly
    54,000 residents to just over 34,000. The already small black population dwindled by
    around 1,000 people, to just 3,452. Meanwhile, the white population increased by around
    18 percent, to nearly 33,000 people, while the median household income increased from
    $53,000 in 2000 to just over $62,000 in 2015, bumping up to nearly $71,000 just two
    years later.

10 Debates were particularly heated surrounding M. Fishman & Co.'s purchase and at-
    tempted eviction of one of the city's last single-room occupancy hotels, the Milshire
    Hotel, which coincided with a building proposal for a very different single-room-
    occupancy living space: a "transit-friendly" development of sixty-three "micro-
    apartments" to be built exactly one-half mile to the southeast of the shuttered hotel.
    Made up primarily of 438-square-foot studios, the units were projected to be rented for
    $1,200 in a neighborhood whose median monthly rent hovers around $800. For resi-
    dents opposing the development, the combatting experiences of the Milshire's closing
    and the proposed micro-apartment development showcase how the neighborhood is
    being physically built to accommodate white hipsters attracted to the area.

11 The Mega Mall has long been home to Latinx-owned, operated, and frequented small
    businesses. The worry is that not retaining some aspects of the Mega Mall culture will
    cement the new development as an eminently white space. As one activist explained at a
    May 2015 meeting, "We would encourage the alderman and the developers to envision
    that 10 percent [affordable housing requirement] as a floor rather than a ceiling, which
    would go a long way to keeping families in this city and keeping our neighborhood
    diverse." Darryl Holliday, "Everything You Need to Know about the First Mega Mall
    Development Meeting," *DNAinfo Chicago*, May 8, 2015, http://www.dnainfo.com

/chicago/20150508/logan-square/everything-you-need-know-about-first-mega-mall
-development-meeting.

12 "Is Chicago's Logan Square Neighborhood Now the Hipster Mecca of the Midwest?,"
Chicago Advocate, June 16, 2014. Another, homemade, antigentrification poster plastered throughout Logan Square calls attention to how the pace of development in Logan
Square is spurred by Marc Fishman (whose photo is on the flyer, which someone has
drawn over to make him out like the devil) to the detriment of people who, for a variety of reasons, can't keep up, including "working students, 95 year old retiree, working
mom, you?" A handwritten note added to the flyer reads, "We were kicked out of our
home of 7 years so Fishfuck could double the rent to **$2600/month.**" The flyer and
this note point to Fishman's practice of serving thirty- and sixty-day eviction notices to
displace residents who can be replaced by higher-paying ones, and slyly interpolates the
person reading it. "Support Diversity in Logan Square," it reads. "Artists, blue collared,
minorities, retirees, disabled . . . which are you . . . replacing?"

13 Nick Salvato, *Obstruction*, 100. Much has been made about the pace of neoliberalism.
See, for example, Hartmut Rosa's works and the robust conversation around acceler-
ationism that is extremely Western, industrialized, and masculinist and, as such, has
dominated much conversation.

14 Sarah Sharma, *In the Meantime*, 139.

15 Sarah Sharma, *In the Meantime*, 134.

16 See, for example, Mechal Sobel, "Early African-American Attitudes toward Time and
Work," 183–99; and Mark Michael Smith, *Mastered by the Clock.*

17 An early version of this chapter appeared as an article in *GLQ* and goes into more detail
about black people's awareness and management of speed itself as a terrain of power
through which claims to (and rejections of) belonging, citizenship, and perhaps the
very category of the human can been registered and asserted. The analyses of work
slowdowns that Angela Davis and Deborah Gray White find in the archives of black
slave women, and that Robin D. G. Kelley adroitly covers in the early twentieth century,
are exemplary. Their works about the complex relations black people have long held
to modes of production across periods of forced and "unforced" labor demonstrate
the overt and covert ways that fights for various modes of individual and collective
freedoms, including for legislative, civil, and labor rights, have been waged through
the tactical mobilization of time itself. Kemi Adeyemi, "The Practice of Slowness,"
545–67. See also Davis, "Reflections on the Black Woman's Role in the Community
of Slaves," 1–14; Kelley, "'We Are Not What We Seem,'" 75–112; Kelley, *Race Rebels*;
White, "Female Slaves," 248–61; Jayna Brown's chapter "Letting the Flesh Fly," in particular, in *Babylon Girls.*

18 Slo 'Mo followed on the heels of the popular Chances Dances parties that were hosted
in Wicker Park from 2005 to 2015, ten years in which they hosted three monthly parties
at Subterranean, Danny's Tavern, and eventually the Hideout, and distributed the Critical Fierceness Grant supporting queer artists and the Mark Aguhar Memorial Grant
funding queer artists of color across the feminine spectrum. For more on Chances
Dances, see https://chancesdances.tumblr.com/.

19 Robin James, "Loving the Alien."

20 Robin James, "Loving the Alien."

21 The TIF designation was set to expire in 2021 but was extended to 2022 and might again be extended, as happens with other TIF districts. For example, in 2019, the West Loop Community Organization was negotiating with stakeholders and residents about designating the area a Special Services Area district upon expiration, which would impose a TIF-like tax levy on the region in order to generate revenue for upkeep of the area—likely to the advantage of developers over residents.

22 The second time the party was held, in August 2014, perhaps eight or nine regulars showed up for an event in a room that can hold approximately fifty people. This was far less than the twenty or so regulars who attended the July event.

23 On the particular "masculinist agenda" of urban space, see, for example, Phil Hubbard, "Revenge and Injustice in the Neoliberal City," 665–86.

24 Saidiya Hartman, "The Belly of the World," 171. Hartman crafts this statement in a larger critique of gender in W. E. B. Du Bois's call for a general strike, pointing to the ways that black women's labor is regularly misunderstood as not labor at all. If black women's labor is not understood as such, but they are called upon to strike, how would the world continue to operate? This conversation builds upon Alys Winebaum's own investigations of Du Bois's approach to gender in "Gendering the General Strike," 437–63.

Chapter 2: Where's the Joy in Accountability?

1 Here, Nick and Rae reflect Bettina Judd's theorization, by way of Lucille Clifton, of how joy exists *with* mourning and suffering, and is the practice of tension between light and dark, good and evil, safety and violence. See Judd, *Feelin*.

2 Javon Johnson, "Black Joy in the Time of Ferguson," 180. On the digital circulation of joy as resistance, see Ashley Weatherford, "The Year in Black Joy"; Jessica Lu and Catherine Knight Steele, "'Joy Is Resistance,'" 823–37.

3 David Román, "Dance Liberation," xvi. Emphasis added.

4 Fiona Buckland, *Impossible Dance*, 7.

5 In his discussion of "The Spot," Marcus Anthony Hunter describes the ways that black people use the nightclub space to generate material opportunities for one another, even strangers, from job opportunities to child care options. Hunter, "The Nightly Round," 165–86.

6 "There were different heavy college promoters and we would go to their parties. All the parties that we would go to like that, they were for people of color by people of color but it was like frat parties. So, you just have a whole bunch of fraternity guys, they'd start stomping around, sorority girls start clapping their heels. And you're just like, 'OK, can I dance for two seconds here? And I'm not going to be a part of y'all's song. Put your elbows down girl. Leave me alone,'" says Ca$h Era.

7 Crawford, "Yours in Blackness," 81.

8 Javon Johnson, "Black Joy in the Time of Ferguson," 180. On the pedagogical formations of joy, black and otherwise, particularly in performance studies context, see Quenna L. Barrett, "Setting the Stage for Black Choice," 1–15; and Elizabeth Currans, "Utopic Mappings," 90–102.

9 A lot has been written about black social dance, and about the physical and social choreographies of the circular formation, in particular. To begin your longer reading practice, consider starting with the ring shout: Katrina Dyonne Thompson, *Ring Shout, Wheel About*; and Art Rosenbaum, *Shout Because You're Free*. Folks have tracked ring shout gestures (which are performative engagements with the conditions of enslavement and confinement) to the cypher in a variety of ways. See, for example, three of Katrina Hazzard-Donald's texts: *Jookin*; "The Circle and the Line," 28–38; and "Dance in Hip Hop Culture," 505–16. For thinking around the cypher, in particular, see Imani Kai Johnson's essay "Battling in the Bronx" (62–75), which is an extension of their dissertation (and forthcoming book project); and Johnson, "Dark Matter in B-Boying Cyphers."

10 In reviewing field notes and interviews, I realized that Ayana was actually one of the women dancing in this moment—a moment that her friend Jayla referred to in saying, "Like that girl you was dancing with, damn near got her pregnant!" To which Ayana responded: "Shorty was nice. I'm ready to connect with her on Tinder."

11 Buckland, *Impossible Dance*, 80.

12 Ramón Rivera-Servera, "Choreographies of Resistance," 271.

13 Understanding the Chicago Renaissance has to go hand in hand with understanding Chicago's place in the Great Migration, and *a lot* has been written on both. The foundational portrait of black life in Chicago during this era is St. Clair Drake and Horace R. Cayton, *Black Metropolis*. See also Davarian L. Baldwin, *Chicago's New Negroes*. For focus on the Chicago Rennaissance, in particular, see Darlene Clark Hine and John McCluskey, eds., *The Black Chicago Renaissance*; Richard A. Courage and Christopher Robert Reed, eds., *Roots of the Black Chicago Renaissance*; and Robert Bone and Richard A. Courage, *The Muse in Bronzeville*.

14 "About," 16" on Center, accessed January 9, 2021, https://www.16oncenterchicago.com /about.

15 Brandi Summers, *Black in Place*, 3. Emphasis in original.

16 Summers, *Black in Place*, 26.

17 Robert Sharoff, "University of Chicago Works on Its Neighborhood," *New York Times*, October 23, 2012, https://www.nytimes.com/2012/10/24/realestate/commercial /university-of-chicago-helps-revitalize-53rd-street-retail-district.html.

18 Teona Williams, "For 'Peace, Quiet, and Respect,'" 504.

19 Davarian Baldwin, "'The 800-Pound Gargoyle,'" 86.

20 On the founding and early development of the University of Chicago, see Robin F. Bachin, *Building the South Side*.

21 On the fluid links between what was happening on and beyond the University of Chicago, and an extremely detailed overview of the policy planning and implementation that the university wielded, see LaDale Winling, "Students and the Second Ghetto,"

59–86. Winling builds upon this essay in a larger study of the entanglements of federal policy and university development in *Building the Ivory Tower*.

22 There is so much to be said about just how fucked up university operations are, and how devastating they can be to the social and cultural fabric of the cities and towns they take over. Google the university closest to you and see how they make their money (How do they grow their endowment? Who do they invest in? Where do alumni donations go?); see how they treat their faculty and graduate students (How often are their contracts renewed? What do they get paid? Are they unionized?); see what their real estate holdings are (it'll depress you); and see who owns their security force, how they interface with the municipal police, and if their security policies and protocols are publicly available (they're not.). For further reading, see, Henry A Giroux, *University in Chains*.

23 Teona Williams, "For 'Peace, Quiet, and Respect,'" 501.

24 A prime example is how the university bought the Checkerboard Lounge in 2003 and moved the blues bar from Bronzeville to Hyde Park in the name of preserving cultural heritage. It relocated the bar in the newly redeveloped Harper Court, a commercial and service multiplex that anchors the neighborhood's revitalized "downtown" core.

25 The 53rd Street TIF was established in 2001 and will extend to 2025.

26 Sharon Zukin, whom Summers also cites, elaborates on the entwined material and symbolic shaping of urban space in *The Cultures of Cities* and in *Naked City*. This work, as is the case for much urban studies scholarship, is in direct and indirect conversation with Jane Jacobs's foundational text, *The Death and Life of Great American Cities*.

27 Jason Hackworth, *The Neoliberal City*, 3.

28 Sam Binkley, *Happiness as Enterprise*, 4–5.

29 Sara Ahmed writes, "To consider happiness as a form of world making is to consider how happiness makes the world cohere around, as it were, the right people." *The Promise of Happiness*, 13.

30 Gina Dent, "Black Pleasure, Black Joy: An Introduction," 1.

31 Ahmed, *The Promise of Happiness*, 10. Indeed, texts about Black Joy often posit its utility for combatting the physical and psychic effects of white supremacy, but do so at the risk of exalting heterosexuality and the institutions of marriage and ownership that it is built upon. Drake's "The Marketability of Black Joy," a reading of black film, is not a critical analysis of how Black Joy is financially capitalized upon but a reading of the ways that imaging black marriage can, indeed, be a financially successful enterprise.

32 Rinaldo Walcott, conference presentation, *Scenes at 20* conference, Rutgers University (October 7, 2017).

33 Walcott, conference presentation, 2017. Emphasis added.

34 Walcott, conference presentation, 2017.

35 Grappling with similar questions of accountability within and beyond the party space, Kristen, who organizes the Slo 'Mo party discussed in the first chapter, reflects:

I think one of the things that's really difficult for organizers to navigate is being an intermediary or negotiator. I think that's incredibly challenging. And it's really heavy, and particularly when again, few party organizers are also social workers. . . . So, you may have someone who's a part of your community who says, "Someone has harmed me in this space. And I don't think that they should be allowed, and I'm asking you to not let them be in the space."

And the harm hasn't necessarily happened in your space—because I think that's a different situation. When harm has happened in your space, you have to address it. You have an obligation to. How you address it is sort of a whole other conversation, but it has to be addressed—but when someone or some people have an experience outside of your space, but then they have to figure out how to negotiate that [in the party] space, it's really hard. So, on the one hand you don't want to say, "Hey, that's your shit. You need to figure it out." But at the same time, what role do you have in that? And that can become really subversive because then suddenly you are becoming an intermediary, an authority on judgment or an authority in general, and I think that that's really difficult. So, I don't have the answers to that.

36 Dent, "Black Pleasure, Black Joy," 1.
37 Dent, "Black Pleasure, Black Joy," 1.

Chapter 3: Ordinary E N E R G Y

1 There is a whole host of writing that troubles "normal" within LGBTQ culture and politics. Consider Michael Warner, *The Trouble with Normal*; Dean Spade, *Normal Life*; Jasbir Puar, *Terrorist Assemblages*; and Chandan Reddy, *Freedom with Violence*.

2 On homonormativity, see Lisa Duggan, "Equality, Inc.," in *The Twilight of Equality*, 43–67.

3 Andre Cavalcante, *Struggling for Ordinary*, 21. Writing in a very different context, Liesl Olson similarly argues that "the ordinary is not always transformed into something else, into something beyond our everyday world; the ordinary indeed may endure in and of itself as a 'final good.'" *Modernism and the Ordinary*, 3.

4 The French philosopher Alain Badiou wrote the foremost text on "the event," *Being and Event*. I truly hated reading this book when I first encountered it in graduate school. It represented (and still does) some of the very worst aspects of philosophical thought and academic writing: it is long, dense, overwritten, and obsessed with white men. Sometimes I take pleasure in reading texts like this; they are worlds unto themselves when you commit to immersion. That hasn't ever been my experience with *Being and Event*, though. It's not lost on me that writing this book has returned Badiou to me, made him unavoidable. In this chapter, however, I intentionally sidestep Badiou and try to craft a conversation on the event and the ordinary that is routed through people who are not white men—people who often say the same things that white men say but never get the same recognition. That said, Shane Vogel, who is white, has a wonderful introduction to how Badiou continues to resonate in "By the Light of What Comes After."

5 See, for example, the many rehearsals of the event that catalyzed many of Frantz Fanon's supremely enduring insights—"Look, a Negro!"—and that has informed various strains of black studies.

6 For a detailed reading of how the increasingly neoliberal university manages diversity (and diverse populations) through the management of different identity disciplines, see Jodi Melamed, *Represent and Destroy*; and Roderick Ferguson, *The Reorder of Things*. Katherine McKittrick has an incisive and generous critique about how the production of the (identity) discipline depends upon extremely limited definitions and descriptions of black life, in particular. See McKittrick, "The Smallest Cell Remembers a Sound," in *Dear Science and Other Stories*, 35–57.

7 Kandice Chuh describes this process as facilitating "aboutness" in "It's Not about Anything," 125–34.

8 Shaka McGlotten, "Ordinary Intersections," 45.

9 Kevin Quashie, *The Sovereignty of Quiet*, 4.

10 Quashie, *The Sovereignty of Quiet*, 4.

11 I'm very indebted to the work of Elizabeth Povinelli and Veena Das, whose work, while cited only a handful of times, entirely shaped my abilities to think this thought and write this sentence.

12 "If events are things that we can say happened such that they have a certain objective being," she writes, "then quasi-events never quite achieve the status of having occurred or taken place. They neither happen nor not happen." Elizabeth Povinelli, *Economies of Abandonment*, 13.

13 They are also largely absent from scholarship that uses phrases like "queer," "black queer," and "black queer women" but where "queer" signals a theoretical framework more than a gendered politics of sex.

14 A handful of studies of black queer and lesbian women's nightlives include dissertations such as Michelle M. Carnes, "Do It for Your Sistas"; Nikki Lane, "In the Life, on the Scene: The Spatial and Discursive Production of Black Queer Women's Scene Space in Washington DC"; and Christina Carney, "Making Space in a Militarized Global City: The Racial and Gendered Politics of Producing Space for Black Queer Women in San Diego." This work is preceded by Rochella Thorpe's foundational chapter, "'A House Where Queers Go': African-American Lesbian Nightlife in Detroit, 1940–1975." While not a social sciences project, Leilani Dowell's 2019 dissertation, "Wolf Packs," is about the violent resonance of black queer women venturing into the queer night. Together, this work on the forms and stakes of black queer women's nightlives can be read and assigned alongside documentaries like *Out in the Night*, about the New Jersey 4, which Dowell examines; *Living with Pride*, about Detroit's famed Ruth C. Ellis; *Jewels Catch One*, about the LA nightclub; *Shakedown*, about an underground strip club; and even in parts of the documentary *The Aggressives* and the canonical fictional documentary *The Watermelon Woman*, which touch on the role of the night in consolidating black queer women's identities and communities. This work is produced against the backdrop of an even smaller number of works on black queer and lesbian lives—but not necessarily nightlives—that did the essential first step of taxonomizing queer and lesbian life in

order to clear ground for it to be taken up as an "acceptable" site of inquiry within traditional if not conservative disciplines like Sociology. (See, for example, Mignon Moore's work.) It's fruitful to combine any number of these texts with selections from E. Patrick Johnson's oral history *Black. Queer. Southern. Women.*

15 Christina Sharpe details the ordinary as a site of care throughout *In the Wake* and in her reflection on that book (and other work) in "And to Survive."

16 Liesl Olson, *Modernism and the Ordinary*, 150.

17 Kathleen Stewart, *Ordinary Affects*, 4.

18 Kathleen Stewart, *Ordinary Affects*, 2. Emphasis in original. Lauren Berlant picks this up in her theorizing of the situation.

19 Shaka McGlotten, "Ordinary Intersections," 45. Emphasis added.

20 Black people are like Chekhov's gun.

21 Veena Das, *Life and Words*, 6.

22 Aliyyah I. Abdur-Rahman, "The Black Ecstatic," 344. In this book's introduction, I put pressure on our desire to theorize other worlds where black life might feel more productively lived, as happens to an extent in this essay. Abdur-Rahman's reading of José Esteban Muñoz's queer utopias is at the same time so necessary in the thinking and doing of black queer life.

23 Rankine had been writing in direct and indirect conversation with the late Lauren Berlant, injecting a fuller critique of racism into Berlant's rich discussions of the enduring cruel optimism required to survive late capitalism. The fantasy of the good life is deeply rooted in the historical linking of "good" and "life" to the imbrication of whiteness with capital gains; "the good life" is whiteness itself prevailing through capitalism.

24 Tina Campt, for example, offers the "future real condition" as a grammatical tense and timeplace that hinges on the idea, phrase, and sentiment of "that which will have had to happen." See Campt, *Listening to Images*, 17. The work becomes sitting in the details of this stretched-out timeplace—what Fanon described as the "interval" and Hortense Spillers called the "interstice"—to illuminate the ordinary mechanics of all that happens before the event is even recognizable as such. In *Black on Both Sides*, C. Riley Snorton focuses on the grammar of "the transitive" to investigate such "temporalities of emergence," articulated as a question that I bring to the figures in this book as *when* they might be—a question that suspends ontological assumptions—rather than where they were and are" (xiv, emphasis added). A focus on "where" might lead to descriptions and end points, locatable data that can be aggregated into events around which "black trans" can make sense within the disciplinary conventions of critical thought (conventions that, in turn, depend upon and seemingly demand the besieged and/or dying black queer subject). On the other hand, "when" becomes a key term and operative framework through which Snorton can "find a vocabulary for black and trans life. In this sense, it works to do more than provide a 'shadow history' of blackness in trans studies or transness in black studies. For many, it will not be understood as history at all, but, as with Fanon, *the problem under review here is time*" (xiv, emphasis added). Snorton undoes the assumed relation of black-trans-death-event(-potentiality matrix) that undergirds much conversation within and beyond academic discourse.

Considering black trans life, and how to persist and endure within and alongside it, demands we think differently about narrative time itself, charting the capacity of emergence (the practices of doing the ordinary) rather than its results (the aggregation into events). See C. Riley Snorton, *Black on Both Sides*.

25 Saidiya Hartman, "Venus in Two Acts," 11.

26 Saidiya Hartman, *Wayward Lives*, xiii.

27 Saidiya Hartman, *Wayward Lives*, "Cast of Characters."

28 "The idea is that in encountering an event, and encountering it as a witness or someone who in part suffered by it, one is entitled to an experience, whereas the sheer fact of having access to things in the world, for example, getting a story from another, is quite a different thing." Harvey Sacks, "On Doing 'Being Ordinary,'" 424.

29 In thinking about the beside as an ethical position, I look to Joshua Javier Guzmán's reflections on José Esteban Muñoz in "Notes on the Comedown," 59–68. Across Veena Das's work, she's considered the relationships between ethnography, the ordinary, and ethics. Indeed, Das suggests that our attention to the extraordinary event "is not because the everyday is hard to find but *because it is easy to deflect the difficulty of not being able to see what is before our eyes*." Das, *Textures of the Ordinary*, 11 (emphasis added). In her earlier manuscript, Das similarly suggests that inattention to the ordinary is rooted in a fear of the "unknowability of the world and hence of oneself in it." Das, *Life and Words*, 10. All told, she has been developing an ordinary methodology that considers what it means "to think ethics as expression of life taken as a whole rather than to privilege dramatic moments of breakdown or ethical dilemmas as the occasion for ethical reflection." Das, "What Does Ordinary Ethics Look Like?," 56. I read Das as asking us to pay closer attention to the relationships between our research and how we write it up, as our politics and ethics lie in that movement from experience to text.

30 Katherine McKittrick, *Dear Science*, 39, 44, 45.

31 Katherine McKittrick, *Dear Science*, 12.

32 Savannah Shange, "Black Girl Ordinary," 15.

33 In *Mules and Men* (1935), for example, Zora Neale Hurston reflected on the plays of opacity in the ethnographic encounter. She explained that the black people she encountered in the course of doing her research "are most reluctant at times to reveal that which the soul lives by. . . . The theory behind our tactics: 'The white man is always trying to know into somebody else's business. All right, I'll set something outside the door of my mind for him to play with and handle. He can read my writing but he sho' can't read my mind. I'll put this play to in his hand, and he will seize it and go away. Then I'll say my say and sing my song'" (2–3).

34 Or, put another way: in their verbal and physical engagements with their friend, they created an intentional, active, and engaged audience that recognized and reproduced the value of this choreography with deep roots in global Afro-diasporic communities.

35 On proprietary object relations, see Summer Kim Lee, "Introduction," *Post45*.

36 Sharon P. Holland, *The Erotic Life of Racism*, 3.

BIBLIOGRAPHY

Abdur-Rahman, Aliyyah I. "The Black Ecstatic." *GLQ: A Journal of Lesbian and Gay Studies* 24, nos. 2–3 (2018): 343–65.

Adeyemi, Kemi. "The Practice of Slowness: Black Queer Women and the Right to the City." *GLQ: A Journal of Lesbian and Gay Studies* 25, no. 4 (2019): 545–67.

Ahmed, Sara. *The Promise of Happiness.* Durham, NC: Duke University Press, 2010.

Allen, Jafari Sinclaire. "For 'The Children' Dancing the Beloved Community." *Souls* 11, no. 3 (2009): 319.

Arendt, Hannah. *The Origins of Totalitarianism.* New York: Harcourt, Brace, 1968.

Attoh, Kafui. *Rights in Transit: Public Transportation and the Right to the City in California's East Bay.* Athens: University of Georgia Press, 2019.

Attoh, Kafui. "What Kind of Right Is the Right to the City?" *Progress in Human Geography* 35, no. 5 (2011): 669–85.

Bachin, Robin F. *Building the South Side: Urban Space and Civic Culture in Chicago, 1890–1919.* Chicago: University of Chicago Press, 2004.

Badiou, Alain. *Being and Event.* Translated by Oliver Feltham. New York: Continuum, 2005.

Bailey, Marlon. *Butch Queens Up in Pumps: Gender, Performance, and Ballroom Culture in Detroit.* Ann Arbor: University of Michigan Press, 2013.

Bakare-Yusuf, Bibi. "I Love Myself When I Am Dancing and Carrying On: Refiguring the Agency of Black Women's Creative Expression in Jamaican Dancehall Culture." *International Journal of Media and Cultural Politics* 1, no. 3 (2005): 263–76.

Baldwin, Davarian L. *Chicago's New Negroes: Modernity, the Great Migration, and Black Urban Life.* Chapel Hill: University of North Carolina Press, 2007.

Baldwin, Davarian L. "'The 800-Pound Gargoyle': The Long History of Higher Education and Urban Development on Chicago's South Side." *American Quarterly* 67, no. 1 (2015): 81–103.

Barrett, Quenna L. "Setting the Stage for Black Choice: Theatre of the Oppressed as Container for Resistance, Black Joy." *Pedagogy and Theatre of the Oppressed Journal* 2, no. 1 (2017): 1–15.

Betancur, John. "The Politics of Gentrification: The Case of West Town in Chicago." *Urban Affairs Review* 37, no. 6 (July 2002): 780–814.

Binkley, Sam. *Happiness as Enterprise: An Essay on Neoliberal Life*. Albany: SUNY Press, 2014.

Blair, Zachary Shane Kalish. "Machine of Desire: Race, Space, and Contingencies of Violence in Chicago's Boystown." PhD diss., University of Illinois Chicago, 2018.

Bone, Robert, and Richard A. Courage. *The Muse in Bronzeville: African American Creative Expression in Chicago, 1932–1950*. New Brunswick, NJ: Rutgers University Press, 2011.

Briffault, Richard. "The Most Popular Tool: Tax Increment Financing and the Political Economy of Local Government." *The University of Chicago Law Review* 77, no. 1 (Winter 2010): 65–95.

Brown, Jayna. *Babylon Girls: Black Women Performers and the Shaping of the Modern*. Durham, NC: Duke University Press, 2008.

Buckland, Fiona. *Impossible Dance: Club Culture and Queer World-Making*. Middletown, CT: Wesleyan University Press, 2002.

Butler, Chris. *Henri Lefebvre: Spatial Politics, Everyday Life and the Right to the City*. London: Routledge-Cavendish, 2012.

Campt, Tina. *Listening to Images*. Durham, NC: Duke University Press, 2017.

Carnes, Michelle M. "Do It for Your Sistas: Black Same-Sex-Desiring Women's Erotic Performance Parties in Washington D.C." PhD diss., American University, 2009.

Carney, Christina. "Making Space in a Militarized Global City: The Racial and Gendered Politics of Producing Space for Black Queer Women in San Diego." PhD diss., University of California San Diego, 2016.

Cartier, Marie. *Baby, You Are My Religion: Women, Gay Bars, and Theology before Stonewall*. New York: Routledge, 2014.

Cavalcante, Andre. *Struggling for Ordinary: Media and Transgender Belonging in Everyday Life*. New York: New York University Press, 2018.

Chambers-Letson, Joshua. *After the Party: A Manifesto for Queer of Color Life*. New York: New York University Press, 2018.

Chicago Advocate. "Is Chicago's Logan Square Neighborhood Now the Hipster Mecca of the Midwest?" June 16, 2014.

Chow, Emily, Christopher Groskopf, Joe Germuska, Hal Dardick, and Brian Boyer. "Reshaping Chicago's Political Map: Race, Ward-by-Ward." *Chicago Tribune*, July 14, 2011. http://media.apps.chicagotribune.com/ward-redistricting/index.html.

Chuh, Kandice. "It's Not about Anything." *Social Text* 32, no. 4 (Winter 2014): 125–34.

Cohen, Cathy. "Deviance as Resistance: A New Research Agenda for the Study of Black Politics." *Du Bois Review* 1, no. 1 (2004): 27–45.

Conquergood, Dwight. "Performance Studies: Interventions and Radical Research." *Drama Review* 46, no. 2 (Summer 2002): 145–56.

Conquergood, Dwight. "Performing as a Moral Act: Ethical Dimensions of the Ethnography of Performance." *Text and Performance Quarterly* 5, no. 2 (1985): 1–13.

Courage, Richard A., and Christopher Robert Reed, eds. *Roots of the Black Chicago Renaissance*. Urbana: University of Illinois Press, 2020.

Crawford, Romi. "Yours in Blackness: Blocks, Corners, and Other Desire Settings." *NKA* 34 (2014): 80–89.

Currans, Elizabeth. "Utopic Mappings: Performing Joy." *Obsidian* 41, nos. 1–2 (2015): 90–102.

Daniel-McCarter, Owen. "Us vs. Them! Gays and the Criminalization of Queer Youth of Color in Chicago." *Children's Legal Rights Journal* 32 (2012): 5–17.

Das, Veena. *Life and Words: Violence and the Descent into the Ordinary*. Berkeley: University of California Press, 2006.

Das, Veena. *Textures of the Ordinary: Doing Anthropology after Wittgenstein*. New York: Fordham University Press, 2020.

Das, Veena. "What Does Ordinary Ethics Look Like?" In *Four Lectures on Ethics: Anthropological Perspectives*, edited by Michael Lambek, Veena Das, Didier Fassin, and Webb Keane, 53–126. Chicago: HAU Books, 2015.

Davis, Angela. "Reflections on the Black Woman's Role in the Community of Slaves." *Black Scholar* 3, no. 4 (1971): 1–14.

DeGooyer, Stephanie, Alastair Hunt, Lida Maxwell, and Samuel Moyn. *The Right to Have Rights*. New York: Verso, 2018.

Delaney, Samuel. *Times Square Red, Times Square Blue*. New York: New York University Press, 1999.

Dent, Gina. "Black Pleasure, Black Joy: An Introduction." In *Black Popular Culture: Discussions in Contemporary Culture*, edited by Gina Dent and Michele Wallace, 1–19. Seattle: Bay Press, 1992.

Dikeç, Mustafa. "Justice and the Spatial Imagination." *Environment and Planning A: Economy and Space* 33, no. 10 (2001): 1785–1805.

Dowell, LeiLani. "Wolf Packs: U.S. Carceral Logics and the Case of the New Jersey Four." PhD diss., City University of New York, 2019.

Drake, Simone. "The Marketability of Black Joy: After 'I Do' in Black Romance Film." *Women, Gender, and Families of Color* 7, no. 2 (2019): 161–81.

Drake, St. Clair, and Horace R. Cayton. *Black Metropolis: A Study of Negro Life in a Northern City*. Chicago: University of Chicago Press, 1993.

Duff, Cameron. "The Affective Right to the City." *Transactions of the Institute of British Geographers* 42, no. 4 (2017): 516–29.

Duggan, Lisa. *The Twilight of Equality: Neoliberalism, Cultural Politics, and the Attack on Democracy*. Boston: Beacon Press, 2003.

Dunye, Cheryl, dir. *The Watermelon Woman*. New York: First Run Features, 1997. 84 min.

Fenster, Tovi. "The Right to the Gendered City: Different Formations of Belonging in Everyday Life." *Journal of Gender Studies* 14, no. 3 (2005): 217–31.

Ferguson, Roderick. *The Reorder of Things: The University and its Pedagogies of Minority Difference*. Minneapolis: University of Minnesota Press, 2012.

Fitz, C., dir. *Jewel's Catch One*. Brooklyn, NY: Cinema Guild, 2017. 85 min.

Forstie, Clare. "After Closing Time: Ambivalence in Remembering a Small-City Lesbian Bar." In *Queer Nightlife*, edited by Kemi Adeyemi, Kareem Khubchandani, and Ramón H. Rivera-Servera, 130–42. Ann Arbor: University of Michigan Press, 2021.

Ghaziani, Amin. *There Goes the Gayborhood?* Princeton: Princeton University Press, 2015.

Gibson, Diane. "Neighborhood Characteristics and the Targeting of Tax Increment Financing in Chicago." *Journal of Urban Economics* 54 (2003): 309–27.

Gieseking, Jack. "Dyked NY: The Space between Geographical Imagination and Materialization of Lesbian-Queer Bars and Neighbourhoods." In *The Routledge Research Companion to Geographies of Sex and Sexualities*, edited by Gavin Brown and Kath Browne, 1–17. New York: Routledge, Taylor and Francis Group, 2016.

Gieseking, Jack. *A Queer New York: Geographies of Lesbians, Dykes, and Queers*. New York: New York University Press, 2020.

Giloth, Robert, and John Betancur. "Where Downtown Meets Neighborhood: Industrial Displacement in Chicago, 1978–1987." *Journal of the American Planning Association* 54, no. 3 (1988): 279–90.

Giroux, Henry A. *University in Chains: Confronting the Military-Industrial-Academic Complex*. New York: Routledge, 2015.

Glissant, Édouard. *Poetics of Relation*. Translated by Betsy Wing. Ann Arbor: University of Michigan Press, 1997.

Godreau, Isar P. *Scripts of Blackness: Race, Cultural Nationalism, and U.S. Colonialism in Puerto Rico*. Urbana: University of Illinois Press, 2015.

Green, Kai M. "The Essential I/Eye in We: A Black TransFeminist Approach to Ethnographic Film." *Black Camera* 6, no. 2 (2015): 195.

Greene, Theodore. "Gay Neighborhoods and the Rights of the Vicarious Citizen." *City and Community* 13, no. 2 (2014): 99–118.

Guzmán, Joshua Javier. "Notes on the Comedown." *Social Text* 32, no. 4 (121) (Winter 2014): 59–68.

Hackworth, Jason. *The Neoliberal City: Governance, Ideology, and Development in American Urbanism*. Ithaca, NY: Cornell University Press, 2007.

Hae, Laam. *The Gentrification of Nightlife and the Right to the City: Regulating Spaces of Social Dancing in New York*. New York: Routledge, 2012.

Haley, Sarah. *No Mercy Here: Gender, Punishment, and the Making of Jim Crow Modernity*. Chapel Hill: University of North Carolina Press, 2016.

Hamera, Judith. *Dancing Communities: Performance, Difference, and Connection in the Global City*. New York: Palgrave Macmillian, 2007.

Hammonds, Evelynn. "Black (W)holes and the Geometry of Black Female Sexuality." *differences* 6, nos. 2–3 (1994): 126–45.

Hanhardt, Christina. *Safe Space: Gay Neighborhood History and the Politics of Violence*. Durham, NC: Duke University Press, 2013.

Hankin, Kelly. *The Girls in the Back Room: Looking at the Lesbian Bar*. Minneapolis: University of Minnesota Press, 2002.

Hartman, Saidiya. "The Belly of the World: A Note on Black Women's Labors." *Souls* 18, no. 1 (2016): 166–73.

Hartman, Saidiya. *Scenes of Subjection: Terror, Slavery, and Self-Making in Nineteenth-Century America*. New York: Oxford University Press, 1997.

Hartman, Saidiya. "Venus in Two Acts." *Small Axe: A Journal of Criticism* 26, no. 26 (2008): 1–14.

Hartman, Saidiya. *Wayward Lives, Beautiful Experiments: Intimate Histories of Social Upheaval.* New York: W. W. Norton and Company, 2019.

Harvey, David. *Rebel Cities: From the Right to the City to the Urban Revolution.* London: Verso, 2012.

Harvey, David. "The Right to the City." *International Journal of Urban and Regional Research* 27, no. 4 (2003): 939–41.

Harvey, David. "The Right to the City." *New Left Review* 53 (September–October 2008): 23–40.

Hazzard-Donald, Katrina. "The Circle and the Line: Speculations on the Development of African-American Vernacular Dancing." *Western Journal of Black Studies* 20, no. 1 (1996): 28–38.

Hazzard-Donald, Katrina. "Dance in Hip-Hop Culture." In *That's the Joint! The Hip-Hop Studies Reader*, edited by Murray Forman and Mark Anthony Neal, 505–16. New York: Routledge, 2004.

Hazzard-Donald, Katrina. *Jookin: The Rise of Social Dance Formations in African-American Culture.* Philadelphia: Temple University Press, 2010.

Hesse, Barnor. "Marked Unmarked: Black Politics and the Western Political." *South Atlantic Quarterly* 110, no. 4 (2011): 974–84.

Hine, Darlene Clark. "Rape and the Inner Lives of Black Women in the Middle West: Preliminary Thoughts on the Culture of Dissemblance." *Signs* 14, no. 4 (1989): 912–20.

Hine, Darlene Clark, and John McCluskey, eds. *The Black Chicago Renaissance.* Urbana: University of Illinois Press, 2012.

Hirsch, Arnold R. *Making the Second Ghetto: Race and Housing in Chicago, 1940–1960.* Chicago: University of Chicago Press, 1998.

Holland, Sharon Patricia. *The Erotic Life of Racism.* Durham, NC: Duke University Press, 2012.

Holliday, Darryl. "Everything You Need to Know about the First Mega Mall Development Meeting." *DNAinfo Chicago*, May 8, 2015. http://www.dnainfo.com/chicago /20150508/logan-square/everything-you-need-know-about-first-mega-mall -development-meeting.

Holmes, Nathan. *Welcome to Fear City: Crime Film, Crisis, and the Urban Imagination.* Albany: SUNY Press, 2018.

Hong, Grace Kyungwon. *Death beyond Disavowal: The Impossible Politics of Difference.* Minneapolis: University of Minnesota Press, 2015.

Hubbard, Phil. "Revenge and Injustice in the Neoliberal City: Uncovering Masculinist Agendas." *Antipode* 36, no. 4 (2004): 665–86.

Hunter, Marcus Anthony. "The Nightly Round: Space, Social Capital, and Urban Black Nightlife." *City and Community* 9, no. 2 (June 2010): 165–86.

Hurston, Zora Neale. *Mules and Men.* New York: HarperCollins, [1935] 1990.

Isoke, Zenzele. "Black Ethnography, Black(Female)Aesthetics: Thinking/Writing/ Saying/Sounding Black Political Life." *Theory and Event* 21, no. 1 (2018): 148–68.

Iveson, Kurt. "Social or Spatial Justice? Marcuse and Soja on the Right to the City." *City* 15, no. 2 (2011): 250–59.

Jacobs, Jane. *The Death and Life of Great American Cities*. New York: Random House, 1961.

James, Robin. "Loving the Alien." *New Inquiry* 9 (October 22, 2012). Accessed March 5, 2018. https://thenewinquiry.com/loving-the-alien/.

Johnson, E. Patrick. *Black. Queer. Southern. Women*. Chapel Hill: University of North Carolina Press, 2018.

Johnson, Imani Kai. "Battling in the Bronx: Social Choreography and Outlaw Culture among Early Hip-Hop Streetdancers in New York City." *Dance Research Journal* 50, no. 2 (2018): 62–75.

Johnson, Imani Kai. "Dark Matter in B-Boying Cyphers: Race and Global Connection in Hip Hop." PhD diss., University of Southern California, 2009.

Johnson, Javon. "Black Joy in the Time of Ferguson." *QED: A Journal in GLBTQ Worldmaking* 2, no. 2 (Summer 2015): 177–83.

Judd, Bettina. *Feelin: How Creative Practice and Pleasure Politics Make Black Feminist Thought*. Evanston, IL: Northwestern University Press, forthcoming.

Keeling, Kara. *The Witch's Flight: The Cinematic, the Black Femme, and the Image of Common Sense*. Durham, NC: Duke University Press, 2008.

Kelley, Robin D. G. *Race Rebels: Culture, Politics, and the Black Working Class*. New York: Free Press, 1994.

Kelley, Robin D. G. "'We Are Not What We Seem': Rethinking Black Working-Class Opposition in the Jim Crow South." *Journal of American History* 80, no. 1 (1993): 75–112.

Kennedy, Elizabeth Lapovsky, and Madeline D. Davis. *Boots of Leather, Slippers of Gold: The History of a Lesbian Community*. New York: Routledge, 1993.

Khubchandani, Kareem. *Ishtyle: Accenting Gay Indian Nightlife*. Ann Arbor: University of Michigan Press, forthcoming.

Lambek, Michael, Veena Das, Didier Fassin, and Webb Keane. *Four Lectures on Ethics: Anthropological Perspectives*. Chicago: HAU Books, 2015.

Lane, Charneka. "In the Life on the Scene: The Spatial and Discursive Production of Black Queer Women's Scene Space in Washington, DC." PhD diss., American University, 2015.

Lane-Steele, Laura. "Studs and Protest-Hypermasculinity: The Tomboyism within Black Lesbian Female Masculinity." *Journal of Lesbian Studies: Tomboys and Tomboyism* 15, no. 4 (2011): 480–92.

Lee, Summer Kim. "Introduction: Someone Else's Object." *Post45* (December 19, 2019). https://post45.org/2019/12/introduction-someone-elses-object/.

Lefebvre, Henri. "The Right to the City." In *Writings on Cities*, translated and edited by Eleonore Kofman and Elizabeth Lebas, 147–60. Oxford: Blackwell Publishers, 1996.

Lipsitz, George. *How Racism Takes Place*. Philadelphia: Temple University Press, 2011.

Lu, Jessica, and Catherine Knight Steele. "'Joy Is Resistance': Cross-Platform Resilience and (Re)invention of Black Oral Culture Online." *Information, Communication and Society* 22, no. 6 (2019): 823–37.

Macek, Steve. *Urban Nightmares: The Media, the Right, and the Moral Panic over the City*. Minneapolis: University of Minnesota Press, 2006.

Madison, D. Soyini. *Critical Ethnography: Method, Ethics, and Performance*. 2nd ed. Thousand Oaks, CA: SAGE, 2012.

Manalansan, Martin F., IV. "Race, Violence, and Neoliberal Spatial Politics in the Global City." *Social Text* 23, nos. 3–4 (Fall–Winter 2005): 141–55.

Marcuse, Peter. "From Critical Urban Theory to the Right to the City." *City* 13, nos. 2–3 (2009): 185–97.

Martin, Allie. "Sonic Intersections: Listening to the Musical and Sonic Dimensions of Gentrification in Washington, D.C." PhD diss., Indiana University, 2020.

McGlotten, Shaka. "Ordinary Intersections: Speculations on Difference, Justice, and Utopia in Black Queer Life." *Transforming Anthropology* 20, no. 1 (2012): 45–66.

McKittrick, Katherine. *Dear Science and Other Stories*. Durham, NC: Duke University Press, 2021.

McKittrick, Katherine. *Demonic Grounds: Black Women and the Cartographies of Struggle*. Minneapolis: University of Minnesota Press, 2006.

Melamed, Jodi. "Racial Capitalism." *Critical Ethnic Studies* 1, no. 1 (2015): 76–85.

Melamed, Jodi. *Represent and Destroy: Rationalizing Violence in the New Racial Capitalism*. Minneapolis: University of Minnesota Press, 2011.

Michelman, Frank I. "Parsing 'a Right to Have Rights.'" *Constellations* 3, no. 2 (1996): 200–208.

Mitchell, Don. *The Right to the City: Social Justice and the Fight for Public Space*. New York: Guilford Press, 2003.

Moore, Mignon R. "Lipstick or Timberlands? Meanings of Gender Presentation in Black Lesbian Communities." *Signs: Journal of Women in Culture and Society* 32, no. 1 (2006): 113–39.

Mumford, Kevin J. *Interzones: Black/White Sex Districts in Chicago and New York in the Early Twentieth Century*. New York: Columbia University Press, 1997.

Muñoz, José Esteban. *Disidentifications: Queers of Color and the Performance of Politics*. Minneapolis: University of Minnesota Press, 1999.

Muñoz, José Esteban. "Feeling Brown: Ethnicity and Affect in Ricardo Bracho's *The Sweetest Hangover (and Other STDs)*." *Theatre Journal* 52, no. 1 (2000): 67–79.

Natalie P. Voorhees Center for Neighborhood and Community Improvement. "Appendix: The Socioeconomic Change of Chicago's Community Areas (1970–2010)." October 2014. https://voorheescenter.red.uic.edu/wp-content/uploads/sites/122/2017/10/Appendix-Oct-14.pdf.

Ngai, Sianne. *Ugly Feelings*. Cambridge, MA: Harvard University Press, 2005.

Olson, Liesl. *Modernism and the Ordinary*. London: Oxford University Press, 2009.

Orne, Jason. *Boystown: Sex and Community in Chicago*. Chicago: University of Chicago Press, 2017.

Pattillo, Mary. *Black on the Block: The Politics of Race and Class in the City*. Chicago: University of Chicago Press, 2010.

Pattillo, Mary. *Black Picket Fences: Privilege and Peril among the Black Middle Class*. Chicago: University of Chicago Press, 2013.

Povinelli, Elizabeth. *Economies of Abandonment: Social Belonging and Endurance in Late Liberalism*. Durham, NC: Duke University Press, 2011.

Puar, Jasbir. *Terrorist Assemblages: Homonationalism in Queer Times*. Durham, NC: Duke University Press, 2018.

Purcell, Mark. "Citizenship and the Right to the Global City: Reimagining the Capitalist World Order." *International Journal of Urban and Regional Research* 27, no. 3 (2003): 564–90.

Purcell, Mark. "Excavating Lefebvre: The Right to the City and Its Urban Politics of the Inhabitant." *GeoJournal* 58, no. 2 (2002): 99–108.

Quashie, Kevin. *The Sovereignty of Quiet*. New Brunswick, NJ: Rutgers University Press, 2012.

Ramos-Zayas, Ana. *National Performances: The Politics of Class, Race, and Space in Puerto Rican Chicago*. Chicago: University of Chicago Press, 2003.

Ramos-Zayas, Ana. *Street Therapists: Race, Affect, and Neoliberal Personhood in Latino Newark*. Chicago: University of Chicago Press, 2012.

Rancière, Jacques. "Who Is the Subject of the Rights of Man?" In *Wronging Rights? Philosophical Challenges for Human Rights*, edited by Aakash Singh Rathore and Alex Cistelecan, 168–86. New York: Routledge, 2004.

Rankine, Claudia. *Citizen: An American Lyric*. Minneapolis: Graywolf Press, 2014.

Rankine, Claudia. *Don't Let Me Be Lonely: An American Lyric*. Minneapolis: Graywolf Press, 2004.

Reddy, Chandan. *Freedom with Violence: Race, Sexuality, and the US State*. Durham, NC: Duke University Press, 2011.

Rivera, Maritza Quiñones. "From Trigueñita to Afro-Puerto Rican: Intersections of the Racialized, Gendered, and Sexualized Body in Puerto Rico and the US Mainland." *Meridians: Feminism, Race, Transnationalism* 7, no. 1 (2007): 162–82.

Rivera-Servera, Ramón H. "Choreographies of Resistance: Latina/o Queer Dance and the Utopian Performative." *Modern Drama* 47, no. 2 (2004): 269–89.

Rivera-Servera, Ramón H. "Musical (Trans)Actions: Intersections in Reggaetón." *Trans: Revista Transcultural de Música* 13 (2009): 1–13.

Rivera-Servera, Ramón H. *Performing Queer Latinidad Dance, Sexuality, Politics*. Ann Arbor: University of Michigan Press, 2014.

Román, David. "Theatre Journals: Dance Liberation." *Theatre Journal* 55, no. 3 (2003): vii–xxiv.

Rosenbaum, Art. *Shout Because You're Free: The African American Ring Shout Tradition in Coastal Georgia*. Athens: University of Georgia Press, 2012.

Rosenberg, Rae. "The Whiteness of Gay Urban Belonging: Criminalizing LGBTQ Youth of Color in Queer Spaces of Care." *Urban Geography* 38, no. 1 (2017): 137–48.

Sacks, Harvey. "On Doing 'Being Ordinary.'" In *Social Action: Studies in Conversation Analysis. Studies in Emotion and Social Interaction*, edited by Maxwell J. Atkinson and John Heritage, 413–29. Cambridge: Cambridge University Press, 1984.

Safransky, Sara. "Rethinking Land Struggle in the Postindustrial City." *Antipode* 49, no. 4 (2017): 1079–100.

Salkind, Micah. *Do You Remember House? Chicago's Queer of Color Undergrounds.* New York: Oxford University Press, 2019.

Salvato, Nick. *Obstruction.* Durham, NC: Duke University Press, 2016.

Scott, James C. *Domination and the Arts of Resistance: Hidden Transcripts.* New Haven, CT: Yale University Press, 1990.

Shabazz, Rashad. *Spatializing Blackness: Architectures of Confinement and Black Masculinity in Chicago.* Chicago: University of Illinois Press, 2015.

Shange, Savannah. "Black Girl Ordinary: Flesh, Carcerality, and the Refusal of Ethnography." *Transforming Anthropology* 27, no. 1 (2019): 3–21.

Sharma, Sarah. *In the Meantime: Temporality and Cultural Politics.* Durham, NC: Duke University Press, 2014.

Sharoff, Robert. "University of Chicago Works on Its Neighborhood." *New York Times,* October 23, 2012. https://www.nytimes.com/2012/10/24/realestate/commercial/university-of-chicago-helps-revitalize-53rd-street-retail-district.html.

Sharpe, Christina. *In the Wake: On Blackness and Being.* Durham, NC: Duke University Press, 2016.

Sharpe, Christina. "And to Survive." *Small Axe: A Journal of Criticism* 22, no. 3 (2018): 171–80.

Small, Mario Luis. "Is There Such a Thing as 'The Ghetto'? The Perils of Assuming That the South Side of Chicago Represents Poor Black Neighborhoods." *City* 11, no. 3 (2007): 413–21.

Smith, Brent C. "The Impact of Tax Increment Finance Districts on Localized Real Estate: Evidence from Chicago's Multifamily Markets." *Journal of Housing Economics* 15 (2006): 21–37.

Smith, Mark Michael. *Mastered by the Clock: Time, Slavery, and Freedom in the American South.* Chapel Hill: University of North Carolina Press, 1997.

Smith, Neil. "Giuliani Time: The Revanchist 1990s." *Social Text* 57 (1998): 1–20.

Smith, Neil. *The New Urban Frontier: Gentrification and the Revanchist City.* New York: Routledge, 2005.

Snorton, C. Riley. *Black on Both Sides: A Racial History of Trans Identity.* Minneapolis: University of Minnesota Press, 2017.

Sobel, Mechal. "Early African-American Attitudes toward Time and Work." In *Time in the Black Experience,* edited by Joseph K. Adjaye, 183–99. Westport, CT: Greenwood Press, 1994.

Spade, Dean. *Normal Life: Administrative Violence, Critical Trans Politics, and the Limits of Law.* Durham, NC: Duke University Press, 2015.

Spear, Allan H. *Black Chicago: The Making of a Negro Ghetto, 1890–1920.* Chicago: University of Chicago Press, 1967.

Spillers, Hortense. "Mama's Baby, Papa's Maybe: An American Grammar Book." *Diacritics* 17, no. 2 (1987): 65–81.

Stewart, Kathleen. *Ordinary Affects.* Durham, NC: Duke University Press, 2007.

Summers, Brandi T. *Black in Place: The Spatial Aesthetics of Race in a Post-Chocolate City.* Chapel Hill: University of North Carolina Press, 2019.

Taylor, Keeanga-Yamahtta. *Race for Profit. Justice, Power, and Politics.* Chapel Hill: University of North Carolina Press, 2019.

Teska Associates. "Fullerton-Milwaukee Tax Increment Financing Redevelopment Plan and Project. Chicago, 1999. Revision No. 2, December 1999. Amendment No. 1, December 2004. Amendment No. 2, February 2011." https://www.chicago.gov /content/dam/city/depts/dcd/tif/T_087_FullertonMilwaukeeAmendment2.pdf.

Thiel, Julia. "One Bourbon, One Scotch, and 20 New Hipster Bars." *Chicago Reader,* August 28, 2013. https://www.chicagoreader.com/chicago/logan-square-new-bars -analogue-robert-haynes-henry-prendergast/Content?oid=10746020.

Thompson, Katrina Dyonne. *Ring Shout, Wheel About: The Racial Politics of Music and Dance in North American Slavery.* Urbana: University of Illinois Press, 2014.

Thorpe, Rochella. "'A House Where Queers Go': African-American Lesbian Nightlife in Detroit, 1940–1975." In *Inventing Lesbian Cultures in America,* edited by Ellen Lewin, 40–61. Boston: Beacon Press, 1996.

Vogel, Shane. "By the Light of What Comes After: Eventologies of the Ordinary." *Women and Performance: A journal of feminist theory* 19, no. 2 (2009): 240–60.

Walcott, Rinaldo. Conference presentation. *Scenes at 20* conference, Rutgers University, New Brunswick, NJ, October 7, 2017.

Warner, Michael. *The Trouble with Normal: Sex, Politics, and the Ethics of Queer Life.* Cambridge, MA: Harvard University Press, 2000.

Weatherford, Ashley. "The Year in Black Joy." *The Cut,* December 9, 2016. https://www .thecut.com/2016/12/2016-in-black-joy-beyonce-simone-biles-and-more.html.

Weinraub, Leilah, dir. *Shakedown.* 2018. 72 min.

Welbon, Yvonne, dir. *Living with Pride: Ruth Ellis @ 100.* 1999; Chicago: Our Film Works. 60 min.

White, Deborah Gray. "Female Slaves: Sex Roles and Status in the Antebellum Plantation South." *Journal of Family History* 8, no. 3 (1983): 248–61.

Whitley, Sa. "The Collective Come-Up: Black Queer Placemaking in Subprime Baltimore." PhD diss., University of California, Los Angeles, 2020.

Williams, Teona. "For 'Peace, Quiet, and Respect': Race, Policing, and Land Grabbing on Chicago's South Side." *Antipode* 53, no. 2 (2021): 497–523.

Winebaum, Alys. "Gendering the General Strike: W. E. B. Du Bois's Black Reconstruction and Black Feminism's 'Propaganda of History.'" *South Atlantic Quarterly* 112, no. 3 (2013): 437–63.

Winling, LaDale. *Building the Ivory Tower: Universities and Metropolitan Development in the Twentieth Century.* Philadelphia: University of Pennsylvania Press, 2017.

Winling, LaDale. "Students and the Second Ghetto: Federal Legislation, Urban Politics, and Campus Planning at the University of Chicago." *Journal of Planning History* 10, no. 1 (2011): 59–86.

Woods, Clyde. "'A Cell Is Not a Home': Asset Stripping and Trap Economics in Central City East/Skid Row, Part 2." In *Black California Dreamin': The Crises of California's African-American Communities,* edited by Ingrid Banks, Gaye Johnson, George

Lipsitz, Ula Taylor, and Daniel Widener, 191–99. Santa Barbara, CA: UCSB Center for Black Studies Research (2012). https://escholarship.org/uc/item/63g6128j.

Woods, Clyde. "Les Misérables of New Orleans: Trap Economics and the Asset Stripping Blues, Part 1." *American Quarterly* 61, no. 3 (2009): 769–96.

Zukin, Sharon. *The Cultures of Cities*. Cambridge, MA: Blackwell, 1995.

Zukin, Sharon. *Naked City: The Death and Life of Authentic Urban Places*. New York: Oxford University Press, 2010.

INDEX

radical Elsewheres, 33–34
Rae: on Black Joy, 63; on burnout, 125–26; on community, 140; on dancing, 67; on Hyde Park, 83; labors of, 123; on ownership, 92; on responsibility, 62, 93–95; on restorative justice, 91
Ramos-Zayas, Ana, 146n25
Rankine, Claudia, 107–8, 157n23
Rauner, Bruce, 21
Reagon, Bernice Johnson, 17
responsibility and accountability, 62, 64, 75, 79, 90–95
restorative justice, 89–90, 91
restrictive covenants, 9–10
revanchist city, the, 9, 10, 13
rights in the neoliberal city, 7, 8–15
rights to the city, 19–23, 147n38
Rogers Park, 45, 46
Roman, David, 66

safety and security, 78, 93–95
Salvato, Nick, 43
Sarah, 55, 56
Sasha, 51
Save Our Boulevard, 43
Scott, James, 147n42
segregation, housing, 9–10
segregation, violent, 86
self-reflexivity, 24–25, 27, 117
Serena, 15, 76, 77, 78, 92
sexual abuse, 89
Shange, Savannah, 109–10
Sharma, Sarah, 43–44
Sharpe, Christina, 157n15
Shayla, 142
Slippery Slope, 39–40, 50–55, 57–58, 131
Slo 'Mo: community building at, 131; demographics of, 40; location of, 16; nomenclature of, 28, 149n1; significance of, 5, 60–61; at the Slippery Slope, 39–40, 50–55; at Soho House, 56–57; at The Whistler, 45–50, 58
slowness: aesthetic of, 57; concept of, 41; at Old Gold, 59; significance of, 5, 60–61, 131; of Slo 'Mo, 45–50; slow jams, 40; temporal aspects of, 43–44

smallWORLD, 103
Smith, Neil, 9
Snorton, C. Riley, 157n24
social media, 65, 76, 89, 126, 138
SoHo House, 56–57
South East Chicago Commission, 82
South Loop, 16
South Side, 15, 34, 36–37, 81–84, 85, 143n2
spatial politics, 7, 11–12, 13, 33
Special Services Area, 152n21
speed and neoliberalism, 43, 151n17
Spillers, Hortense, 157n24
sponsorships, 127
staff training, 124, 133–34
stereotypes of blackness, 85–86
Stewart, Kathleen, 107
straight, the term, 149n1
suburbanites, 56
Summers, Brandi, 81
sustainability and profitability, 123–24, 127–28
Swag Surfin', 69
Swoon, 103, 123

Tantrum, 16
Target, 3, 144n5
Tax Increment Financing (TIF), 41–42, 83, 84, 152n21, 154n25
Taylor: on the "black woman," 29–30; on community, 137, 140; on dance, 141; on E N E R G Y, 114, 116; on feeling, 142; on intimacy, 138, 139; on outsiders, 78; on Party Noire, 68, 69
tech bros, 56
temporal inequities, 43–44
terminologies, 28–32, 149n2
Tess, 13, 30–31, 68, 86, 137
Textures of the Ordinary (Das), 158n29
This Black Girl, 1–3, 22, 32–38
Thorpe, Rochella, 145n15
TIF (Tax Increment Financing), 41–42, 83, 84, 152n21, 154n25
Tori, 97, 101–2, 127, 134, 135
Tori Photography + Design, 103
Tracy: on alcohol, 135; on exhaustion, 122; interest of, 139; on politics, 21; politics of, 22;

www.ingramcontent.com/pod-product-compliance
Lightning Source LLC
Chambersburg PA
CBHW050651270326
41927CB00012B/2979